Dead of Winter Meetings

SCORNED & BELOVED

with Canadian Eccentrics

BILL RICHARDSON

KNOPF CANADA

PUBLISHED BY ALFRED A. KNOPF CANADA

Copyright © 1997 by Bill Richardson

All rights reserved under International and
Pan American Copyright Conventions. Published in
Canada by Alfred A. Knopf Canada, Toronto, in 1997.
Distributed by Random House of Canada Limited, Toronto.

Page 341 constitutes a continuation of the copyright page.

Canadian Cataloguing in Publication Data
Richardson, Bill
Scorned & beloved : dead of winter meetings with
Canadian eccentrics

ISBN 0-676-97079-6

1. Eccentrics and eccentricities - Canada - Biography.
I. Title.
II. Title: Scorned and beloved.

FC25.R52 1997   920.071   C97-9309883
F1005.R52 1997

Printed and bound in the United States of America

First Edition

For Wallace

• • •

"Scorned as Timber, Beloved of the Sky"
Title of a painting by Emily Carr

"Sometimes, however, a trip across
the country is just a trip across the country."
Rick Salutin, *The Globe and Mail*, Sept. 20, 1996

Contents

ELLY MAY
Entertainer, Toronto
GLENN GOULD
Pianist, Toronto
GLENN GOULD'S NEIGHBOURS
Tenants of Mount Pleasant Cemetery, Toronto
ANNA BROWNELL JAMESON
Art Historian, Nineteenth-Century Travel Writer
JOHN HENRY LEFROY
Nineteenth-Century Surveyor
GEOFFREY PIMBLETT
Restaurateur, Queen Impersonator, Toronto
ESTHER BRANDEAU
Cross-dresser, Traveller, Quebec City
SARAH EMMA EDMONDS
Bible Salesman, Civil War Veteran, Cross-dresser, New Brunswick
CHAS. S. ROBERTSON
Elocutionist, Kenabeek, Ontario
GRENVILLE KLEISER
Master of the Universe and Author, Fifteen Thousand Useful Phrases
DAME EDITH SITWELL
Author, English Eccentrics
CHARLES DOMERY
Remarkable Glutton
ST. SIMEON STYLITES
Pillar Sitter
ST. SIMEON SALUS
Fool for God, Tectonic Clairvoyant, Dog Walker
CHARLES HENRY DANIELLE
Dancing Master, Costumier, Proprietor of Octagon Castle, Paradise, Newfoundland
S. G. COLLIER
Undertaker, St. John's
FREDERICK A. BRAZILL
Heir to Charles Henry Danielle, Paradise
CLARENCE WAUGH
Friend of Charles Henry Danielle
PIERRE-LÉON AYOTTE
Farm Labourer, Trousers-Phobic, Ste-Geneviève-de-Batiscan, Quebec
WILLIE FRANCIS FRASER
Learned to Dance in a Dream, Deepdale, Cape Breton Island
MRS. JOYNER
Struck by Lightning, Souris, Manitoba

MR. JOYNER
Her Husband, Souris
EDDIE R. SOURIS
Genealogist, Mouse Fancier, Traveller, Toronto
ST. MODOMNOC
Apiarist
FRED SAUER
Inventor, Charlottetown
GEORGE DOWIE
Convicted Murderer, Poet, Charlottetown
FRANCIS LONGWORTH
Sheriff, Charlottetown
NOAH
Flood Survivor, Wildlife Conservationist
NOAH'S FAMILY
Also on the Ark
MOGUL
Elephant
SAMUEL BEAN
Preacher, Physician, Cryptographer, Wellesley, Ontario
MERIT BEAN
Curmudgeon, Yarmouth
JEROME
Amnesiac, Double Amputee, Meteghan, Nova Scotia
ARTHUR THURSTON
Historian, Collector, Pigeon Keeper, Yarmouth
CAPTAIN REED
Commander of the Ill-Fated Royal Tar, *Saint John*
KEITH PELTON
Actor, Burned to Death with a Curling-Iron, Yarmouth
TONY CURTIS
Actor, Hunk
ROBERT GOULET
Singer, Hunk
JEAN ST-GERMAIN
Inventor, Mystic, Pyramid Builder, St-Simon-de-Bagot, Quebec
ALEX KOLANSKY
The Mad Trapper of the Whiteshell
NICK KOLANSKY
His Brother, Portage la Prairie
MARGARET MCDONALD
Muskrat Slayer, Cobden, Ontario
NELLEE JESSEE REID
Farm Labourer, Cross-dresser, Englehart, Ontario
JACK AND DONNA WRIGHT
Cat Fanciers, Kingston

JACK MARRIOTT
Photographer, Philosopher, Composer, Farmer, Cat Lover, Port Williams, Nova Scotia

JOB
Resident of Heaven

JEAN-PAUL SARTRE
Existentialist

PAUL WUKETSEWITZ
Known as Paul Bog, Petersfield, Manitoba

MICKEY DONOHOE
Paul Bog's Neighbour

HECTOR MACKENZIE
Fiddler, Tour Guide, New Glasgow, Nova Scotia

K.
Hermit, Nova Scotia

GABRIEL DRUILLETTES
Jesuit, Quebec

LAURA KAY PROPHET
Seer, Duck Fancier, Vancouver

SYLVIE LONGPRÉ
Barbie Enthusiast, Repentigny, Quebec

THE GREAT ANTONIO
World's Strongest Man, Montreal

BILL JAMIESON
Collects Shrunken Heads, Toronto

JOE DELANEY
Scarecrow Maker, Cheticamp, Cape Breton Island

CLYDE FARNELL
Artist, Decorator, Cornerbrook, Newfoundland

ALEXIS LAPOINTE
Half Man, Half Horse, La Malbaie, Quebec

LETITIA J. REID
Graduate, 1928 Marvel School of Cosmetology, Regina

THE MARVEL GIRLS
Her Classmates

LILLIAN ALLING
Walked from New York to Siberia

DAVID CURNICK
Teacher, Film Maker, Robin Hood Fan, Vancouver

EMILY CARR
Painter, Writer, Victoria

Fugue

So, you want to write a fugue,
You've got the urge to write a fugue,
You've got the nerve to write a fugue,
The only way to write one is to plunge right in and write one.
So go ahead.
    — Glenn Gould, "The Anatomy of Fugue"

Elly May's eyelashes are beautifully groomed and expertly attached. Longer than long. Fracturers of time and space. Exquisite, extravagant receptors. At any minute they might register a distant seismic trembling, or crackle with radio waves beamed over light-years from a remote and intelligent corner of the universe. If you were to see one out of context — flaccid and strewn across the bar, say — you might mistake it for one of those cunning brushes waiters use, postprandially, for clearing crumbs from tables. When Elly May bats her lids, which is often, they generate a breeze that sets the candle flames to shimmying. These, as the inquisitor said to the heretic, are holy lashes. Everything about their architecture — their anti-gravitational sweep, their unlikely heft, their evidence of the divinely inspired human inventiveness we call Art — funnels attention heavenward. If a single, highly individuated snowflake were to precipitate itself from the grey forge of the December clouds, tumble down angle over unique angle, and expire, meltingly, on the thoughtfully combed expanse of one of these wide rakes, they would achieve transcendence. Mere lashes no longer, they would become Poetry. Unalloyed Poetry.

Elly May's eyes are brown and uncommonly wide. They may owe their preternatural dilation to the effort required to keep half a kilo of synthetic fur aloft. Or, it might be nothing more than one of the discreetly athletic requirements of voguing.

"Have you seen my Bette Davis?" she asks. I shake my head. We have only just met. I haven't had the chance to plumb her repertoire of tricks, which is evidently steppe-like in its expansiveness. It doesn't matter a jot that our acquaintance is so freshly minted. Elly May lowers her eyes to half-mast and lasers me with the same "where the hell have you been" regard she used when I asked her her name. It is surely no accident that avid is the mirror image of diva. As divas go, Elly May is the quintessence of avidity. She is accustomed to having her reputation parade before her, preceding even her hyperextended and feathery ocularia. She sighs the sigh of the worn-out and the righteous. In me, she sees, she has her work cut out for her.

"Then watch."

She stands, opens the full-length fur coat her mother gave her last year for Christmas. She squares her hands — her nails are magenta, her fingers festooned with gaudy, multifaceted glass bijoux — on her hips. They are so narrow, those hips! Even so, they are scarcely contained by the shiny vinyl swatch of her black miniskirt. It is a frock of her own design, and she says it began its life on earth as a tablecloth. No matter. It more than suits her. She looks like a million bucks. Elly May stretches her neck. Elly May angles her head. Elly May lifts her chin, and achieves the seemingly impossible by widening her eyes further still. She flares her nostrils to such cavernous good effect that I find myself momentarily thinking of the Chunnel. Every movement is acid-etched and arch. She lifts her fag to her lips, sucks, exhales both smoke and the inevitable camp expostulation.

"What a dump!"

New Year's Eve, 1996. Toronto, Ontario. "Dump" would be the operative word. Canada's largest city is labouring under the weight of its second meaningful snowfall in twenty-four hours.

The pavements are encumbered with soggy, treacherous slop, neither slush nor snow nor ice. The Inuit must have a name for it, but there is no noun in English. The language is lacy with such inadequacies. Speak, and you hear your own wind whistling through the lacunae. In this neither-here-nor-there climatic moment, when thaw and freeze battle for hegemony of the air, what aspires to snow hangs somewhere between liquidity and quiddity. Revellers, fishtailing after the sexy bait of midnight, squoosh and slip through the same weepy, abortive, churlish stuff that blighted the land God gave to Cain.

Here and there around the city, it must be said, are untrodden Edens, landscapes that are simply like picture prints from Currier and Ives. I spent a cheerful afternoon in the anaesthetically named Mount Pleasant Cemetery, where the snow dusting the graves and markers was a shroud (what else?), unblemished save for the ungual calling-cards of a few of the city's more contemplative deer. I had come to the cemetery on the first day of my travelling not to fawn, but to pay homage to Glenn Gould. His is a complex portfolio: pianist, composer, nocturnalist, pill popper, actor, documentarist, genius, legend, dead man, academic growth industry, eccentric. As I am the well-raised son of a very good mother, I phoned ahead to check on his availability.

"Good morning, thank you for calling Mount Pleasant Cemetery."

A male voice, warm and welcoming, but mercifully not unctuous.

"Good morning. I'm calling to confirm that Glenn Gould is interred at Mount Pleasant."

"Okay. Just a second while I change screens. I'll have to get out of 'point of sale.'"

I had not before this minute taken into account how computers have altered even the reassuringly pallid complexion of the funeral business. It was not a rosy dawning. Something shifted, then withered in and around my left chest. I knew in that moment that my life would never again be quite the same. Indeed, not even my death would be as I had imagined it.

"There we go! Now, you said Gould? That would be G - O..."

His voice trailed off into orthographic uncertainty. I gave him the spelling of both family and Christian name, and also provided the year of death.

"Nineteen eighty-two," I intoned, hoping I sounded appropriately sepulchral.

The tell-tale tapping of keys. A tense, digitized silence.

"Yup!" came the merry reply, jigging over the fibre-optic filaments that lay between us. "Here he is! Section thirty-eight, lot ten-fifty."

"Thank you. Can you tell me how long it takes to get there by cab? I'll be coming from downtown."

"Golly! I wouldn't know about that. You see, I'm from Whitby."

"Ah."

What else could I say? For I have never been to Whitby. For I detected in his voice something melancholy and confessional. For I could think of no other rejoinder.

"That was swell," I tell Elly May. And it was. I've seen more than a few Bette Davis impersonations in my time, and hers surely was among the best.

"And this," she says, clamping a full nelson on my attention, "who's this?"

She gives her frosted mane — a wig which has been teased until it is on the threshhold of outrage — a haughty toss, and follows through with a vixen moue. It is not a lot to go on, but I can't bear the idea of disappointing her.

"Can I see it again?"

She sighs the sigh of the afflicted and obliges.

"Oh. Oh, golly. Uh — is it Tina?"

"Baby!" she cries and smacks her palms with glee. "Oh, baby, you are so right! Tina! And I do Billie, and Sarah, and Aretha. I do Dionne, too. Did you know I did Dionne for Dionne once? It was at the Sheraton in Hamilton. I was entertaining there, just a one-night thing, just a favour for a friend, you know. I sang 'I'll Never Love This Way Again' and 'Do You Know the Way to San José.' Oh, you know, baby, I do them all, all the Dionne songs. 'That's What Friends Are For,' of course. Anyway, after I'd gone to my dressing room, there was this knock on the door, and there was my friend and she said, 'Elly May, I've brought you a surprise.' Well, I thought it would be a little brooch, you know, maybe a few roses, something like that. But no. She steps back, and standing there is Dionne Warwick. I mean, *Di*-onne *War*-wick! And you know what she said to me? She said, 'Honey, you do me better than I do me.' And I'll tell you, the both of us standing there, it was like we were two energies becoming one. Yes. Yes. Dionne Warwick. Hey, you want a cigarette?"

I demur, tell her I've quit, pick up her pack of Export A's with its "Smoking Can Kill You" warning, and study the grim chemical analysis.

"Wow. That's a whack of tar."

"Yeah, baby, but you know I need that tar. It keeps me looking the way I do. If I didn't have that tar, I'm afraid I'd wake up some morning looking like a little white boy and we couldn't have that! Uh-uh."

She takes a long drag and looks at me closely in the dim light.

"Hey. You know what you can do for those crow's feet? Spirit gum. You just put a little spirit gum around your eyes and it'll smooth those wrinkles away. You try it. You'll see."

Elly May, one of Dame Veracity's crueller handmaidens, had a point. My complexion is not without furrows. Mind, she wasn't seeing me at my moisturized best. The drying environs of Mount Pleasant had not bestowed anything like a benefice on my epidermis. If you visit this cemetery — and one day before you die you must — you should take a moment to stop at the office and pick up one of the easy-to-follow walking-tour maps. I squinted through cold-fogged lenses and tripped a hot fandango in the doorway, coaxing the snow from my boots' deep treads. The sweet fellow from Whitby was nowhere to be found, but an equally well-disposed woman named Mary Angel — it said so on the decorative plaque on her desk — happily gave me the guide to the graves of the erstwhile worthwhile and presently absent. Over the years, Mount Pleasant has been thickly sown with establishment skeletons. Here lie politicians, military types, industrialists, kingpins of commerce: rich white guys and their wives and families, all gone to seed. Timothy Eaton, William Lyon Mackenzie King, and Sir William James Gage are here. So are the Masseys, whose Greek revival mausoleum is a real showpiece. If it were transplanted wholesale to an upscale neighbourhood like Forest Hill, or Westmount, or Shaughnessy, it would handily fetch a price in the seven figures. Such ornate memorials are rare in this tony bone drop where, by and large, a Presbyterian austerity prevails: thoughtful, timeless design for a thoughtful, timeless place. *Life may be transient, darling, but taste is forever.*

Fresh air. Bright day. I was in a perambulatory mood. I took my time finding section thirty-eight, lot ten-fifty, gladly wandering the ploughed paths that bracket the ploughed-under. The Boylens. The Conways. The Millers and the Pattersons. The Staines. I marvelled at the commendable restraint of those epitaph writers who had resisted doing something whimsical with the Paynes, the Aikens, the Youngs, the Stillmans. To say nothing of the Scores. I passed by the insulin-discovering team of Banting and Best, and the well-tamped mound of Dr. Alan G. Brown, the inventor of Pablum. I turned the hackneyed phrase "the dead of winter" over and over in my mouth, contemplating how it took on a new flavour as I skirted the tombs of the Ballards, the Breckenridges, the Boultons, the Bennetts, the Blodgetts. There were the Greens. There were the Hills, whom not even the sound of music could revive.

And so I walked among the dead for an hour or more before I steered my ramble through neighbourhoods that were largely Asian, and finally found, masked by snow and a concealing wreath, the sought-after plot. The Gould memorial is tasteful and unassuming: a simple stone with a classic border — trailing roses — surrounding the most laconic of family summations.

Gould

Florence E.

July 26, 1975

Beloved Wife Of

Russel H. Gould

November 22, 1901 – January 4, 1996

Their Dearly Loved Son

Glenn H. Gould

October 4, 1982

He may have been one of the century's great pianists, but the exigencies of filial piety prescribe that he spend eternity with bottom billing. It is a modest memorial for so extravagant a talent. There is a small marker nearby, etched with the melancholy aria from the *Goldberg Variations*. Otherwise, nothing beside remains. All that is Gould is not glitter.

It had just gone noon. The snow, though not at all deep, was reasonably crisp and absolutely even. Its tracklessness was evidence that I was the family's only hogmanay visitor. I tried, unsuccessfully, to call to mind the specifics of the Scots tradition called "first footing." Does it not bode ill to find a fair-haired man on your stoop at the turning of the year? Here was fodder for concern. Then again, for the Goulds at least, how much worse can it get? A fledgling, graveside Sitka spruce — the very wood used in piano manufacture — cast a long shadow over the hallowed ground. A crow claxoned. A hardy, omniscient songbird whistled, "I see, I see, I see," in descending minor thirds. A jogger trotted along the nearby trail. She waved. I returned her salute. A funeral party of twenty-one vehicles, seventeen of which were minivans, followed a hearse into the nether reaches of Mount Pleasant. Then everything was still. All you could hear was the ripening of the day and the slow dancing of happy shades. The crematorium across the way was quiet, its chimneys cool.

Elly May jettisons smoke into the air at a forty-five-degree angle. She coughs and says, "Hey, baby. Who told you smoking was bad for you? Huh? Who told you? That's just what everybody wants you to think. Me, I'm fifty-one and it isn't hurting me. That's because I won't let it. You got to make up your own mind about this stuff, you know? Because everyone's different. Those lines around your eyes. You know what causes them? Worry. You're worried all the time. I can see it. I'm watching your face and I can see it. You get worried and you sort of screw up your face all tense-like, and you end up with those lines. You're worried about money. Worried about work. Worried about what people might think. You're worried about smoking. Ha! Me, I'm my own person, so I just don't pay any attention to that crap. I do what I like in this world, you hear what I'm saying? It's this way with me, baby. You can call me and call me, but chances are you won't find me at home and that's because I'm going to be out doing just exactly what I like, which is having fun with my friends. I won't stop having fun till they put me in my coffin. Hell, you can come and visit me then! I'll roll over! I'll make room!"

Graveyard visiting is a particular penchant, a "never the twain shall meet" recreation. You like it or you don't. It can be a great frustration to travel with someone who is otherwise disposed in this regard. It's annoying for the one to be forever pulling over so that the other can caper through the corpse field, and just as irritating for the aficionado of the fallen to be pulled away prematurely from his pleasures by a tooting horn or the short-tempered bark of impatience. I am of the mind that it's one of those aspects of being, like blood type, for which two people should be tested before they form a serious attachment. Conversion is not a realistic prospect. Those who are ill disposed towards a cemetery tour are unresponsive to tactics of suasion. For them, it will never be transcendent, never anything more than a dull break from the road; and is possibly a symptom of a dangerous morbidity. We who like nothing better than a cadaverous meander cite any number of reasons for our enthusiasm. Genealogical research. Historical curiosity. The challenge of creating spontaneous fictions by filling in the blanks between birth and death. Incipient necrophilia. Me, I embrace the pointlessness of the enterprise. When I stroll among headstone, angel, and virgin, it is almost never with a specific goal or soul in mind. I am merely enjoying the business of being. If I had to isolate a purpose, I would say it is to rinse my mind clean with a wash of names — McCleary, Woo, Seaton, Anderson, Brandt. The faceless, anonymous dead. Their random dates. The nullity of their requirements. Now and then I'll be struck by the way a wreath or flower offers up the tacit proof that memory and love are active agents in the battered world. Sometimes I might be visited by a line from *Hamlet*, or by a glimmer of something like perspective. But this is nothing I long for, nothing I crave; which is all to say that visiting Mount Pleasant with the specific intention of dropping in on Glenn was an aberrant moment in the history of my relationship with the dead.

I think it was in the worthy pages of *Reader's Digest* — with its tales of valour at sea and good clean jokes, its subtle tips for keeping the magic in a marriage and biographical sketches of Joe's organs — that I first heard about Glenn Gould. I would have been nine or ten years old at the time, just beginning to read material that was not meant specifically for children, and just learning that I harboured a fondness for music. I suppose it was because I came across his story at this developmental stage — when the world was presenting itself on a new set of terms — that it made such an impression and stuck with me. It was full of anecdotes attesting to Gould's many peculiarities. Much was made of his penchant for dressing in a heavy coat and gloves in the heat of summer, of his idiosyncrasies and rituals in the recording studio and on the concert stage. The *Digest* detailed his unnerving need to vocalize while he played, of the guttural baritone that rumbled beneath the melody like an improvised continuo line. I read about the long, warm baptism to which he treated his arms and hands before every performance, and about the battered chair he always used when playing. His father had tinkered with it, sawing, filing, and nailing, altering it to his genius son's specifications so that he could enjoy an easier relationship with gravity when he was wooing the gods with his virtuoso tinkling. The writer of this article recounted one of Gould's appearances with the New York Philharmonic, a performance of Brahms' Concerto in D Minor, and how Leonard Bernstein grew ever more vexed with the young Canadian's bizarre requirements, especially the way he kept the orchestra waiting while he adjusted his seat, taking forever to settle on a physical angle of attack. "Perhaps we could slice an inch off your *derrière*, Mr. Gould," said the fretful maestro. (Or words to that effect. I remember it only because it was the occasion of my first learning the word "derrière.") There were disagreements between soloist and conductor that were even more fundamental. Gould's interpretation was so very *outré*, so entirely abstracted from the traditional and time-tested conventions of performance that, before the concert, Bernstein publicly disassociated himself with what was to follow. Nonetheless, he is reported to have said after the fact, "There's no doubt about it. That nutcase is a genius."

Standing graveside, I fired up my Walkman and listened to an interview Gould gave in 1958, three years after the release of the Columbia recording of the *Goldberg Variations* had made him a huge international star. His conversational style is fluid and tangential, fugal really, an intricate braiding of ideas, conveyed on the buoyant and nuanced voice of an aesthete. He's confident, brash, funny at times, an expert mimic. He's unpredictable, unapologetic, uncompromising in his views — which are fascinating, sometimes infuriating. It's a wonder that anyone so young can be so self-possessed, so anchored in his opinions. Sometimes, his arrogance makes you want to say, "Oh, Glenn! Blow it out your *derrière*!" He's just so damn fussy with his tight-assed litany of wills and won'ts. He plays Chopin only in weak moments. The only operas he cares to hear are those by

Mozart and Strauss. Verdi makes him squirm, Puccini makes him squiggle. He never goes to concerts unless they are given by friends and he has to attend for diplomatic reasons. The tedious social obligations of touring exhaust him, just exhaust him. And as for performing itself — well, it is a vastly overrated enterprise. Still six years away from famously turning his back on the concert hall, he is even now staking out his preference for making recordings over giving live performances. The microphone, he finds, is a benevolent presence, but an audience is troublesome, inhibiting, and applause is misleading, sometimes even vicious. In the studio, there is no one to answer to, no one to please but oneself. Already he is envisioning the day when he will be able to achieve hermitage through the sanitary distancing made possible by technology.

He is not all prickly self-absorbtion, though. He is quite endearing when he speaks of his love for Canada. London, New York, Paris: any of those cities would be available to him, but Canada is not a place he'd care to abandon. When he says he feels something like a sense of debt to his homeland, I can't help but think how uncommon it has become to hear the country spoken of with tenderness, with passion even, in a moment that isn't fuelled by crisis. He is tired, he says. The demands of being Glenn Gould have drained him. Half-jokingly, he tell his interviewer that someone of his age can hardly sustain the rigorous pace required of sought-after artists. It's a peculiar remark for someone who is just twenty-six. In the here and now, it takes on a patina of irony, for in a relative way Gould was already middle-aged. He couldn't have known it, could never have imagined dying at fifty, a cerebral hemorrhage taking him down, one last big flash from the brain, an explosion of circuits, and then he was bound for the earth.

Gould once said that Toronto was among the few cities in which he could find peace of mind. A little less than a century before his birth, the English writer and art historian Anna Brownell Jameson, who possessed an *amour propre* of at least

Gouldian proportions, was not so well pleased. When she arrived from New York around Christmas-time, 1836, she wrote, "I see nothing but snow heaped up against my windows, not only without but within; I hear no sound but the tinkling of sleigh-bells and the occasional lowing of a poor half-starved cow, that, standing up to the knees in a snow-drift, presents herself at the door of a wretched little shanty opposite, and supplicates for a small modicum of hay." Nor was the English surveyor and military man John Henry Lefroy any more impressed a few years later. Even after he spent the better part of two years doing magnetic surveys in the western and northern hinterlands, Toronto failed to tug at the iron filings of his heart. In January 1845 he wrote to his sister Isabella that the city was socially deficient. "There is so little that deserves the name of conversation, so much egregious trifling, so much which makes me ashamed of my folly if I join in it, that I seldom leave a party without some secret self-reproach....The great defect in the lady society of Toronto, especially the young lady branch of it, is the want of character. There are very few who possess any one distinguishing taste, acquirement, or characteristic. One cannot be surprised at this considering the deficiencies of the colony in subjects and schools of taste, but it reduces conversation to trifles and matters of the moment."

Anyone seeking reassurances that the lady society of Toronto has come a long way in the 150 years since these two early travellers set down their impressions would need only spend New Year's Eve with Elly May and company at Pimblett's. This Cabbagetown restaurant and bar has the genial, slightly down-at-the-heels, flocked-wallpaper look of a cluttered Victorian bordello. It is chock-a-block with taxidermy: stag heads, tick-filled ducks, and mounted fish. There is a dusty Canada goose whose wings are spread in a sad posture of flight, and the goose forges a curious link between Elly May and Messy May. Messy May was a Vancouver drag queen. She reigned in days of yore. She is said to have invited friends for Christmas dinner and neglected to procure the requisite fowl. Messy May was unfazed. Resourceful to the nth degree, she simply doffed her heels, slipped on a pair of serviceable flats, and hustled her way along Robson Street to Stanley Park. There, any number of geese were floating about on Lost Lagoon. She surveyed the possibilities. She selected a bird that would look better on a platter than it did on the pond. Somehow, she dispatched it. Don't ask me how. The story is hazy on this point. Messy May trotted home with her prize under her arm. She plucked it as she went, scattering the feathers behind her. The police, alerted to the felony, simply followed the trail of discarded plumage. Not for nothing was she called "Messy."

At Pimblett's, a couple of cats, self-contained and still animate, wander from table to table, heedless of city by-laws. No one seems to mind. Everywhere you turn there are pictures of monarchs, past and present. One wall is hung with paintings of bathers, very Aubrey Beardsley. There are a couple of magnificent chandeliers, some imposing fireplace surrounds and mantels, a suit of armour, odds and ends of statuary, and *tchotchkes* too plentiful to name. The furnishings, the dishes and flatware, all the various trappings have a look of proud salvage. Much the same can be said for the clientele. Pimblett's patrons are an eclectic bunch. It's a popular gathering spot for monarchists, for transvestites, for transsexuals, for gay and straight Torontonians alike. Elly May is here to strut her stuff as one of three performers in the prelude to the midnight drag show that is a Pimblett's New Year's Eve tradition of long standing. She has changed costume five or six times now, first shedding her fur and black vinyl for a sequinned sheath, then for a skimpy little lamé number. She watches with some disdain while one of her colleagues varnishes her nails. "Oh her," she says, *sotto voce*, though perhaps not quite as *sotto voce* as absolute discretion might require, "she thinks she looks like Anne Murray. Does she look like Anne Murray to you? Ha! I don't think so!"

Well. Maybe Anne Murray on a bad day. Maybe Anne Murray after a lengthy bout with Asian flu. But so what? Put her on the stage and crank up "Snow Bird" or "Danny's Song," and disbelief will quickly settle into a state of blessed suspension. No one would dispute that Geoffrey Pimblett, the cheerful, eponymous owner of the joint, looks remarkably like the Queen. He has togged himself up in a gown and a sash and a tiara — one of several regal headpieces he has crafted out of soup tins and a prismatic array of costume jewellery. The queen get-up is one he likes to trot out on festive occasions and high holy days such as this. He often sports it for gay pride parades, or for special events staged by the Cabbagetown merchants' association. Tonight, his regalia is rather more slapdash than he would like. He has lingered too long in the kitchen, dishing up huge servings of roast beef, Yorkshire pudding, and trifle. Between times, he has been nipping over to the computer to make last-minute amendments to his New Year's speech. "Come on, old queen, move along," he mutters while navigating through his many tasks, and while hurrying to change. He is unable to locate a pair of matching gloves, and has to discard his falsies as they make the zipping of his frock impossible. Even so, he looks very much the part. He has no need of a wig as his own slate-coloured and very full head of hair is a fine approximation of the bob we see pictured on so many stamps and coins.

Elly May and company rise up on their spikes and teeter downstairs to the bar to do their show, while Geoffrey, alias Betty Windsor, takes the stage in the upper room that is the restaurant proper. There is prolonged applause when the queen mounts her dais. She crooks her arm and acknowledges her people with an understated wave. She adjusts her tiara and launches into her address. Something is awry with the queen's sound system. Everyone cranes forward, straining to hear. These are words worth hanging on, her insights, her benisons. Her lips move, but all we hear is Marilyn Monroe coming through the floorboards from the bar below. She is singing "Diamonds Are a Girl's Best Friend." The queen adjusts her paste diadem and takes it all in stride. She is too noble and well practised to let a little gaffe like this hang her up. Appearance counts for everything. Resilience is all. She soldiers on, not appearing to mind that she has lost her audience, that they have returned to attacking their trifle and to gossiping among themselves. Outside, it is snowing like blazes.

Glenn Gould tolerated Toronto well enough, but he loved the country north of the city, around Lake Simcoe. He loved it especially in the winter, when the trees were stripped down and careless of their secrets; when the cottagers were absent and the icy stillness in the air made the place seem all the more remote. In winter, at Lake Simcoe, it was the heated *froideur* of the music of Sibelius that spoke to him most ringingly. I would be hard-pressed to think of something more crystalline and lovely than Gould's performance of the andantino from Sibelius' Sonatine in E Major. It is heart-centred music, full of longing, moving beyond telling. If you listen to his recording, you will hear how he inhabits not just every note, but every space between every note. You can't help but believe that, in the moment of its playing, the whole structure of the piece, all its gentle mathematics, was as necessary to him as oxygen.

You would think better of me, I'm sure, if I could tell you it was the andantino, or even *Finlandia*, I thought to hum by way of tribute as I left his grave on this winter afternoon, on this last day of the year, with the clockwork Earth already rocketing closer to the sun. But the song that came to my mind and mouth was one made famous by a singer for whom Gould had a certain wry and surprising fondness, Petula Clark. I looked around to make sure I was alone and unobserved. I sang "Downtown," badly, but with all the feeling I could muster:

> Just listen to the music of the traffic in the city
> Linger on the sidewalk where the neon signs are pretty,
> How can you lose?

The words thudded among the markers, sterile seeds on stony ground. My breath was the colour of a ghost. I clapped my hands together when I was done, thinking just to warm them, but the addled whacking rang out like the saddest applause the world has ever heard. It was time to say goodbye. It was getting late. Elly May, whom I had yet to meet, was studying her wardrobe, making hard and necessary choices. She was saying to herself, "Oh, baby, how can you lose?" while her closet shimmered and the day turned grey. Soon, she would settle on her vinyl miniskirt, wrap herself in her fur, kiss her mother goodbye. "Don't be late, son," the old lady would say. And Elly May would answer, "Don't be late yourself." She'd angle her wide-brimmed hat and pull it down low, give herself a final once-over in the mirror, bat her lovely lashes approvingly, and step out into the deepening dark, the deepening snow. Soon, all the city's neon would come into its own. As would Elly May. The night would grow heavy with possibility. And downtown was where it would happen. And downtown was where she needed to go.

Before We Go Further,
a Parenthetical Word

Pride and self-disgust served her
like first-aid surgeons on the battlefield.
— Grenville Kleiser, *Fifteen Thousand Useful Phrases*

I admit I have my hypocrisies. I can't deny that I maintain a running subscription to certain double standards. That I see these lapses for what they are, and acknowledge them, mitigates nothing. Such detached and self-critical lucidity gets me nowhere. I consider my imperfections. I know the sticky welling of remorse. Then, I continue on my merry, duplicitous way. I risk compounding the interest on whatever disdain this deficiency earns me by revealing that I am also godless. Perhaps it would be more precise to say I don't seek the sponsorship or intervention of a god who is affiliated with one of the major fraternities. I've been that way for years now. In fact, the one behavioural arena in which I stand resolute and steadfast, where hypocrisy is forbidden to enter, is my refusal to attend church, other than to put in an appearance at occasions that are largely social: weddings, funerals, concerts, fowl suppers, white elephant sales, and so on.

I am especially committed to this staunch and Calvinistically dour principle of non-attendance on high holy days. On those occasions I actually have to make a study of avoiding the place. For reasons of personal history, and because I like a crowd, and because I know all the verses to "O Come, All Ye Faithful," even the one about "Lo, he abhors not the Virgin's womb," I can count on feeling the strong tug of churchiness on Christmas Eve. I resist giving in to it. I can't bear the idea of being one of those fair-weather Christians who turns up when the living is easy. I figure that if I am not able to find my way clear to accepting some of the basic tenets of Christian belief, and I am not; if I can't carry the salvationist teachings of the faith in my heart on a day-by-day basis, and I can't; then I hardly deserve the pew space I'd usurp by putting in an appearance just when everything is so campy and garish and sodden with ceremony that it actually verges on being fun. A ritual is a ritual. It deserves respect in and of itself. You dishonour it if you take part with anything less than full and unqualified intent, and to do so wreaks havoc on the old karma. If it has no more meaning for you, has no more impact on your being and thinking than, say, yet another viewing of *It's a Wonderful Life*, then what's the point?

I suppose it's been ten years since I last did the Christmas Eve thing. I went with friends to an Anglican cathedral where all the observances are quite high church. I sat in the balcony and watched it unfold from above. I remember how, at the beginning, the choir and the celebrants and the sub-celebrants and associate sub-celebrants proceeded up the aisle, engulfed by the effulgent from the swinging censers, their progress measured by a heartfelt bellowing of "Joy to the World." Among them was a man I knew, a queen of high degree, who was also a very respectable high-school English teacher. He was in his glory. He had been given what I imagined to be a plum assignment, which was to carry the crucifix. He held it high before him, with the same expression on his puss that I had seen a few weeks earlier when I had been to his house for dinner. He had come to the table from the kitchen with a dessert soufflé that had risen so beautifully it had the look of a sacred relic. On Christmas Eve, as then, his pace was grave and stately, and with his long robes, white and red, hiding his footwork, he seemed almost to float, as though on water, towards his rendezvous with the Father, the Son, and the Holy Ghost. (Come to think of it, in candid moments he had often professed a fondness for threesomes.)

Now, this was a man who managed to be both prim and craggy at the same time. He was regimental in his bearing, and possessed a steely-eyed regard and stiff-upper-lip demeanour that has rarely been seen since the days of the Raj. In a personal ad he would describe himself as "straight-looking, straight-acting," and for all his fastidious prissiness, he was. He professed an aversion to displays of effeminacy, and wouldn't on a bet have donned such gay apparel as a slinky sheath festooned with sequins and bugle beads. However, studying him from above, noting how carefully he had arranged his hair to hide the beginnings of male-pattern baldness, I felt I understood the deeper reason he took so active a role in this pageantry, rather than contenting himself with the sidelines, and the status of believing observer. I felt sure that I was witnessing an act of sartorial sublimation. Some deep-seated urge to disport himself in garments with such beautiful names as camisole, negligée, peignoir, or in a gown of taffeta or of lace worked in colonnades and gussied up with flounces or in peau-de-soie, was satisfied by this wonderfully pompous display of chasuble, surplice, and cassock. Were he drawn to the Church for reasons of faith alone, straightforward attendance and adherence to rules and regulations would have scratched his religious itch. But no. He wanted a more visible and theatrical role. He wanted the assistance and complicity of the costume department. More than anything else, he wanted to swaddle himself in bright ecclesiastical drag and go for an after-dinner mince at midnight mass. And here he was, fully engaged. Oh, his countenance might have been a study in devotion, but I knew very well there was a smirk of delight bubbling not far below his sneer of cold command. He was working hard to keep it from breaking through and shattering his marmoreal visage. And why should he not be delighted? He was doing what he'd always craved. He was wearing a dress in public, and getting away with it, too. Not only that, his swishing was sanctified by the highest authority, by God himself. It was definitely a case of whirl without end, amen. I was seized by one of those uncontrollable fits that usually come over me at funerals when the kitsch of mourning becomes too much to bear. I had to make a great show of coughing into the Book of Common Prayer, in order to suppress my laughter.

I'm sorry I've burdened you with this. I've told you things that will make you think the less of me. But we are going to go on a long trip together, and you might as well know I am evil, evil, evil. Evil right to the core.

Not evil exactly, but certainly suspect, was Esther Brandeau, who got herself into hot water by preferring trousers to frocks and who declined to affiliate herself with the Church. Esther is popularly said to be the first Jew to arrive in Canada. She also bears the weight of being one of our first recorded cross-dressers. She was a pioneer of gender-role subversion. An early confounder of conventions of costume, Esther paved the way for the likes of Elly May, as well as for Sarah Emma Edmonds, who was born in New Brunswick in 1841. Sarah dressed as a boy from early childhood, and when she left home to take up work as an itinerant Bible seller, it was as Franklin Thompson that she went door to door. Franklin was also her *nom de guerre* when she enlisted as a private with Company F, 2nd Michigan Infantry, during the American Civil War. She served with distinction, survived the conflict, went on to marry and to raise three children, moved to Texas, and eventually revealed the truth of her soldier-boy identity. She was awarded, by a special act of Congress, a civil war pension, and was the only woman ever to receive one.

Esther was not so well compensated. When she put into the port of Quebec in September 1738, on board the ship *St. Michel*, she was dressed as a man, a boy really, and had successfully passed herself off as "Jacques La Fargue." Exactly how the ruse was discovered — a wrestling match, a bunk-room glimpse, an unwarranted interest on the part of Jacques in feminine hygiene products — I can't say. What is sure is that Esther, when her true identity was revealed, was hauled before the local administration, and that a prolonged tizzy ensued.

And no wonder. Everything about her was wrong, plain wrong. Everything about her was unsettling. For one thing, there was her religion. Jews were forbidden by decree to set foot in the colony. And then there was the question of her inappropriate choice of wardrobe. A proper woman of the day might have come down the gangplank dressed modestly and practically in a sacque dress, apron, petticoat, and mob cap. She might have accessorized the ensemble with a neat little fichu, delicately knotted at the neck. But no, not Esther, who was presented to the intendant, Hocquart, and the naval secretary, Varin, clothed in standard eighteenth-century mariners' duds: the all-purpose linen trousers known as "slops," a jacket, a waistcoat, a body shirt, a leather hat, and shoes with wide silver buckles. They peppered her with *pourquois*, and the story she had to tell about her life as a boy was a regular pageant of misrepresentation.

To everything there is a beginning. Diane Tye, who teaches in the Folklore Department at Memorial University in St. John's, Newfoundland, wrote her dissertation about "local characters" in her own home town of Amherst, Nova Scotia. In her data gathering, she noted the way her informants would isolate a specific event, often a mishap or trauma, and identify it as the trigger or fuse that detonated some neighbour's quirk or eccentricity. So-and-so was perfectly "normal" until such-and-such happened. Until he was gassed in the trenches. Until her fiancé stood her up on their wedding day. Until the barbecue was struck by lightning. And so on. Dr. Tye observed that finding such a hook on which to hang a peculiarity provides a comfort, of a sort. Not only does it offer an explanation as to the underlying reasons behind perceived aberrance, it also reinforces the sense of inclusivity within community. We acknowledge that someone has veered from the well-furrowed path. We seek to know why. We find a way to accommodate the unusual behaviour that is theirs by virtue of some external intervention, either deliberate malevolence or accidental mishap. And we receive the tacit assurance that we, too, will be taken care of, should we be gassed, dumped, or struck by a bolt from the blue, and find ourselves derailed as a consequence. In the case of Esther, the agents of change appear to have been a shipwreck and a ham sandwich. Here is the substance of her story, contained in a document signed by Varin, "Commissaire de la Marine," and dated September 15, 1738.

"This day…appeared Esther Brandeau, aged about twenty years, who embarked at La Rochelle as a passenger dressed in boy's clothes, under the name of Jacques La Fargue, on the vessel *St. Michel*, Sieur de Salaberry commander, and declared her name to be Esther Brandeau, daughter of David Brandeau, a Jew, trader, of St. Esprit, diocese of Daxe, near Bayonne, and that she is of the Jewish religion; that five years ago her father and mother placed her on a Dutch vessel, *Captain Geoffroy*, in order to send her to Amsterdam, to one of her aunts and to her brother; that the vessel having been lost on the bar of Bayonne, in the moon of April or May, 1733, she was happily brought safe to shore with one of the crew; that she was received by Catherine Churiau, a widow living at Biaris; that two weeks thereafter she started, dressed as a man, for Bordeaux, where she shipped as a boy, under the name of Pierre Alansiette, on a vessel commanded by Captain Bernard, destined for Nantes, that she returned on the same vessel to Bordeaux, and there shipped again in the same capacity on a Spanish vessel, *Captain Antonio*, for Nantes; that on reaching Nantes, she deserted and went to Rennes, where she took service as a boy at the house of one Augustin, a tailor, where she remained six months; that from Rennes she went to Clissoy, where she took service with Récollets as a servant and to run messages; that she remained three months in the convent and left without warning for St. Malo, where she found shelter at the house of a baker named Seruanne; that she next went to Vitré to get a place there and entered the service of Sr. de la Chapelle, an ex-captain of the infantry; that she left the situation because her health rendered her unable to watch the said Sr. de la Chapelle, who was always sick; that when returning to Nantes, and when one league from Noisel, she was taken for a thief and confined in the prison of Noisel aforesaid; that she was set free, after twenty-four hours, because it was found that a mistake had been made; that she then went to La Rochelle, where assuming the name of Jacques La Fargue, she took ship as a passenger on the said vessel, *St. Michel*.

"Upon which declaration we called upon the said Esther Brandeau to state for what reason she had so concealed her sex during five years. Whereupon she said: That when she escaped from shipwreck and reached Bayonne, she entered the house of Catherine Churiau, as above stated; that the latter made her eat pork and other meats the use whereof is forbidden among the Jews, and that she thereupon resolved not to return to her father and mother in order that she might enjoy the same liberty as the Christians."

In all my days, I have never once tried to conjure the forbidden flavour of liberty, but I can't imagine that it would ever register on my tastebuds as bacon. Why would it? Mine was a WASPy, Sunday-joint kind of upbringing and I was never estranged from the delights of pig flesh. Still, I wonder if Esther might not have been teasing her tribunal with her "give me pork chops or give me death" story, might not have been prevaricating, just a little. Surely the greater freedom was to be found in cutting herself loose from the shackles of girlhood, concealing her sex to safeguard herself against interference and tampering, and then taking to the road. A few months here, a few months there, another name, another situation, no ties to bind her, no fixed address. The allure, especially to a young person with a bent for adventure, could not have been so very different in the eighteenth century from today.

Perhaps by the time Esther reached Quebec, she had decided that the advantages of a Christian life didn't outweigh the dreary prospect of blistering her fingers on a rosary. In spite of her professed desire to enjoy the same freedoms as were accorded trinitarians who didn't give a hoot what they ate, Esther resisted the idea of conversion. She stayed in the colony a year, yawning at the priests who tried to instruct her, and generally proving herself a thorn in the hides of the governors, who didn't know what to do with her. She was lodged with nuns, she was put up in private homes, she was surrounded by the day-to-day rituals and trappings of Catholic devotion, but she resolutely refused to take the plunge. Her résumé, as cited above, suggests that she might have had difficulty applying herself to employment for any length of time. Hocquart and his cronies found her fickle and flighty, for sure, and finally they just gave up and packed her back across the Atlantic on *Le Comte de Matignon*. There is no record of what she wore as a going-away ensemble. No one can say what she did or became. France absorbed her. We can be confident, I think, that somehow she got by. If nothing else, she had learned the importance of keeping her options open. She hadn't spent all that time shipboard without learning something about navigating her way through the trickier shoals, and the older she got, the more confident she became that the tired old restrictions didn't apply in her case. There was nothing she couldn't do.

"Tell me," asked the boy, looking up from his Torah studies, "why you have never grown a beard like the other rabbis?"

"For the same reason Moses never grew wings. God gives to each of us only as much as we require. And not a whisker more. Now hush."

And the child went back to his scroll, well satisfied. He didn't care what the others said, wouldn't heed their suspicious whisperings, or believe for even a second those stories about covert cutlet gobbling. This was a holy man, and as far as he was concerned, no one could ever be as good and as wise as Reb Brandeau.

Begin

As men strip for a race,
so must an author strip for the race with time.
— Grenville Kleiser, *Fifteen Thousand Useful Phrases*

Imagine yourself stretched supine in a wintery field. This is
Frostian snow, man. What words best describe it? Deep. Lovely.
Dark. Though not necessarily in that order. You have given in
to the childish impulse to make an angel, and now you lie quietly, bisecting a seraph of your own sculpting, hardening your
hearing to the siren cries of cryogenics. You study the sky, study
the indolent vapouring of two clouds through the blue and
recumbent air. Within the grey striations of one cumulus puff
you can make out the word ECCENTRIC. In the other, you are
sure you can discern the comforting label CANADIAN. Slowly,
slowly, they drift together. Each cloud absorbs the woolly mass
of the other. There is a low rumble, a suspenseful pause, and
then a gentle tumbling-down of names. When first I lay on my
back and saw those clouds collide, Glenn Gould's was the second name to fall to earth. Chas. S. Robertson came first. I never
met Chas. S. Robertson, never met any of his family. I have only
the most circumstantial of evidence that once upon a time —
round about sixty years ago — he lived in Kenabeek, Ontario.
His is the name and that is the town stamped on the inside
cover of a book which is now mine, a flea-market find. The
book, *Fifteen Thousand Useful Phrases,* was written in 1917 by
Grenville Kleiser. What a glorious moniker to trail! Grenville
Kleiser! He was, according to the information on the jacket, the

author of a great many texts which must have been intended mostly for elocutionists, or other *belles-lettres* dabblers. I mean such books as *Similes and Their Use, How to Read and Declaim, How to Argue and Win,* and *Humorous Hits and How to Hold an Audience.* I have not seen these fruits of his labour, but I'd bet none is as stirring, as juicy, as the book which is a bond between me and Chas. S. Robertson. *Fifteen Thousand Useful Phrases: A Practical Handbook of Pertinent Expressions, Striking Similes, Literary, Commercial, Conversational, and Oratorical Terms, for the Embellishment of Speech and Literature, and the Improvement of the Vocabulary of Those Persons Who Read, Write, and Speak English.* Fifteen thousand! An outlandish claim, but true! Not, understand, that I have taken the time or trouble to count and verify. What? Grenville Kleiser beef up the stats? I think not! Anyone called Grenville Kleiser deserves to be trusted, deeply, unconditionally, and always. Just imagine the work of it — Herculean! — assembling 15,000 phrases, all of equal utility; phrases that the happy reader can use to liven up business talk. Day-to-day talk. Literary talk. And so on.

A drowsy murmur floats into the air like thistledown.

Languid streams that cross softly, slowly, with a sound like smothered weeping.

Theories sprouted in his mind like mushrooms.

She flounders like a huge conger-eel in an ocean of dingy morality.

Each is a gem! And there are 14,996 more just like them!

Chas., who had the book before me, marked the phrases he found most useful. The pages are dense with his check marks and underlinings. Here and there he added a date. I wish I could have seen him on May 7, 1932, waiting on tenterhooks for his chance to insinuate *quaking and quivering like a short-haired puppy after a ducking* into any old conversation. Only a month before, he had amazed those around him by referring to *buried hopes rising from their sepulcher.* Over the course of 1933, he was able to embrace such circumlocutions as *into the purple sea the orange hues of heaven sunk silently* and *jealousies and animosities which pricked their sluggish blood to tingling.* But it was on July 8, 1934, that poor Chas. experienced his Grenville Kleiser–inspired apotheosis. It was on that day that Chas. let a simile be his umbrella. Or so it would seem. Dozens of phrases in the book are marked with that date. What was it that pushed him over the margins of the merely reasonable? What dark angel possessed his throat? By my reckoning — which, in the absence of contemporary accounts, I base on his annotations — he must have said:

> *Dear as remembered kisses after death, hers the loveliness of some tall white lily cut in marble, splendid, but chill. Her hair dropped on her pallid cheeks like sea-weed on a clam. Like Death, who rides upon a thought, and makes his way through temple, tower and palace; or, like a caged lion shaking the bars of his prison, shadowy faces, known in dream, pass as petals upon a stream. Bronze-green beetles tumbled over stones, and lay helpless on their backs with the air of an elderly clergy-man knocked down by an omnibus. Thy brown benignant eyes have sudden gleams of gladness and surprise, like woodland brooks that cross a sunlit spot. My love for thee is like the sovereign moon that rules the sea. The days have trampled me like armed men. Thou must wither, like a rose. This life is like a bubble blown up in the air. Your tongue is like a scarlet snake. Like two doves —*

July 8, 1934. It must have been quite a day in the life of Chas. S. Robertson, late of Kenabeek, Ontario, for it is the last date entered in *Fifteen Thousand Useful Phrases*. I can just see how Chas. spat them all out at once at the church picnic, stopping the box-lunch auction and the three-legged race, stopping everyone in his tracks, stopping them with his fragrant vomiting. And then he would have dropped his lemonade and just expired from the beauty of it all.

They didn't bother to hold an inquiry into his dramatic demise. It was obvious to everyone that plain old ecstasy did him in. Life was cheap back then, up there, and no one much saw the point in asking a lot of damn-fool questions when all was as clear as clear could be. They knew what to do. They closed his eyes. There was no need to soften his mask by curling his mouth into a smile. In fact, his last expression was one of such delighted goofiness that they had to rearrange his features so he looked more decorous, more appreciative of the gravity of the moment. They carried him home, dressed him in his one decent suit, and laid him out in his parlour. Word spread. Neighbours dropped by to pay their respects. It was generally agreed that he looked at peace. Several even remarked how the strawberry spot on his left cheek was less angry in death, which wasn't surprising since Chas. had tended towards the florid in life. Some of the ladies brought over pies and casseroles and jellied salads. It was a demonstration more of custom than of charity; there was no one so grief-stricken as to wring comfort from eating to excess. Chas. lived alone. He had not been in the habit of having people round, had not encouraged visitors. Hardly any of the mourners could think of when they'd last been invited to his place. A simple house. Neat. They were glad to see he'd kept it up, that he hadn't let things slide since his wife up and left with that Bible salesman all those years ago. No one knew how to track her down, and they wouldn't have thought it appropriate to contact her even if they did. She'd always had a wild way about her. Some recollected that he had a sister, but she had moved to California and had come to a bad end. Some thought she might even have been divorced. Poor Chas.! He'd had bad luck with women, that's all there was to it. His life had been touched by sadness. Still, it was a tidy death, as deaths go.

Fifteen Thousand Useful Phrases was on the kitchen table where last he left it, held open by the butter dish. Someone leaned over and read aloud the whole of the phrase Chas. had marked but had not managed to fully utter, his last amen, the interrupted coda of his glorious incantation. *Like two doves with silvery wings, let our souls fly.*

"You know," said Joseph Flanagan, who was Chas.'s nearest neighbour, "he was straight as an arrow till he got hold of that book."

"Till it got hold of him, you mean." That was Ethel Parker who had as much right to say so as anyone, since she had made a point of inviting Chas. over for Christmas and Easter dinners until her own husband had died, after which it wouldn't have been seemly. She picked up the book, opened it randomly, and read out one of the marked similes.

Rage, rage ye tears, that never more should creep like hounds about God's footstool.

A sour pill, that one. Ethel pursed her lips and handed it over to Joseph, who also read aloud.

Me on whose heart as a worm she trod.

And passed it on. One by one, the good folk of Kenabeek located a phrase Chas. had found useful. One by one, they spoke his eulogy.

Silence now is brooding like a gentle spirit o'er the still and pulseless world.

Her heart has grown icy as a fountain in fall.

Sorrowful eyes like those of a wearied kine spent from plowing.

The dead past flew away over the fens like a flight of wild swans.

Suddenly snuffed out in the middle of ambitious schemes.

All my life broke up, like some great river's ice at touch of spring.

He snatched furiously at breath like a tiger snatching at meat.

Life had been arrested, as the horologist, with interjected finger, arrests the beating of the clock.

They did not, when they were through, feel they knew him any better. His life had been a puzzle. When all was said and done — and now it was — there wasn't much to be gained from piecing it together. They buried Chas. on Sunday, and before the week was done they had cleared out his house. There was not much worth keeping. The remnants of his wife's wardrobe — curiously, he'd held onto a few of her things — and some of his more colourful shirts were earmarked for the quilting circle. His chipped butter dish, his several plates and shaving mug, and his few books went for jumble. *Fifteen Thousand Useful Phrases* was purchased at a church sale just before Thanksgiving by someone's city cousin, an English teacher who happened to be visiting and wasn't acquainted with its sad history. She thought it might have some utility in the classroom. For a while, it did. Then, it travelled. It must have had many owners in the interim between then and now, but it will never have another during my lifetime. I number it among my treasures. I will never let it go. As near as I know, it is the only memorial to Chas., one of this country's great, if little-celebrated, oddballs.

When I began confiding to friends, acquaintances, and colleagues that I planned to investigate and write about the lives of some Canadian eccentrics, a disconcerting number of them arched speculative brows and asked, "Are there any?" That they had never heard of Chas. S. Robertson or Grenville Kleiser was neither astonishing nor disappointing. These gentlemen are my personal heroes. For me, they *are as amusing as a litter of likely young pigs.* Although I believe they merit wider attention than they have received, I accommodate the sad and present certainty that they are long since *gone like a glow on the cloud at the close of day* and are pivotal to no one's mythology but my own. However, it surprised and rather pained me to have my project and its broader possibilities so summarily dismissed, *as ruthlessly as the hoof of a horse tramples on a rose* by chums who are, in the main, *fresh and unworn as the sea that breaks languidly beside them.* I read in my friends' supercilious rebukes the subtext that I was setting out on a fool's errand; that the concepts "Canadian" and "eccentric" were wholly foreign to each other and would find no point of intersection. I stress that these initial consultants were not dolts. They were — they are — good people, *as delightful to the mind as cool well-water to thirsty lips.* They are responsible people, vigilant citizens, conscientious taxpayers, bearers of degrees from accredited post-secondary institutions, holders of enormous mortgages taken on for five-year spans at reasonable rates. They are people with mutual funds, people who flock to seminars on how best to squirrel away their hard-earned moolah for their retirements, which they plan to begin in their mid-fifties. They are dedicated consumers of culture. Oh hell, they are middle-aged, slightly jaded, somewhat educated, faintly agnostic, mostly pink-skinned city dwellers. They are people of my own tribe and they had disappointed me. For them, the phrase "Canadian eccentric" was oxymoronic, an exemplum of mutual exclusivity, *as unapproachable as a star.* It was strange, depressing even, to see implicit in this flippancy the way they subscribed to the frayed old notion that Canadians have a genetic propensity to eschew individualism, that we aspire as a nation only to a passive uniformity, that we trail clouds of blandness behind us where'er we walk, that we are a self-effacing folk: mildly humorous, peace-keeping, maple-tapping, syrup-sucking, snow-fort–building rustics. Meek? Sure! Proud to be! But we'll have our reward, by cracky! It'll take a team of apocalyptic horses to keep us from inheriting the Kingdom of Heaven, bucko, just you wait and see!

"Are there any?" I would echo the doubters, feeling in the moment *companionless as the last cloud of an expiring storm whose thunder is its knell.* "Well, what about Glenn Gould?"

"Oh. Yes. Well. Him. I suppose Gould, yes. And Mackenzie King. He was quite odd, wasn't he? Something to do with spiritualism, or his dog, or his mother, or Hitler. What was it? Did his mother have an affair with Hitler? Did *he?* And then there was Emily Carr. She kept that monkey. Gould, King, Carr. Who else? Well, there's always my uncle. He's a real case. He spends every weekend going to lawn sales, looking for back issues of *Majesty* magazine. He never buys anything else. His basement is stacked, floor to ceiling, with *Majesty* magazine. He also likes to speak in rhyming couplets. Of course, he was born in England. That's the place to find eccentrics!"

That England holds a world monopoly on eccentricity was another refrain I often heard sung as I began to make my discreet domestic inquiries, *like a moral lighthouse in the midst of a dark and troubled sea.* I would not for one second think of drawing bead on the tenet that the old sod (an endearment to which I myself aspire) has proved itself, over the last thousand years or so, a rich loam for the cultivation of human curiosities. I doubt that any social precipitate other than one that has oozed up over the centuries in Britain could have produced such outstanding examples of eccentricity as those catalogued by Edith Sitwell in her aptly odd (and aptly titled) book, *English Eccentrics: A Gallery of Weird and Wonderful Men and Women.* To read her florid prose is rather like coming home to discover that one's favourite old auntie has mistakenly eaten a whole plateful of hash brownies and is free-associating all over the attic. Cutting a wide swath through a rich trove of sources — dispensing, by and large, with the tedious convention of acknowledging them — Dame Edith tells the story of Mr. Jemmy Hirst, a tanner who went hunting on a bull, with pigs instead of hounds, and who kept his coffin in his dining room and whose eventual funeral procession was attended by pipers and fiddlers. Their music sustained the exertions of the eight stout widows who bore the pall. Widows were engaged in this labour only because eight willing old maids could not be found. It was old maids he'd hoped to employ. She recounts dozens of other remarkable lives, including that of Lord Duffus, who was spirited away by fairies and found himself in the wine cellar of the King of France; and the reprobate Squire John (Mad Jack) Mytton, who liked to go duck hunting in the nude, and who set his nightshirt on fire to cure himself of hiccups.

So much weirdness has flourished in England's green and pleasant land that it sets a standard which is hard to match, let alone beat. What tales can Canadians trot out that will not pale to invisibility when held up against such flamboyant exploits detailed by Dame Edith? More *outré* still is the cast assembled by Henry Wilson and James Caulfield in a sadly neglected Victorian tract called *The Book of Wonderful Characters: Memoirs and Anecdotes of Remarkable and Eccentric Persons in All Ages and Countries.* What does Glenn Gould with his summertime overcoat and agitated humming have to say to Francis Battalia the stone-eater, or to Joseph Capper the enemy of flies? What are Emily Carr's spiny strangenesses compared with those of Eve Fleigen, who lived on the smell of flowers? And can Mackenzie King, who merely talked to the dead, so much as hold a flickering candle to Charles Domery, the remarkable glutton?

Domery was a Pole by birth and a soldier by profession. He fought for the French, was captured by the English after one of those overwrought Napoleonic confrontations, and brought as a POW to Liverpool. His dietary insatiability attracted the attention of his captors, and little wonder. His appetites were legendary. As an enlisted man, he would supplement his camp rations with whatever he could find that was remotely edible. He would graze on four or five pounds of grass every day. In one year, he is reported to have stuffed himself with 174 cats (skinned). His face was badly scratched, as he did not always scruple to kill them before ingesting them. He ate rats. He dined on dogs. He was observed, after the pitched battle that brought about his ship's surrender to the English, to pick up another man's leg — it was not attached, as it had been shot off — and to gnaw on it contentedly until it was snatched away by a sailor of more refined sensibility, who chucked the offal overboard. It was nothing to Domery to wolf down, in a single sitting, a bullock's liver, three pounds of candles, and a few pounds of beef.

Curious to see just how much grub this ravenous prisoner could put away without doing himself harm, a committee from the English Admiralty — made up, we must suppose, largely of men with too much time on their hands and unfettered access to the larder — conducted an experiment. On September 17, 1799, at 4 a.m., Domery was awakened and allowed to chow down on four pounds of raw cow's udder. At the more respectable hour of 9.30 a.m., a small consortium of doctors and captains assembled and watched their prisoner go at breakfast in earnest.

"There was set before him five pounds of raw beef, and twelve tallow candles of a pound weight, and one bottle of porter; these he finished by half-past ten o'clock. At one o'clock there was again put before him five pounds of beef and one pound of candles, with three bottles of porter; at which time he was locked up in the room, and sentries placed at the windows to prevent his throwing away any of his provisions. At two o'clock he had nearly finished the whole of the candles, and a great part of the beef, but had neither evacuation by vomiting, stool, or urine; his skin was cool, and pulse regular, and [he was] in good spirits."

Glenn Gould, for his part, ate a moderate, low-fat diet.

"Aha!" my considerate detractors would cry, assailing me with *windy speech which hits all around the mark like a drunken carpenter.* "Our point exactly! We rest our case! Devotion to tofu is admirable, but not nearly so tasty a lure as a slab of raw bullock's liver. And while we're scattering nails in your path, let's ask another troublesome but necessary question. What do you mean by 'eccentric,' anyway? To define 'eccentric' don't you need to define 'normalcy'? Surely that puts you in the express lane to peril."

The words of the wise fall like the tolling of sweet, grave bells upon the soul. What could I do but shrug and let them fall? I had already made up my mind to proceed. In my heart of hearts, I never doubted for a second that all I had to do to drag up instances of eccentric people and places in Canada was to cast a wide-enough net. I was as confident as Christ at Tiberias that it would come back teeming. If there is one thing I've learned over the years I have spent listening to, and now and again working for, the radio services of our public broadcaster, the CBC, it is that the numbing onslaught of information, the noisy parade of news and commentary to which we are daily subjected, has not dulled our need to flesh out the verb "to be."

We are a people — or at least there are numbers of people among us — who like to take stock of our lives, to wrap them up and give them away as stories. There is still a hunger for narrative in the land, and all the anecdotal evidence presented to me over the years suggests we are as fond of receiving such gifts as we are of giving them. I have sometimes been in the happy and privileged position of having a pulpit from which to encourage such an exchange. Demonstrate an interest in the real and everyday lives of real and everyday people, and demonstrate that you will honour their lives simply by taking them seriously, and the stories will come, *fluent as a rill that wanders silver-footed down a hill.* I have learned enough about the imperative of narrative to know, or to be able to predict with some accuracy, that if you open yourself up to hearing the stories we like best to tell — the stories about the people in our families or neighbourhoods who distinguish themselves by their peculiarities, who perplex and delight us because they are so different from us — then willing tellers of tales will present themselves, and in numbers *impressive as a warrant of arrest for high treason.* Canada itself is so unlikely a proposition — this long, thin band of bickering population strung out necklace-like in clusters mainly across the southern reaches of a hugely ponderous land mass — that it wouldn't be so much of a stretch to attach the sobriquet "eccentric" to the political entity as a whole.

While no one, on anything like serious reflection, could cleave for long to the ridiculous credo that this is a country held together by a thin paste of devotion to monochromatic geniality, a country that by its very nature is inimical to displays of eccentricity, it would also be a mistake to think that the ferreting-out of stories scribbled in the margins will necessarily add an attractive gloss to our ideas of nationhood. Shout "eccentric" often enough into the air, and the words of John Stuart Mill will come walloping back as an echo. In *On Liberty* he wrote, "Precisely because the tyranny of opinion is such as to make eccentricity a reproach, it is desirable, in order to break through that tyranny, that people should be eccentric. Eccentricity has always abounded when and where strength of character has abounded; and the amount of eccentricity in a society has generally been proportional to the amount of genius, mental vigour, and moral courage it contained. That so few dare to be eccentric marks the chief danger of the time."

This is good stuff, delicious to cite and self-contained, exactly the sort of high-humanist pith a librarian would stitch up as a sampler, or a civil-liberties agency would get silk-screened onto tea towels or T-shirts to sell at fund-raisers. Because John Stuart Mill said it, and because most of us know that we should recognize his name even if we can't say particularly why, we impute to his sloganeering the quality of authority. Why? After all, he was only writing and it isn't as though writing doesn't have its own dumb-ass exigencies. He was as concerned with the balance and music of his words, as concerned with their aesthetic impact as he was with illuminating the Truth. Whatever *that* might be. He was riffing. He was on a roll. He was in love with the sound of his own sermonizing voice in his own head, and anyway he had a reputation to sustain. Opinion spewing was his whole *raison d'être*. What's more, he had bills to pay. He had a publisher sending threatening letters. He'd spent the advance. He had a headache, he was constipated, the milk was sour, the coal was gone, the cat knocked over the inkpot, the maid was surly, he thought he might have syphilis, God only knows, and 150 years later we nod sagely and say "Hmmmm. Yes. Yes."

I don't think there's any more reason to run Mill's flag up the pole and salute it than there is to embrace the like-minded but lesser-known words of Henry Wilson and James Caulfield, who attained the specious sanctity of print when they compiled the aforementioned *Book of Wonderful Characters*. It was their opinion that "we have nearly lost all, and are daily losing what little remains of our individuality; all people and all places seem now to be alike; and the railways are, no doubt, the principal cause of this change. For railway stations, all over the world, seem to have a strong, we might almost call it family, resemblance to each other...." No doubt the railways led to a certain homogenization, as did the expanding network of adequate roads, as did the proliferation of cars, as did the emergence of the many mind-grasping tentacles of media. Any agent that brings us closer together carries with it a certain pressure to conform. We are deeply social creatures, and we resist the urge to do anything that might set us apart from the group. But that same agent also bears on its back the opposite number, which is the more theatrical urge to stand apart from the throng. I am, I am, I am, beats the labouring heart. We harbour alongside our need to belong, perhaps in lesser measure, a need to assert selfhood; it is part of us, it is in our blood. We find a way to do it, even if only through so mild and private an expedient as wearing our underwear inside out. There is no one who could not be called, in some way, eccentric. A few are taken over by it. A few make it a life's work. They are conspicuous, easy to see. But look hard enough, and at just the right angle, and you will find other stories. They are everywhere. For my purposes, for better or worse, it is the stories that matter, in and of themselves. My responsibility is to query, to find, to listen, and to tell. I leave it to others to extrapolate clues as to the state of the nation.

I untoothed the venomous question of definition, that is, What does "eccentric" mean?, by shrugging it off. I have chosen not to worry about it. This was not so much a product of intellectual laziness — although I would never deny that my deficiencies of brain are many and that their number is on the rise — as it was of a decision not to be prescriptive or proscriptive, not to limit the field by presenting a series of fixed and numbered dots which, if joined, would make the picture of an eccentric. The dictionary was a sufficient anchor for me. "Eccentric." From the Latin *eccentricus*, out of the centre. Also the Greek *kentros*, the centre, and *ek*, out of. What could be more succinct or descriptive? I would search out stories of people whose lives veered away from the comfortable middle ground. I would collect stories of both the living and the dead. I would be broad in my definition of "Canadian," since the historical record is thick with names of personages whose extraordinary adventures took place somewhere in the country we now call Canada, and are of necessity part of our collective story, but who were not by nationality Canadian. I dispensed right away with any idea of all-embracing inclusivity. Even if such an inventory were possible, the end product would prove to be little more than an annotated list, possibly supplemented by illustrations, which is a snore-provoking prospect if ever there was one. Instead, I chose to rely on my favourite research methodology, which is to leave everything to chance and simply pay attention to rumour. I would inflate a trial balloon, inscribe it with a question, and float it right across the country. Who do you know who is or was eccentric? Feel free to nominate yourself. That would be the extent of my specificity. Whatever names were forwarded by those scattered individuals who just happened to hear of the project in whatever way and had the time or inclination to contact me would serve as the basis for my investigation. My job would be to check out reported sightings. I knew full well that the imperfections in such a technique would make social scientists and ethnographers run screaming from the room. So be it, I thought. They can write their own damn books to their own pernickety standards. Furthermore, I decided I would visit as many of the nominees as possible, which would require that I travel across the country. Considerations that were purely practical and professional dictated that I would do this during the months of January and February. While this is not the season most ideally suited to tripping about north of the 49th parallel, and while there was a general consensus among those most likely to benefit materially from my death that I was mad to even think about such an undertaking, I went ahead and booked the time off work. I got a post office box. I got an e-mail address. I gassed up the balloon, tested the prevailing winds, and sent it off. I sat back and waited for word.

The first letter to arrive came from an anonymous source in Regina. I transcribe it here in its every detail:

Today everybody who is CULTURED and EDUCATED is an eccentric, that is what I am called, because 90% of Canadians are uncultured and uneducated as well as unsophisticated and unrefined.

Canadians fuck into every hole they can get a handle on, kill their offsprings, murder and steal by breaking into other people's houses. THAT is CANADIAN CULTURE, and everybody who is vice from this and a bit sophisticated on top of it is an eccentric, because he does not fit into the norm.

So, here you are! Now you know Canadian eccentrism! And everybody is ridiculed by wearing necklase, earrings and a proper outfit is laughed at and called an ECCENTRIC.

Beside, what do you want with other people's stories? to make money by publishing a book from other people's material and gaining from it. You are a mental burgelar.

The veiled future bowed before me like a vision of promise. Any doubts I might have entertained about the viability of the project were blasted out of the clear blue sky with this finely nuanced missive from the heartland. *They broke into pieces and fell on the ground, like a silvery, shimmering shower of hail.* There was nowhere to go from here but up. I called the airline. I booked a ticket (one-way) to Toronto. I bought a pair of long johns and some Bermuda shorts. I polished my St. Christopher medal and began to collect all the Glenn Gould tapes I could muster. Before I knew it, December was at an end. *The gloom of winter dwelt on everything.* It was time to begin.

A Folly in Paradise

...a fool layeth open his folly.
— Proverbs 13:16

I am Sleep's courtesan. His slave. His talisman and harem favourite. His elected slut and tart *du jour*. Don't ask how this came to pass, what I did to merit his attentions. I have no idea. It was nothing I asked for. I can only suppose that Sleep, passing others by, spotted me in the cradle and sniffed some ineffable quality that made his loins boil over. He stopped. He kissed me. He made me his. My one true lover. Lusty autocrat. Irascible demagogue. Unkind master. He metes out his humiliations willy-nilly, whether I'm at home or in the most public of circumstances. He'll have his way with me at a lecture or a play or a movie. At a dinner party, where I might turn from my interlocutor and fall face forward into the *crème caramel*. He has even intervened while I'm making love. He'll come calling any old time at all to assert his randy primacy. He is rapacious, voracious. Insatiable. I adore him. I hate him. I wouldn't have it any other way.

Sleep loves to travel. Buses, cars, trains, planes, it doesn't matter a damn. Directly we're in motion, my dauntless companion is all over me, suffocating me with caring. The poor sod sitting next to me, in 27B, has no idea that I am being raped as we climb towards 35,000 feet. How could he? I'm the soul of decorum. I neither struggle nor flinch. My seat-back is upright, my tabletop securely fastened. The *ceinture de sécurité* is neatly cinched. Everything tuckable is tucked. There are no outward signs of my appalling circumstances. This is a pity, for if my assigned partner in altitude understood all that was unfolding beside him, he would surely be more tolerant of the incursions of this stranger who lolls on his shoulder, trickling spittle and fetidly exhaling.

En route from Toronto to St. John's, Newfoundland. The year is new. The day is cold. The sky is clear. Somnolent before the wheels leave the tarmac, I dream that we are passing through the ghost of Glenn Gould. I know with a vain oneirocritical certainty that this is so, even though there is nothing about the apparition that's reminiscent of Gould in his terrestrial incarnation. His ghost is more "Star Trek" than Dickens, a vast and amorphous protoplasmic film. It is suspended in the stratosphere, like a jellyfish in a tidal pool. Phantoms are said to wander, but there is nothing transient about this spectre. No, it is fixed longitudinally in space. This is its permanent address. Exempt from even momentary appropriation, it doesn't care to budge or sidewind. The nose cone of the plane penetrates its midriff and it neither dissolves nor shatters nor rends, but stretches on and on, a kind of indefatigable taffy, dimensionless, self-regenerating, complete, linking the tangible earth with the limitless sky. Its only response to penetration is sonic: not a Jacob Marley rattling of chains, but a spill of voices, an articulate cascade like the one Gould orchestrated in his celebrated radio documentary, *The Idea of North*. It was a brilliant concept, a fugal composition for voices that was revolutionary in its day and remains both startling and wholly unlistenable, an aggregative and aggravating weave of narratives. Rising above the babble, I hear two clear phrases in a voice that might be my own. Old land, new country. Old land, new country. Then, the flight attendant's chirpy and reviving interrogative: Peanuts? How could so significant a ghost be exorcised with so mundane a spell? Much to the relief of 27B, I lurch awake and take the snack, wrest open the recalcitrant cellophane with my teeth, and down the pale, stale nuggets in a single gulp.

The word "saline" surfaces in my fudgy brain, borne along

on the salty wake of aftertaste. "Saline" morphs to "Salus," which comes from the Greek *salos*, which means foolish. "Salus" was the descriptor given to one of the St. Simeons. There were several of these, the most famous being the pillar-sitting hermit St. Simeon Stylites, who is said to have lived for thirty-seven years in the desert on a platform he installed atop a column. Originally, his pillar was ten feet tall. As word of his exploits got out, he was swarmed by copycat hermits, all of them eager for a piece of the action. The *arrivistes* were a nuisance. They set up their own columns in Simeon's sandy backyard and threatened his solitude. They intruded on his silence. They lobbed plea after plea in his direction. They wanted shortcuts to enlightenment. They wanted construction hints. There was nothing for it but to undertake renovations. Simeon built his pillar higher. And higher. And higher still. By the time he was done and his burnished soul was sundered from his flesh, he had a commanding view of the surrounding dunes from an altitude of sixty feet.

St. Simeon Salus is a lesser character in the Roman martyrologies. He was born in Egypt, round about 522, and lived a solitary life in the Sinai for twenty-nine years. Eventually, when he was about sixty, he made his way to the Syrian city of Emesa. There he had a ready audience for the antics that would one day make the hagiographers sit up and take note. Unlike his brother Stylites, he didn't tempt gravity. Nor would anyone have called him grounded. He was just about as flighty as they come. He became a fool for God. He could be seen wandering about the streets of Emesa, dragging a dead dog on a rope, babbling happily to himself, eating dirt. One day, thanks to that internal seismic measuring device with which cats and holy men are blessed, he sensed a terrible earthquake in the offing. He walked through the town, rapping with a lash on various columns (none of which, as near as we know, was sustaining the weight of high-flying hermits), and saying to them, "Thus saith the Lord: you will stay standing. Thus saith the Lord: you will fall down." And sure enough, when the earthquake rocked the foundations of Emesa in 588, it was with the columns just as Salus had said it would be. Iconographers have pictured him surrounded by children. The little ones watch wide-eyed while he huffs into a sixth-century balloon. Balloons, pillars, earthquakes, a willing fool: it all makes for an engaging story, but what I like best about Simeon Salus is that his feast day is July 1. Canada Day. Oh, Canada. There. Look. In the window, a pale, transparent face. My own, of course. Not so much a ghost as a Salus balloon caught up in the jet stream. Below, a curve of earth, an accidental amalgam of mineral and water, a blotter onto which we've spilled the idea of a country. A fool's paradise. The idea of north.

My mind canters in a pre-Newtonian corral. Laws of motion? Elementary concepts of physics? Feh! Don't even speak to me of such high-school fripperies! I choose to believe that a plane stays aloft because of an act of collective will. If, for even one second, all we passengers were to abandon our belief that these several tons of metal are capable of sustaining us at this height, we would plummet to earth like a buckshot-riddled mallard. And this country where I've been pleased to live my whole life long, and above which now I hang, is likewise nothing more than an act of imagination, of irrational belief. In these latter days, we're not much given to taking sustenance from imagination. We'd rather a diet of proof. We'd rather see and name every rivet. Nonetheless, the country holds. Against every reasonable expectation, and on the strength of imagination alone, so far, it holds. Old land. New country. I mouth these words to my shivering, exiled *doppelgänger*, close my eyes, and drift.

Whatever his other gifts, it must be said that Sleep is a lousy mime. Death is the only charade he can successfully pull off. Since Sleep left his vampire love bites on my neck when I was still floating in the rushes — and since I have been all these years his tasty bit, his cherished piece of tail — I have very often had to sit through performances of his single party piece. Little wonder, considering these influences, that I was precocious when it came to courting intimations of mortality. Anyone would think my mother had spent her pregnancy reading the drearier sermons of Donne. As a child, I would spend many happy hours imagining the circumstances that would see me pulling up to the door of the Hotel Terminus. A solitary soul, I played a private game. On hot summer afternoons, when the unhaltered south wind bucked its way over the flatlands, when I was bored with the more savoury recreations of dashing through the sprinkler and peeing onto anthills, I would position myself upright in the middle of the lawn, extend my arms to their fullest width, and spin around and around and around, a tubby gyroscope, before surrendering to the depredations of gravity. I'd collapse onto that well-tended square of green and urbanized prairie, let it absorb my giddiness while the vertigo-inducing inner-ear fluids splashed and settled in their delicate, Eustachian canals. I'd stare up at the same thin stretch of timpanic blue through which now I fly: a screen behind which God sat, conniving with His angels. To see them face to face! What a tempting prospect! So many questions would be answered. I would lie there and imagine my death, would turn face downward and inhale the earth, and think of all the possible ways and means of achieving ending, all the grim and pleasant catalogue.

How and where and why would it happen? A brakeless bus, a limping heart, a stumble on a high cliff, a rusty nail, irascible hiccups? Yes, even that was possible. I knew, for I'd seen it. When next-door Mr. Magnuson came down with the hiccups one morning, he and his wife just supposed he was drawing the wages of gobbling his oatmeal. No one would have guessed that before the week was out he would dig his own grave with his intemperate gulping, that he would hick [sic] the bucket without ever having recourse to Squire Mytton's drastic pyrotechnic therapy. Oh, yes. You didn't have to look far to see that Death would come. When and how were the only variables. I was full of childish impatience to know. Let it happen now, I would think, now, when I am as happy as this! But here I am, decades later, telling the tale. Dig in childhood's littered midden and you'll find the shards of shattered wishes. Come to think of it, I never got a pony, either.

The irony is that now that I am of an age when arteries can be counted on to implode, when rogue tumours (always the size of a golf ball or grapefruit) could rear up and overthrow the body's careful government, I am entirely unprepared for that great day's dawning. If this buoyant craft were to shudder and fall, achieving homonymic unity with the plain, I'd perish intestate. I've left no instructions, other than having once muttered something on the radio about how I'd rather be planted than incinerated. This prompted a woman from Qualicum Beach to send a note saying she hoped I would persevere in this line of thinking. Cremation, she told me, "is a horrid, painful happening. The extreme heat burns all your aura which will be the support, ground, in your new existence. No guardian angel can help you. It is your will which is supremely Godly. The two most awful acts God and heavenly angels cannot do anything about are suicide and cremation."

Heavens to Betsy! There are days when it's worth your life to open the mail. Still, it's always a good idea to hedge your bets. What if she was right? I had never bothered to pass the scoop along to someone with the power to influence the disposition of my remains. What were the chances my court-appointed executors would find her letter among my effects and put two and two together? I would put them on a par with the chances that, should I die in a car wreck, the celebrant at my service would think to speak the only words I care to have uttered in such an eventuality: He suffered and died under Pontiac pile-up.

"It is better to be ready to die and live than to die and not be ready," said Professor Charles Henry Danielle, whose end days were an encomium to just such morbid preparedness. He was born in the United States, but severed his links with the earth in Newfoundland. The Professor — for that is what he was called, both fondly and derisively by the people among whom he landed as an exotic alien and to whom he was always an object of considerable curiosity — died not where but as he wished. He boarded the coach for heaven at Octagon Castle, the eight-sided palazzo he had designed as a resort and erected on a pond near Irvine station, which was next door to Paradise, which was then about two hours by train from St. John's. He died in his own bed, with his customized coffin in an adjacent room. Danielle was a true Son of Salus, a *fin-de-siècle* crank who just managed, like Queen Victoria, to overlap the new century. His spirit flew the coop in the spring of 1902, when he was seventy-one and a half years old to the day, and just a couple of months shy of launching his seventh season as the island's most celebrated hotelier.

It was neither an unexpected nor an untimely death. He himself had predicted it, and with eerie accuracy. A pioneer in the art of public relations, he customarily distributed, free of charge, a descriptive booklet, detailing for prospective customers the many delights afforded by a visit to the Octagon. "Pleasant rooms are provided, with a liberal table, and tourists may find here a peaceful home for a brief or a prolonged stay. The views from the Octagon are at once extensive and beautiful. A landscape for twenty miles in extent is presented to the eye, including Conception Bay, in which may, far into the Summer, be seen icebergs, and lovely lakes, meadows and forests, with all the lights and shadows by which the sun lights up this beautiful land." And so on. At the end of the 1901 edition of his pamphlet, the Professor offered this adumbration: "It is more than probable, this spring booklet…will be the last from my pen that the intelligent public of Newfoundland will ever be amused at, or a lot of others disgusted with. I am a victim and a sufferer from a VERY BAD CASE of valvular heart trouble, and cannot live long, according to all medical opinions and my own knowledge of my condition….CHAS. H. DANIELLE. Octagon Castle. May 1st, 1901."

None of his readers was taken aback at this news. None was surprised. How could one expect otherwise? He had already hung on for more than his allotted span of three score and ten. He was living on borrowed time. The bloom was gone from his rose. Anyway, it was well known round about that Danielle's relationship with robust good health was at best flirtatious. Certain prophylactic measures might have sustained him. Anyone in his situation who had a vested interest in continuance could abjure activity, give himself over to leisurely days and tranquil nights punctuated by herbal infusions and recuperative meditations. But the Professor, a veteran showman, was undeterred by the thickening and slowing of his own vapours. In the best tradition of the show going on, he averted his gaze from the imminence of his ending. He welcomed excursionists from near and far to his castle for one last summer. As always, they came. As always, there was a crowd. The Professor was partial to self-aggrandizement through statistics, and by his own figuring and boasting: "The Octagon covers 3,750 square feet of ground; it has 10,180 square feet of inside floor surface. Allowing 18 square inches for each person, it can shelter 6,756 persons at one and the same time. There are 420 chairs in the Octagon and more are ordered. There are 84 windows in the Octagon, and 43 doors. The 3 lower front rooms are paneled, 4 feet from the floor, with 344 panels. There are 9,979 running feet of moulding in the building. Every foot of this moulding the Professor has gone over with 3 coats of Aspinal's enamel. It took 1,040 yards of wall cotton to cover the walls of the various rooms, and over 25,000 tacks to hold it there; 5,480 blocks of the best wallpaper cover the walls — no two blocks being alike. There are curiosities and artistic draperies to be seen at the Octagon that are to be seen nowhere else in Newfoundland, or at few other resorts on earth."

Oh, the measuring, the hammering, the fumes from the Aspinal's enamel! His poor old wheezing heart! By his reckoning, 9,927 visitors had come to the Octagon during the 1900 season, and he expected to entertain at least that many in this, his final go-round. Madness for a man in his condition! Surely his doctor told him so, surely even the servants, over whom he ran roughshod, ventured a word. He was heedless of their counsel. He forged on. All summer long he worked to ensure that the outdoor fêtes and picnics of the various societies, clubs, lodges, Sunday schools, and churches he suffered to come unto him went off without a hitch. Not only did he treat them splendidly when they arrived, but he immortalized their outings by stitching up "large Satin Banners, elaborately embroidered and bespangled in gold and silver [and bearing] symbolic letters of the gatherings they commemorate, so all may be read." Failing though he was, he didn't break with his custom of entertaining the Church of England orphans, turning over the grounds to them on a given afternoon, and sending them away with fond memories and pockets full of sweets. The Anglican teachers came to the castle, as was their custom. Temperance societies turned up, reassured by his promise that they would find the Octagon "as free from the sight, sound, taste or smell of spirits as the WCTU...the Bar-room and Wine-room will be locked and sealed if they but express the wish." The Odd Fellows put into port, as did the Dudley Lodge of the Sons of England, whose party numbered 200 people, and whose sentiments were in no way prohibitionist. "JOLLY DAY AT THE OCTAGON" read the next day's newspaper headline, and the accompanying story makes it clear that the verb "to stint" had been stricken from every Son of England's lexicon for the day. Directly the Sons (and, one imagines, their female adjuncts) arrived, they broke into teams and went at a football match "as if their lives depended on it." They played cricket, too, "the contesting teams being formed by W. Edney and J. Harris. Here, it was hard to decide who won for in the midst of the game tea was announced. Needless to say the Professor had done his best and was eminently successful. The delicacies obtainable at this season were soon disposed of and with appetites sharpened by the clear pure air of the country, full justice was done." They stayed late into the night, dancing to music provided by Professor Powers' band, and didn't allow their host to retire until well after midnight. They sang patriotic songs all the way home.

However deleterious the effects of these wee-hour revels on the Professor's leaky valves, it surely did the SOE a world of good to come to the Octagon and romp with such careless abandon. Ever since the century turned, the papers had been full of nothing but dreadful news. The Boer War. The Boxer Rebellion. The seductive, subversive whisperings of confederationists.

The world! The world! It was more than a healthy heart could bear, never mind one constricted and worn by years of hard work and disappointment. The Professor took in all this news — he must have read the papers, if only to scan them for news of himself — and still he pressed on. He wrote a little poem that made his life seem a regular breeze:

> Just six things are requisite
>   To make the Octagon sunny,
> One is a cook, that is a cook,
>   The other five are money.

Of course, there was much more to it. Simply inspecting the quality of the dusting would tax the strength of a young and healthy man. His was a house of many mansions. The ceiling in the rotunda was thirty feet high. There was a private dining room, a reading room, a smoking room, a music room, a bagatelle room, a card room, and a barn with room for eight horses. To prepare himself for his last innkeeping summer on earth, the Professor had supervised the construction of seven new salons, including "a Blue Chamber, a Pink Chamber, a Yellow Chamber, a Crimson Chamber, and a Lace Chamber, all true to their names and elaborately embellished. There is not a room in the Castle that is not furnished in satin draperies, with gold and silver trimmings. Even the rooms in the servants' quarters have satin window lambrequins, while their beds have the same spring, wool, and hair mattresses and furnishings as the rooms in the Octagon itself." The servants were an ongoing concern and required his vigilance. They were so well schooled in the domestic arts — taught by Danielle himself — that other grasping agencies were forever trying to lure them away with ridiculous offers.

Horticulture brought its demands and influence to bear. The Professor oversaw the cultivation of seventy-five gallons of strawberries, from choice new varieties of American plants, as well as the tending of the gardens that made it possible for the kitchen shelves to groan under the weight of 800 pounds of home-made jams. He made a daily tour of inspection to check on his four cold-storage plants to see that the hundred tons of lake ice he had put in store was sustaining itself against the beating of the August sun. Likewise, he ascertained that the miraculous beverage-cooling device he had installed — and there was not another one like it anywhere in Newfoundland — was keeping its frosty promise. Angered by accusations that he was watering down his milk, he issued a sensible disclaimer that his dairy herd, by way of some grievous congenital defect, had developed overly porous hides, thus allowing water in. To safeguard against future leakage of rain into their milk, he had tiny bovine-friendly roofs constructed for their use. These he caused to be strapped onto the backs of the willing cows.

Summer took a powder. One morning he woke up, and it was *gone like tenants that quit without warning.* The touristic flood slowed to a trickle. He caught up on his correspondence. He continued to write away to fabric companies for free samples, continued to plan how he would use their swatches to do over yet another room. With enough cunning, you could project the impression of tremendous opulence and wealth and do it on the cheap. Illusion, illusion, that was the thing! It was the promise and possibility of illusion that had sustained him, all these years. Now, however, his body was overtaking his will. It was a long winter. The Professor's powers dwindled steadily. According to his obituary in the St. John's *Evening Telegram*, he was under the constant care of Dr. Mackenzie, but was always acutely cognizant that his long-term prospects were far from cheery. He knew full well "that there was no medical agent that could save him, and had therefore made all preparations for his burial. His system became greatly weakened by lack of sleep. One peculiarity of his disease was that, when in a lying position or sleeping, a suffocating sensation would come in the throat, of which the sufferer is always in dread. On Thursday evening last there was a relapse and the Professor knew he could never rally again....Mr. S. G. Collier was called to the Octagon to receive instructions as to the burial. His casket was made by himself and was a magnificent piece of work."

The splendour of the coffin was well known and amply celebrated, and not just in St. John's or Carbonear or Harbour Grace, either. *Scenic Magazine*, published in Portland, Maine, had given over precious column inches to describing the Byzantine grandeur of Danielle's château, and of his coffin in particular. In an article published shortly before the Professor's death — too soon, really, for him to have enjoyed whatever tourist dollars that might have found their way to his counting-house on account of it — an American reporter draws back the curtain on what was certainly the most widely touted of the Octagon's many features. On the building's third floor, he writes, "is a large, square room that is kept locked; it is called the mortuary chamber. It is draped in black velvet embroidered in gold. In the center of this room is a catafalque, covered with black velvet trimmed in white satin, on which rests the most elaborate casket the writer has ever seen. The casket is covered with black satin beautifully embroidered in gold, while the interior is upholstered with 7,800 white satin shells. A fluted satin pillow filled with eiderdown is at the head, while a white satin shroud and golden slippers lie within, ready for the body of the strange man. All this burial outfit is the work of the man it is waiting for. At the head of the casket, hanging upon a wall, is a gilt frame encircling a sheet of paper on which is written, 'In the back of this Frame will be found Full instructions to be followed Immediately after my Death.'"

The Professor's hour came and went. The document was dislodged from the frame, and not for the first time, either. Vandals had snitched it on at least two previous occasions, had stolen the record of his wishes away and snickered at it with their friends in some foul-smelling bar. "Full," as it turned out, was too slight a word to bear on its back the heft of his instructions. They were the work of a controlling sensualist, a man who wanted more than anything to be both an active participant in his own laying-out and chief mourner at his own funeral. Mr. S. G. Collier, the undertaker, who had been a regular visitor to the Octagon over the years, who was indeed the president of the Dudley Lodge of the Sons of England, followed the five pages of instructions in their every finicky particular.

"1st My Body to be washed & dressed in a suit of new cotton Underclothing & a White top shirt & collar, the white Satin Shroud, which buttons up the back, in dressing the body do not roll it over with the face on the Table or bed, but place a pillow under the Head."

He furthermore admonishes that they be "careful that the mouth is closed with the head resting on a Pillow. Tie the feet with a bandage, so they will be upright & not spread....During the days & nights of my 'Waking' I particularly request & Hope there will be *none* of the Unseemly & out-of-place mirth which is too often a part of the last solemn rites here in Newfoundland."

Poor Danielle! A devout Christian, and an artist to boot, stranded on this barren rock, with no one to keep him company but a legion of party-mad, spirit-swilling, loutish heathen. He died on the first of May, and was shortly thereafter consigned to the clay. (Mercifully, his sustaining aura was spared the damaging heat of ovens.) On the day he reverted to dust, a Sunday, there were still tattered, wind-whipped ribbons, bright as flames, unbraiding themselves from various poles on various greens. Nubile Newfoundland maidens had wrapped them there, had capered and twined at the very hour of his leave-taking. None of them, we can safely guess, gave the embittered, dried-up man in his folly in Paradise a second's thought as she pranced around and around the phallic columns. The light touch of flesh as they passed under one another's arms made them long for a more significant pressing, for heat, for salt, for the taste of something like cod. His systems were shutting down, one after the other. He had just heart enough left to worry that some slatternly visitor — for this had been known to happen, and more than once, too — had climbed into his coffin during this time of his indisposition, had failed to wipe her shoes, had soiled the silken scallops. The cheek of it! The wench who would do such a thing was no better than the common trash who had snatched photographs from the wall and torn them into pieces; had stolen his silver jug, marked "Royal." All this had happened in his own home, under his very nose. Who knew what might be transpiring as he lay there, fighting for air. He would have clutched at his throat, had he had the strength to lift his hand. He felt himself suffocating, and this time it was for real. He tried to call out, but his voice was lost in the rattle that says finis. Somewhere nearby, the cool virgins skipped and twirled and sang "Tra la," and all the while their young blood simmered.

The funeral cortège was to come down Prescott Street. One can't help but feel sorry for Daniel Mulrooney, a sergeant of the Western Fire Station, who was buried on the same day. Officers came out for him, came out in all their regalia, and they tolled the fire bell, too. But Mulrooney's obsequies paled before the hoopla accorded the Professor, whose dying was acknowledged by the presence of representatives of the bar, the bench, the professions, commerce, the press, and many, many run-of-the-mill citizens. Oh, there was a crowd! Perhaps the organ grinder who had recently arrived from Port-aux-Basques with his monkey played to keep them all amused while they lined the pavement and waited. There was a long delay before the procession hove into view. Fathers held their children in the air so they could catch a glimpse of the man of the hour — his full head of hair, his imperious nose, his artistic beard, his spotless shroud — through the coffin's glass top. The neglected May Day ribbons crackled in the air as the spectators oohed and aahed at the splendour of it all. The ribbons still snapped as they headed home for tea. Some — no more than a few — might have reflected on the irony that, while the old fellow's death and disposal were incendiarily innocent, his life on earth had been dogged by fire. Fire would trail his legend, too, like a comet's tail. Thirteen years later, in circumstances some would call "mysterious," the Octagon would burn to the ground, and the stories of the enigmatic Danielle would be hauled out again, and undergo the fond regilding accorded to oft-told tales.

Octagon Castle was the last of Danielle's several Newfoundland hurrahs. It was opened in a grand ceremony held on June 18, 1896. *The Evening Telegram* recorded it as "a red-letter day....Sir Wm. Whiteway [the premier of the colony] formally declared it open in the afternoon, at 4.30, in a few happy words in which he paid tribute to the manner in which the genial professor had exercised his energy and taste in placing such a lovely resort at the service of the public....The wish of all seemed to be that success and prosperity might attend this venture of Mr. Danielle, to which the professor responded in his own inimitable manner. The gathering was immense, and the professor ably sustained his reputation as a caterer of the first water. Mr. Vey took some excellent photos of the proceedings. Prof. Powers' band discoursed sweet strains during the evening. Everybody and his wife was there, and boating and other amusements were indulged in during the day. We trust that this will be the commencement of a long reign for the 'Octagon' as one of the best holiday resorts that this country possesses, and a boon that the tired worker of this city will not forget to appreciate."

That Danielle was able to broker the construction of so stately a pleasure dome — the total cost was more than $20,000 — and that he could attract so sizeable and so eminent a crowd to its opening tell us something about his standing in the community. Keenly aware that he had a reputation to sustain, he spared no expense to equip the Octagon with every sybaritic accessory. Visitors stepped from the fresh Atlantic breeze into a torrid opium dreamscape, the rooms festooned with — in Danielle's own words — "hundreds of yards of satin, thousands of yards of tinsel, and hundreds and thousands of spangles." Of particular note was the honeymoon suite, described in one finely observant contemporary account as "a bower of satin, lace and plush, all dazzling in gold and silver, while on the bed is a quilt composed of small shells of satin, of every imaginable color, adroitly put together, each shell overlapping the other, like the scales of a fish, and not a stitch is visible. It took 2-1/2 years to complete this quilt; it contains 8,500 yards of satin and is valued at $700."

There were 19,832 individual pieces of fabric in that bedspread. But however splendid the chamber, and however lavish its accoutrements, this intended site of maidenhead disposal became a focal point for the Professor's growing ennui and impatience with the stubborn refusal of the locals to live up to the standards he had set for them. Once, a young and blushing couple turned up at his door. Even though the ink was still wet on their marriage certificate, even though they stood on the cusp of *l'heure exquise*, they showed no sign of being anxious to consummate their union. They lingered overlong by the fire in one of the sumptuous downstairs parlours. Danielle, thinking they surely must be longing to steal away for a night of connubial bliss, but were too delicate to reveal their carnal eagerness, suggested subtly that he might show them where to "find the chamber." The bridegroom simply shrugged the kindness off, saying, "That's all right, sir, just show it to the woman, I'll do mine out the window." At one point, he is said to have thrown up his hands in despair at the paltry receipts he was able to bring in from renting to newlyweds. He declared he would turn the suite over to the rearing of hogs. He could make more money from pig husbandry than from piggish husbands.

Even if Newfoundland in the early years of the century was not populated by women who would fondly remember the night of their deflowering in the beautifully adorned room at the Octagon, the quilt, like the coffin, became an object of veneration and visitation for the castle's many day-trippers. Not only was Danielle a dab hand with needle and thread, not only was he an interior designer and caterer *par excellence*; he was a dancer. In fact, he was a dancer first and foremost. It was in this capacity, and as a teacher of the Terpsichorean arts, that he first presented himself to the people of Newfoundland. The precise date of his glorious advent on the rock is not certain. Michael Francis Harrington, who provided the entry on Danielle in the *Dictionary of Canadian Biography*, and has written about him elsewhere, suggests that he first turned up in St. John's in the 1860s, and that he might have been drawn there by news reports of Cyrus West Field, the quixotic American business-man who around that time was trying to lay a transatlantic cable to the island. While there seem to be no exact data on when and why he came, and how long he stayed initially, it is clear that this first excursion was the beginning of an "on again, off again" love–hate relationship with the place.

He was a man with ambi-tion, he was a man with in-sight, and he was a man with portable skills. He could dance, he could sew, and he was possessed of a zealous, persuasive theatricality. Little is known of his parentage or family. He said he was the youngest of six children, that his parents were Joseph and Isabelle, that he was born in Baltimore on November 1, 1830, and that he took to the boards at an early age. He was on the stage at fourteen,

Charles Henry Danielle as Neptune.

and claimed to have shortly thereafter founded a dancing acad-emy in Chicago. For a time, he worked in Brooklyn as a haber-dasher. By all accounts, he was endowed with evangelistic fervour, and was able to spread a great contagion of enthusiasm for the spectacles he was uniquely equipped to engineer. By

1872, he had dropped anchor in St. John's and acquired, through either lease or purchase, the use of the Victoria skating rink in Bannerman Park, near Government House on Military Road. Danielle was a gifted visionary. He looked into the blade-scarred ice and saw, clearly revealed in the frozen intricacy of its curlicues and whorls, certain signs that the edifice was intended for less pedestrian purposes than, say, curling. He took it over. He installed his enormous collection of costumes, each one a product of his own hand. He hired a printer to do up some posters, and he set about staging the first of the fancy-dress balls that made his name.

He knew from the start that this was a no-fail proposition. He brought his costumes and his haughty demeanour, his slightly Southern accent with its overlay of who-knows-where and his other maddening affectations, and he came to live among fisher folk, farmers, and small-time merchants, among prostitutes and hidebound school teachers, among lunatics. It was perfect! He understood that the rough and jagged surfaces of this place concealed a pliable underbelly and a heart that was soft and ripe for the plucking. His neighbours were cut from the coarsest of cloth, but by simple dint of being human, each and every one of them had a soul. One of the soul's essential properties is that it hungers after brighter shining. What better way to achieve this luminescence than through the arts? And what art could be more elevating than the dance? It was simple! And it was lucrative, too. There was a living to be made, just by working out a simple syllogistic sequence. Advertise yourself as a "Professor of the Terpsichorean arts" and you suggest to the public the possibility of dancing. Once you've created the possibility, you've also created the need. Don't give too much of yourself away. Let it be known through word and deed and rumour that you carry the credentials of one who is exotic, cultured, remote, all of which is to say, someone who is clearly a cut above the *hoi polloi*. Thus, you become a source of fascination and envy. Offer to share, for a reasonable fee, one of the skills that sets you apart from the throng, such as a knowledge of the dance, and you will attract some of the many who want in on your secret. Teach it, and your students will want to show off their new skills, to demonstrate to the world at large how like you they've become. Give them this opportunity through a fancy-dress ball, for which you conveniently will be able to rent the costumes, and *voilà*! Every Bob will clamour to be your uncle.

For six years, the Professor staged his carnivals and taught his classes. No student left his care without being able to execute a credible minuet, quadrille, polka, schottische, or waltz.

For six years, all went swimmingly. Then came the first of the fires that were to punctuate his latter days. On July 16, 1878, someone set the Victoria rink ablaze. Who could have done such a thing? And why? Someone eaten away by jealousy, perhaps. Someone who couldn't abide the sight of others having fun, who didn't know his right foot from his left, someone with an icy heart. All his sets, all his costumes, even his piano, was reduced to smouldering ruins. If there was just one hint of pewter in that black, black cloud, it was that he was insured. He collected his thousand pounds and left Newfoundland. Where did he go? Somewhere he'd be appreciated, that much we can count on. Somewhere the climate was amenable to the licking of wounds. Somewhere you could live comfortably for a long time on a thousand pounds.

Time heals. A Christian man forgives. It was ten years before islanders again had the benefit of his presence among them. His first words, on stepping off the gangplank, were "Is the fire out yet?" At least, this is how they have been recorded in the vast book of his apocrypha. What is sure is that on May 31, 1888, *The Evening Telegram* reported that Professor Danielle, "well and favorably known throughout Newfoundland as a teacher of dancing," had arrived on the steamer *Peruvian* and that he "will soon open classes in dancing and weekly assemblies. He is quartered at the Atlantic Hotel, where he will be pleased to see his old friends and pupils."

A week later, once he was reacclimatized to the reviving slap of the wind and the cobbles of the street; once he had adapted, as any traveller must, and as he was accustomed to doing, to the strange physics of a new hotel room, he went down to *The Evening Telegram* office and placed an ad. It ran, with some variation, for the next three weeks.

From this moment on, the public was kept well informed of Danielle's Terpsichoric progress. On September 1, 1888, the *Telegram* ran a breathless story about the Grand Juvenile Ball the Professor had held at the British Hall, an *amuse-gueule* meant to give the public a foretaste of the glorious feast to come. Danielle himself appeared as "Emperor William," and his pupils were togged up as Joan of Arc, the Queen of the Golden Realm, the Albino Prince, an Amazon, and an Italian Peasant. The paper notes that lucky Master Firth, who must have been a favourite of the moment, or gifted with an especially pretty turn of ankle, had been elected to play the page to Danielle's Emperor.

"The hall," writes the *Telegram*, "was brightly lit up and well ventilated all through the night, and it is needless to say that parents and friends of the pupils — large numbers of whom were present — as well as the young people themselves, were delighted with the evening's exhibition. Indeed, so enchanted were they with the fairy-like scene and the fascinating influences of the occasion, that many remained until midnight, and even then they seemed reluctant to tear themselves away.

"Some people are opposed to this kind of amusement; but, for the life of us, we never could see any great harm in it, when superintended by suitable persons."

Harmless, if superintended. How broad-minded! Doubtless this is what they said about skeet-shooting and fireworks, too. Danielle, we are to understand, was not "suitable," but by and large he was harmless enough. Whatever danger or threat he represented could be mitigated, defused by the presence and intervention of the conventionally respectable. He was an odd duck, amusing, but you wanted to keep an eye on him, just in case. Who could say what he might get up to when your back was turned, and it wouldn't do to leave him alone with the children, who were defenceless and impressionable, both. You could never tell when someone might come along and pipe them out of Hamelin.

The juvenile ball was a feast for the senses, but it turned to dust in the mouth when set next to the main event, the Oriental Ball. For the next several weeks, Danielle extolled the glories of "a mammoth night at the big city rink." The anticipated Babylonian excesses of the evening had *le tout* St. John's slavering with anticipation. This was going to be good! More than 2,000 people attended the event, including Governor and Mrs. Blake. The Governor was overheard to remark that, other than a production or two at the Drury Lane Theatre, it was the finest show of theatrics he'd ever witnessed. The critics waxed orgasmic. "The first tableau — the Japanese legation — was simply inimitable. As the dais slowly revolved, the posing of the different figures had the best possible effect, and during the entire scene the delighted audience frequently expressed their admiration. The second tableau — 'Mary, Queen of Scots,' was very impressive in all its details, especially the reading of the death warrant and the execution.... Not a hitch or disappointment occurred at any stage of the entertainment. Every part was admirably performed...."

When the reviews were in and the costumes put away, Danielle took himself off for a recuperative visit to Halifax. He had a right to be tuckered. He had been burning the candle at every available end. For almost two years he hunkered down, kept a low profile, hammered out the details of his reinvention. His next Newfoundland incarnation would be as a restaurateur. He launched a bistro called The Royal. It was a throbbing success until it was eaten by fire in the great conflagration of 1892 — the St. John's equivalent of London's 1666. It was a concussive blow, but the Professor didn't know the meaning of the word "daunted." Another smaller establishment, The Little Royal, rose from the ashes. In these two eateries, our hero was able to hone his culinary skills and exorcise the twin demons that possessed him: an irrepressible hospitality and an overweening need for executing handiwork. The press, for a time, was on his side. The papers advised the public that "Prof. Danielle, who has the nicest dining parlors in this city, is constantly adding improvements to his establishment, which not alone beautify the place but add to the convenience of his patrons. The skill of the Professor as a designer and decorator is unsurpassed. This fact is admitted by everybody. His latest work is a magnificent piano canopy composed of 90 tablets of different colored silks and satins exquisitely embroidered in gold and silver, no two designs being alike. The effect of this superb piece of work, as one enters the room, is simply indescribable. He has also on exhibition a beautiful mantel drape... which surpasses anything of the kind ever seen in this city. In the same room are some very attractive curtains and lambrequins, also a bed-spread representing the aurora borealis, all the work of the busy hands of the Professor."

Busy hands, it is well known, are not available to do the devil's work. Similarly, it is said that one good reason to build an octagonal house is to soften the corners, so Hell's governor will have no place to hide. It is tempting to speculate that the

Professor, whose energies were superhuman, might have struck a Faustian bargain somewhere along the line. Somewhere in his far-flung travels he cut a deal with old Nick. All that stands between Satan and satin is a single vowel and it is almost certain that, in a moment of weakness, Charles drew a pentangle in the snow and summoned the goatman forth. He said, "Listen here, good fellow. Give me your dancing shoes, and all the shiny fabric my heart desires, and you can have my soul when my body is done with it. You can waltz with me for all eternity, and what's more, you can lead."

"Agreed," said the evil one, who clicked his cloven heels and vanished, leaving sulphurous pocks in the deep, white drifts. And from that day forth, Charles Henry Danielle kept Lucifer at bay with his art and his industry. Not that the devil much cared. If there's one thing he's good at, it's biding his time. He watched Charles Henry at his petit point and laughed. He knew what to do. He had his own recreations. He made up spells by working out anagrams of his quarry's name.

Cheery liars handle Len,
Helena's early children,
Chilled hyenas relearn,
Hen reached Nelly's lair,
Chinese rarely lead NHL.

And he planted contempt and rancour into some prominent hearts. He gave the Professor enemies, caused them to whisper calumnies against him. They called him a fool. One Member of Parliament said his satins and laces were nothing but "refuse." It was more than he could bear. He moved away from the city centre. He built a roadhouse on the shores of Quidi Vidi Lake and called it the Royal Lake Pavilion. Its dining room measured sixty-by-forty feet. It had eight magnificent columns supporting a ballroom overhead. It was a bower of beauty, and what did it get him? Contempt. Hot, unwatered, carbolic contempt.

"I was harassed," he would write in his 1901 booklet,

"hooted at, groaned at and barked at, and suffered nightly acts of vandalish destruction, and my servants were assaulted when getting water from the public lake, and all by the very man from whom I leased the land, and why? Why! because I ran a similar business to his and because I ran it thousands of miles superior to his.

"Then, in 1895, being unable to endure the persecutions at Quidi Vidi Lake any longer and remain outside of the insane asylum, I bought this property, tore down the Royal Lake Pavilion, carted it through town to the railway station, railroaded it and its plant to Irvine station, carted it again to the present Octagon grounds, tore down old buildings, and with a hundred thousand more feet of lumber I erected this magnificent Octagon Castle. Then my real heartaches only began, and they have lasted up to this writing, six years later, and all through ignorant, brutish jealousy."

He must have found more than occasional consolation in the beauty of his castle. Out of wood and glass, he built four storeys, eight sides, three wings, and a mansard roof. Some of the gabled windows were decorated with caribou antlers. He must have found solace in the wrought-iron furnace, which measured seven-by-three-by-three feet, which could boil two barrels at once, for dishwashing. It must have cheered him to stroll about the cricket grounds, and the open-air ballroom, and to consider the lake, which was alive with trout. He did not, however, take kindly to dogs. Dogs weren't welcome at the Octagon. Included on his list of dos and don'ts was "Don't bring any growlers with you; they keep me awake nights... I have [had] two sixty-five dollar satin draperies ruined by the inquisitiveness of dogs and this is enough for me to say, 'No Dogs.'"

He was a man of many parts and a man of many words. What were the last words he uttered, May 1, 1902? Alas, they are not recorded. What was the last sound to make its way through his ears to the still-sensible brain, as the net closed around him? It would have been just his luck to have been assailed by a terrible baying, a delighted howling welling in the throat of what only sounded like a dog. Outside his mortuary chamber, the devil was building a satanic head of steam, gearing himself up to lay claim to his prize.

"At 4.15 p.m. yesterday the news reached town of the death of Charles Henry Danielle, proprietor of the Octagon Castle at Irvine station....The remains will be confined at the Octagon and remain there till 1 p.m. Sunday, when a special train will take it to the West End railway terminus. The casket will be left there, when friends can view the body through the glass lid.... Professor Danielle's death will be regretted by many. He, though eccentric, had many good traits of character and was well-liked by his friends around him. He was very fond of children..."

There was a funeral card. It reads:

One precious to our hearts has gone,
    The voice we loved is stilled,
The place made vacant in our home
    Can never more be filled.
Our Father in His wisdom called
    The boon His love had given;
And though on earth the body lies,
    The soul is safe in Heaven.

He was buried in the Church of England cemetery on Forest Road. I went to find him on the very day I arrived in St. John's. It's a very satisfactory graveyard, a few blocks from downtown, in a beautiful neighbourhood of quiet streets lined with stately homes. There is a wrought-iron gate that growls and clanks, and row upon row of eroding, slanted stones. This is a place where even at noon it's easy enough to believe in hauntings. I trudged along paths steeply banked with snow. I heard a crow, looked up to find it, and saw at the same time, in a hoary, thick-limbed elm, the Fellini-esque vision of three little boys in a simian mood, hanging by their legs from one of its branches, studying me, the blood rushing to their toques. I thought how that would have pleased the Professor, what with his fondness for youth and all. I searched and searched along the rows, but was unable to find the requisite mound. I sought out the sexton. He was hunched over a desk in a small outbuilding office. He reluctantly left his work — he was writing a letter of complaint to someone about a lobster he'd ordered for Christmas that hadn't been up to snuff — and led me where I needed to go. *En route*, he pointed out a gully they call, rather redundantly I thought, "Death Valley." This is a mass grave, an earthen blanket laid over those who were sliced and diced by one of the cholera pogroms that marauded its way with Cossack-like rapaciousness across the island. Whole families were wiped out in a few days. "Even now," he assured me with a dire nod towards the shallow depression, "we won't dig there. Won't risk setting something lose." This proscription may or may not stand up to medical scrutiny, but it certainly excites grunts of understanding and accord from a dark and reptilian corner of the brain.

"To the memory of Charles H. Danielle" is the simple inscription on the marble slab that covers his pretty bones and whatever might remain of the magnificent walnut coffin with its thousands of silken scallops, its golden slippers at the ready, and the Orphean lyre etched on the side. There are those who will tell you that stone absorbs sentiment and, if that is the case, someone who is psychically acute might be able to lay hands on the Professor's flat marker and still discern, especially on a warm day, something of the fever-pitch excitement that surrounded his burial. There were accounts of the event in the daily papers, but it was most lovingly and lavishly described by *The New York Post*. The predominant emotion, they say, was not so much grief as it was curiosity.

A carnival atmosphere pervaded overall as some 10,000 people massed along the processional route. They leaned from windows. They stood on roofs. They hung from telephone poles. They jostled on the sidewalks. Those who had cameras brought them along, and the air was alive with the sound of their clicking. There was a great deal of pushing and shoving. At one point, the bier was almost overturned. Individual will was lost in the clamour of the collective. The crowd began to move. They followed along behind the hearse. They practically pushed down the gates of the cemetery in order to watch the lowering. A vault had been built over the grave. They tore it down, bearing away the bricks as souvenirs of the day. It's a compelling picture, this graveside fracas, though here and there are details that make one question the absolute veracity of the report. For instance, we are told that at the head of the procession was "the Professor's body servant, dressed as a Bulgarian brigand and leading his pet dog." The costume would be absolutely in keeping with Danielle's wishes. But a dog? We think not.

Let us turn our attention towards the question of "the Professor's body servant." A couple of years after he opened the Octagon, the Professor granted an audience to an American journalist, who published the interview under the headline "WHO WILL BE THE HEIR OF THIS NEWFOUNDLAND HERMIT?" The writer caught Danielle in a confessional mood. Solicitous, even. He said, "I am practically all alone out here. When you see me, you see my whole family, and I don't fancy that any one else would take as much trouble with me after I have passed away as I have in anticipation of the actual event.... There is only one thing in the world I want. It would take a heap of trouble from my mind. I am well to do, and probably haven't many years to live. If I only had an heir! I'd like to adopt a well brought up, honest, intelligent American lad who would be a son to me and carry on this property after I am dead."

Enter Frederick A. Brazill, a young man of uncertain provenance. Brazill is a common-enough Newfoundland name, although it is more often spelled with a single "l." In fact, one of

Frederick A. Brazill by Danielle's coffin.

the first Europeans known to have drowned off the Newfoundland coast went by the surname Brazil, and he was so called because he had travelled in South America. It seems unlikely, given the regional prevalence of this family name, that Frederick was an American opportunist who made his way north after reading the Professor's plangent plea. He was more likely a local lad, possibly the son of someone in the SOE who had been an occasional visitor to the Octagon. He was someone in whom the perspicacious proprietor saw qualities he liked and trusted. He was good-looking, that was for sure. In his photos, he projects dapper self-confidence. In one portrait, he holds a smoke in his left hand. He might be a youthful Noël Coward or Ivor Novello or some such matinée idol. He was hired on as the aging Professor's right-hand man, and before long was named his heir. He was left Octagon Castle, "on condition that it be conducted on the same lines as when the Professor was alive." The building was not heavily mortgaged. At the hour of dissolution, his employer's aggregate debt on his $20,000 investment was under a thousand dollars. Brazill was also entrusted with a notebook, the title page of which was inscribed, in the Professor's own handwriting:

Book of Instructions and Information by C.H. Danielle for the guidance of Frederick A. Brazill. Octagon Castle N.F.L. November 14, 1900.

In this book, as clearly as in the funeral instructions he placed in the frame behind his elaborate casket, we read writ large the truth of this man's deeply controlling nature. Death might come for us all, but there are those of us who cannot bear the idea of loosening our grip on the world or on our loved ones. The Professor's written legacy to Frederick includes homely advice as to the handling of servants and the advisability of keeping an adequate supply of firewood on hand in the winter and ice in the summer, as well as more portentous, Polonius-like words of counsel.

Keep this Book in your own possession & in such a safe place as to be able to put your hand upon it at any and all times & let it be your guide in all its bearings.

When death over takes me suddenly or after confinement to Bed, Lock all the doors of all the Rooms in the House & take possession of the Keys, there is no one who has the right to question your authority to do so....

Clear the Reading Room of its tables & chairs and have the body "Laid out" there, the Casket resting upon the Stool & drapery it now rests upon in the Mortuary Chamber. Keep the Body in the House "Waking" over two nights, or if possible for a Sunday funeral as more friends can attend on that day than any other....

My Sisters two Photos tacked to the Wall in my Bedroom, please place under the pillow in my Casket....

Keep Octagon Castle as clean and as reputable as you have known me to keep it. Add as little as possible to it until my Debt is cleared....

Order a wreath of Flowers from Mrs. Stein, to place upon the Casket, for I have few loving friends in this coldhearted country. Oh! how *different* it would be if I could be fortunate Enough to Die in my own country America, there I would be *burried* [sic] beneath flowers.

Mrs. Stein will send the bill to you, & you pay the same....

And so he ended, and so he was buried, with handsome Brazill (evidently) parading before the glass-topped coffin in the guise of a Bulgarian brigand, possibly with an incongruous dog in tow, and with six prominent men of the day — including, once again, the politician William Whiteway — bearing the pall. They walked slowly. They nodded at friends in the crowd. Now and then, one might have winked. They inhaled the pollen from Mrs. Stein's flowers. They tried not to sneeze. They unshouldered their burden, they doffed their hats, they bowed their heads, they said amen, they went home again, and they had supper. Brazill returned to the hotel. For a while, he kept it up. Then he sank without trace. When the Octagon burned in 1915, it was held in the name of R. Fowlow, of Trinity. A Mr. Poole was the proprietor. And that is where the story more or less peters out. More or less.

Most of the extant material about Danielle is housed in the archives of the Centre for Newfoundland Studies at Memorial University of Newfoundland. Bert Riggs, the archivist, has done a very admirable job of cataloguing, describing, and preserving what little remains, materially, of the Professor. However, in the Special Collections division of the St. John's Public Library, locked away in a little cash box, and bound with a pretty ribbon, is a small cache of letters and papers that fleshes out the story ever so slightly. There are two documents in Danielle's hand. One is a sort of work in progress, a rather paranoid account of his investigation into the kleptomaniacal tendencies of his servants. It's next to impossible to wring anything like sense from those pages, but my impression is that he decided to test the honesty of his domestics by leaving thick ham sandwiches and slices of cake round about the Octagon. Having baited the trap, he hid behind the arras, waiting to see who would bite and when and how often. Not surprisingly, these unclaimed foodstuffs didn't linger long. It gave him some satisfaction to see them eaten and to have his suspicions confirmed. There is also a more contained and cogent note, a single page written on the letterhead of Deer Lodge Farm, Montrose, Susquehanna County, Pennsylvania. It is dated September 18, 1881, and is addressed to a Mrs. Waugh. The Professor offers her his condolences. He has just received the news about "*Poor Clarence's* distressing *condition*," and begs her to keep him apprised of details as they emerge about her husband, that is, Clarence, and his unnamed pathology.

The rest of the letters were written in 1902 and 1903, all of them after the pivotal date of May 1, and all are addressed to Mr. Frederick A. Brazill. One is a note from Perry Claude Byron, who lived in New York, and apparently made his living as a theatrical photographer. It is dated September 25, 1902. He wrote, "Been very busy since we got home, have no time for such dances & singing as on that Thursday night when within the Castle's walls, but oft-times think of the fun we had.... Wish Mr. Lunt and I were with you...." From this we can garner that the Castle was not hung overlong with the black crêpe of mourning. There is also a letter from an American relative of the Professor's who wonders if there might not be a bibelot or two coming his way, now that the estate has been settled. The balance of the material, however, consists of letters from one C. H. Waugh, of Pittsfield, Massachusetts. This would be none other than Poor Clarence who in 1881 was laid low by that distressing condition but was luckily able to stave off its more lingering symptoms. We can suppose that Frederick uncovered Waugh's name and address among the Professor's effects, or that his particulars were included by Danielle on a list of those to be contacted after his death. Read through this one-sided correspondence — none of the letters from Brazill to Waugh is to be found here — and you get the sense that Frederick is pressing his benefactor's old friend for biographical details. Perhaps the Professor was as much a mystery to him as he was to any of the throng of 10,000 who mobbed his funeral. On July 12, 1902, Clarence replied to a letter he had received from the new owner of the Octagon:

"Dear Sir: Your interesting letter of July 5, 1902 received this day. The last letter Prof. Danielle wrote me was about two years ago. It was a very pathetic letter, telling me how much he had wept over the loss of my friendship, and how much he had thought of me over all these years. I first met him in Bridgeport, Conn. when I was teaching there, a principal in one of the city's grammar schools in 1866, and have known him ever since. He was a great lover of *men*. He used to hug and kiss them and want to *sleep* with them. I did not like this. But there was much about him I *did* like."

Aha. Yes. Men. Well. Is anyone surprised? Hands up whoever is surprised. Bachelorhood, embroidery, theatrics, tinsel, spangles, costumes, fits of temper, and a career in the hospitality industry: put it all together and the word "symptomatic" comes to mind. On July 16, Clarence wrote:

"I felt sure you would like to know someone well acquainted with Prof. Danielle, for it is best to know all we can of our valued friends. With all his glaring faults, did he have more of them than most of us? We are all imperfect, but in different ways. Our faults are different. For that reason, I exercise the broadest charity towards my fellow men, as I want the same for myself.

"But faults aside, I have always considered Prof. Danielle a *very remarkable man* — superior to nearly all other men. His ability, executiveness, his creative genius and art were sublime. His tender heart and charity to the poor were conspicuous throughout his life.... He in early life was always infatuated with *men* — never women — and these *men* would work on his soft side to get all the *money* they could and then *drop* him — and he gave *freely*. They *bled* him. Only for that he would have become *a very wealthy man*."

Charles Henry Danielle (seated) and Frederick A. Brazill.

It would be neither charitable nor kind, not even in the light of this information about the Professor's attraction to gold-digging bottom feeders, to cast aspersions on the purity of the motives and actions of Mr. Brazill, or to speculate that the Professor might actually have been in love with his ward. Only an outright bounder would wonder aloud whether the hunky Freddy might have had motives that were just ever so slightly on the ulterior side of honourable when he came knocking on the door of the Octagon, with an indulgent look on his face and his kitbag in hand. There is no concrete proof to suggest that he delayed marrying until after the death of his sugar daddy for fear of alienating the Professor's affections, which might have led to his being heaved out of the comfy castle. It is surely nothing more than a coincidence that directly the old man was gone he found himself a willing girl and put the honeymoon suite to its intended purpose. On August 28, 1902, Clarence — who would receive a piece of wedding cake by return mail — sends a note of congratulations to him and to "the dearest little girl in St. John's." In subsequent letters, he recalls how, once upon a time, the touch of his own beloved would send shock waves through him, would make him feel as though he had fallen from a two-storey building. Frederick must always remember that the love of a good woman is the greatest thing a man can have. "The dear creatures come high but we must have them and I never forget that my mother was a woman."

In other letters Clarence speaks of his health. It has remained rocky ever since the unpleasantness of 1881. He has just enough energy to tune and repair pianos. This is an avocation at which he is expert. Perhaps one day, he writes, he'll come for a visit and work his magic on uprights in Newfoundland. Would there be enough paying customers to make a trip north worth his while? In every missive, he always offers up another recollection of dear, departed, mixed-up Charles.

"When the lady and I were stopping at his home for a few days...he had arranged for *me* to sleep with *him*. Every *man* that *visited him* he wanted to *sleep* with him. Not being in the habit of sleeping with *any*one — not with my own wife even, nor with *any* person, I said, 'No, Charles, let me sleep *alone*.' Being short of *beds* he made me one up on the *floor* and I slept there *alone*. I am queer about that — can't sleep with anybody else, male or female."

Mr. Waugh also thanks Brazill for having sent him a copy of Danielle's last booklet. He must have paid special attention to page twenty-six. There he would have read, "I have scrap-books as big as family Bibles, filled to bursting with letters and press opinions, that locate me every day from 1848 until this day — such a record as no other man in this country can show. These records can be seen by any visitor to the Octagon, and, if I am not Charles Henry Danielle, I have stolen his life and records and the question is: Who am I?"

It is the query of a dyed-in-the-wool romantic who must have lived between the lines of stories like "Rumpelstiltskin" and *Parsifal*. He made a show of stanching the sly, suspicious whisperings about his genesis and habits, but his nature was so thoroughly theatrical that he might now and then have seeded with rumour the cloud that hung above his name. Ah, the conundrum of the name! Some mendacious bastard spread it about that "Danielle" was a transmogrification of "Dan O'Neill," a slanderous utterance which moved the Professor to say, "...if my name ever had been Dan Neill or Dan O'Neill, I would have swapped it for a dog, and killed the dog. My full name is Charles Henry Danielle, a much prettier name than Dan Neill.... If I am not Charles Henry Danielle, the question is: Who am I?"

Clarence Waugh — who, let's just come straight out and say it, was one of the all-time great killjoys, and a terrible priss to boot — knew the answer. He was only too happy to blurt it out, in his very first letter to Brazill, crying the truth as triumphantly as the miller's daughter in the fairy tale. Danielle's real name, he crows, was Charles Augustus Everson. He had it on the high authority of the Professor's brother-in-law, a cultured man with whom he was well acquainted. Yes! His real name was — Charles Augustus Everson! "Mr. Overton gave away his secret, and Prof. D. *wrote me* that *that name* was his *true* name.... Charles *wrote* me that he changed his name because he had danced himself into fame under the name of *Charles H. Danielle* and therefore *retained* it *afterwards*. (This was at Chicago.) But he was a born *mystic* and had his own secrets that he kept from his most intimate friends. He had a large cluster ring which he called *diamonds*, when in fact they were only imitations — yet he would *say* they were *genuine*. Of course I could not *trust* his *word* for *this* defect was *born in* him, and he could not be different — could not *help* it.... He could cry like a child over the death of a bird. I have *known* him to weep over the death of a swallow. When I was about to marry he wanted to know if *his* love was not better. He *begged* of me *not to marry*. Of course, *this* showed an *abnormal mind*, but it was *born in* him; and what is *born in* a man will *stay* there till death. But he is dead — God bless him. C.H.W."

The little lake on which Danielle built his castle is still called Octagon Pond. You can take a cab there from St. John's for about $20. You should know, though, that there is precious little to see. A convenience store. A few hangar-like buildings, remnants of the one or two failed attempts to establish some light industry on the grounds where a castle once stood. In a normal January, the pond will be frozen. The snow might have been cleared from a small patch of ice in preparation for a hockey game. The children of Paradise will arrive with their sticks and their pucks and their skates, and chase each other around the crusty water where years and years ago, on an August afternoon, the Church of England orphans paddled, and tortured frogs. You won't be able to guess, from surveying the scene, where the Octagon stood. There is not a single sign of its galleries, its paintings, its banners, its kitchens and its banquet halls where, during any given summer, 2,969 meals would be offered up and 817 chickens and ducks would be roasted and served. Long gone is the guest book in which were inscribed such appreciations as "Excellent, magnificent, unequalled...Out of sight...Of all the places I have seen in the United States and other countries, nothing compares with this grandeur...Ingenuity and taste everywhere displayed...Three cheers for the Professor."

Three cheers for the Professor, who kept close track of numbers, and who by the end of the day had taught dancing in eighty-nine cities and towns to 16,831 persons; who had slept in 912 beds, who had travelled 51,833 miles, who had written

61,390 letters (where are they now?), and who finally managed to boil his life down to something that could be contained in an octagon. He is gone now, gone altogether. There is no sign of him, nor will there be again. His life was smoke and mirrors. No one had to show him how to vanish, and he knew when it was time to go. Stand by Octagon Pond in the winter and think of him inside the eight walls of his soon-to-be immolated palace, that Knossos of Newfoundland. Think of him stitching up his quilts, embroidering his hangings, working at his tatting, sitting at his loom. Think of the pricked fingers, the hunched shoulders, the eye strain, all the suffering in the name of art. Think of him rising from his work and surveying his domain, moving from room to room, looking from each of his eighty-four windows, taking in the magnificent far-off views, the big white fields and the big grey sea. Think of his full and aching heart; his deep, cold loneliness. Think of him listening, listening to see if he could distinguish in the wind the syllabizing hubbub of Beelzebub's desperate and incantatory anagramming:

> Ye learn Hell's red chain!
> Die charnel, Hell yearns!
> A cheery Hell, sinner lad!
> Any Hellish reel, dancer!

Think of him smiling, knowing that, as sure as he was born in Baltimore, the devil could never, not in a million years, guess his secret name.

Devil among the Tailors

But the Spirit of the Lord departed from Saul,
and an evil spirit from the Lord troubled him.
   — I Samuel 16:14

Sad sack Saul, then! An evil spirit come to roost where once the
Lord had lived. This is not the kind of visitation to which anyone would willingly open the door. Even for the King of Israel,
this was a problem. What to do? What to do? It was a lucky
thing for him he could call on David, his personal Mr. Fix-It.
David, the psalm singer. David, the giant killer. David, who was
not only a dab hand with a slingshot, but also a music therapist
with a specialty in exorcizing evil spirits. He knew what his
king needed, and, what was more, he had the skills and materials to bring it off. He picked up his harp. He strummed a
soothing song. Before you could say Nebuchadnezzar, "Saul
was refreshed, and was well, and the evil spirit departed from
him" (I Samuel 16:23).

   The moral of the story is, never underestimate the power of
the harp. It is the instrument of angels, and calms the mind as
surely as a rose-scented breeze from the south. The psaltery will
also do in a pinch, and the timbrel and the trumpet both have
their sanctified uses. As for the fiddle — well, that's an instrument you want to handle with care. Be leery, dearie, of the fiddle. It's not for nothing they call it "the devil's box." They call
it that because it's his invention. He's the one who thought it up.
Are you surprised? You shouldn't be. Figure it. A slab of wood,
strung with four tight filaments of gut. A hank of horsehair to

stroke them till they squeal. Could anyone invent such a device had he not spent the better part of eternity assailed by clouds of sulphur and the screams of the damned? I think not.

The devil made the fiddle and he loved it right away. He never tired of playing it, and would have sawed at it without a break were it not for the administrative demands placed on him by his job. Even when he had to give full attention to the day-to-day running of Hell, he didn't set the contraption down, but carried it on his hip, as a mother carries a baby. It didn't take long before the fiddle came to feel like an extension of his body, an extra limb. He knew it proprioceptively. It became his language, his currency, his passport. He played it while clambering up the smoky flue that was his conduit to the world above. He played it as he wandered the earth, looking for frangible souls he could tempt with a jig or a reel. He played it at the Octagon while the Professor tatted or sewed up his costumes, sequin after sequin. He played it at Frederick Brazill's wedding, bowed all his favourite tunes: "Knocking at the Door," "Hell among The Yearlings," "Joy among The Darkies," and "Big Footed Coon." He laid into "Fat Meat and Dumplings," "Old Mother McCarthy," "Peaches and Cream," and "Soldier's Joy." He tried his hand at "Old Woman at the Well," "Ice on the Pump Handle," "Sugar in the Coffee," and "Ladies on the Steamboat." He teased them a little with "Turkey Knob," and by way of saying goodnight, he treated them to "Speed the Plow." "Speed the Plow" was his favourite. When he played "Speed the Plow," the sparks just flew.

Any fiddler knows that the quick tunes are so much flash and sparkle. They're not without their challenges, they're full of virtuoso turns, but it's the slow and tender melodies that really prove a player's mettle. If you play the fiddle, you know it's the lullabies and laments, with their transparent simplicity, that plumb the depth of your heart, that reveal your essence to the listener. The devil, who has an investment in keeping such qualities concealed, did not care for music with an easy lilt. Too namby-pamby, he said. Too soporific. It might be said that he lacked a sense of occasion, for he'd as readily play "Hogs in the Tater Patch" at a funeral or a christening as he would at a wedding or a barn-raising. Exactly what he played while standing beside the cradle of Pierre-Léon Ayotte is anyone's guess. "Joseph Won the Coated Fiddle" or "Silver Star Hornpipe." What is sure is that the baby didn't like it one little bit. It made him all sleepless and bilious. He erupted into a colicky fit, and that was what gave the devil his entrée.

Pierre-Léon Ayotte, who was born in 1845, spent his life in and around the rural environs of Ste-Geneviève-de-Batiscan, Quebec. It was a no-nonsense kind of place where most people lived off the avails of farming and forestry; where practicality was the byword; where men wore pants, women wore skirts, and that was that. Pierre-Léon distinguished himself from the crowd by wearing a *jaquette*. This was a curious garment that looked, from all accounts, like a nightshirt. It was simple in design, long-sleeved, unadorned except for the buttons that ran up the front, cardigan style. It was about the length of a nightshirt, and hung down over his knees and boot tops. So identified did he become with this get-up that he achieved his nickname, "Jaquette-à-Simon."

That the *jaquette* became his everyday attire grew out of his phobia about wearing trousers, an inconvenient kink dating back to his infancy. It was really his father who was to blame, his father who should have known better. It was he who opened the door to satanic influence. Once it was ajar, even that tiny crack, the fiddling devil couldn't wait to get in there and leave his mark. The story they told around Ste-Geneviève was that Pierre's mother heard her child sobbing in his cradle. She was occupied elsewhere in the house, and shouted to her husband to attend to the baby and his rocking. The elder Ayotte's nerves were on edge. This kid cried all the time, and surely it was a mother's job to comfort her baby. So, he refused. She bristled. They quarrelled. The devil, who likes such a scene, stood by, playing "Good for the Tongue." The baby bawled the louder. Finally, his father threw up his hands in rage and frustration and shouted, "Que le diable le berce d'abord!," which is to say, "May the devil rock him then!" Hell's fiddler required no further invitation. He was in there like a dirty *jaquette*. From then on, the baby's cradle would rock and rock, seemingly of its own volition. The child was pacified, but the house was otherwise thrown into disarray. Dishes would fly from the cupboards, pictures rearranged themselves on the walls, even the barn was seen to shake and tremble, as though it were dancing to the strains of the "Findy Sickle Two Step."

No one doubted whose handiwork this was. Watching Pierre-Léon grow up — which is not to say mature — was like watching the linking of the letters that made the devil's signature. The boy became increasingly bizarre. He began stealing things — common, dumb household objects — and squirrelling them away. It satisfied a need, no one could say for what, least of all Pierre-Léon, who never learned to speak in anything other than a childish lisp. And then there was the question of his clothing, where his predilections were not at all *comme il faut*. He couldn't be made to dress properly. That *jaquette*! Many thought he needed only a stern hand and tried to force him into trousers. The breeches would be ripped to shreds within the hour. It was the devil's handiwork, there could be no doubt about that.

Word of his eccentricities spread and reached the ear of one Hubert Trépanier. He was an unscrupulous promoter, an impresario with an eye for the freakish. He convinced Pierre to run away with him to the circus. They went to New England and got onto the carnival circuit. They fell in with the bearded ladies and the Siamese twins, with the brainless babies floating in bottles, and the giants and the midgets and the man from whose forehead there sprouted horns. As if Pierre didn't know already about men with horns. He was exhibited as one who was possessed by satanic spirits, as the carrier of a cruel curse. "Come See Jaquette-à-Simon, the Man Whom the Devil Forbids to Wear Trousers!"

It was a short-lived adventure. The ruse was transparent. It was easy enough to expose. Some gamblers got together and decided to test the veracity of this outlandish claim. They placed their bets, then laid hold of Ayotte. They dressed him all in white, in a shirt and the hated pants. They blackened his hands with charcoal, they locked him in a room. When he emerged, his suit was in tatters, and dirtied all over with tell-tale soot. The devil's work? The smudges told a different tale. It had all the earmarks of a ruse, and not even a cunning one. Conclusions were drawn. Fingers were pointed. The jig was up, and a jig was what the devil played. "If I Hadn't Been a Fool, I Might Have Been a Lady," I think it was, or maybe "Shake the Bow."

Pierre-Léon must have been relieved. He slipped back into his beloved *jaquette* and hit the road for home. He spent the rest of his life as a labourer, laughed at by some, pitied by others. His reputation continued to grow, and he became in his own lifetime a figure of folkloric fun, a full-blooded fool, a cautionary tale. He died in 1907, at the age of sixty-one. You'll never guess who provided the music at the funeral. He played "Someone's at the Door." He played "Done Gone."

The sad story of poor Ayotte is told in the *Dictionary of Canadian Biography*, and has been recounted in a number of journal articles and novels. Lionel Dessureaux, writing in *Le Mauricien* in 1938, remembers how he became a kind of bogey man, and that the threat of a visitation from La Jaquette-à-Simon was used to quell children who refused to go to sleep. E. Z. Masicotte speculated in 1929 that Ayotte's strange comportment might have been the result of a prolonged childhood fever that left him damaged. Whether or not that was the genesis of his strangeness, I suspect that any qualified diagnostician could, if given all the facts of the case, attach a name to his condition. *A quoi bon?* would be the operative question. Me, I favour the supernatural explanation. I'm content with the fiddling hypothesis. If a reason must be found, it's as good as any other.

For the longest time, the devil kept the fiddle to himself. He was the only one who owned or played one. Somewhere along the line, the instrument fell into human hands. How this happened is anyone's guess, though I imagine it was part of a deal Beelzebub cut to secure the promise of some coal-rich soul he couldn't do without. Over time and use and travel, passed from mortal hand to mortal hand, the fiddle shed most traces of its fiery antecedents. Held to the chins of some players it still sounds like hell, of course, but overall it's taken on a much more benignant quality. In some lives, like that of Willie Francis Fraser, the fiddle has even proved something of a charm.

Mr. Fraser, who is verging on eighty, lives in Deepdale, on Cape Breton Island. He is not celebrated as a fiddler, but rather as an exponent of the related craft of step-dancing. He's been at it all his life and says he's danced in or on every hall, step, and bridge on the island of Cape Breton about ninety-nine times, usually with a fiddle playing along. When he was younger, and still working in the mines, he'd sometimes stay out most of the night dancing, then go underground with just a couple of hours' sleep. Such alacrity and indefatigability make him the artistic heir to Malcolm MacLean, who arrived from Scotland early in the nineteenth century. No sooner had Malcolm seen the shores of North America rise up on the horizon than he hurried below deck and put on his step-dancing togs, donned his top hat, and coattails, and fine buckled shoes. He was a man with a mission. He meant to teach his art to all and sundry in the New World, and it was his intention to launch in the second he stepped onto the pier. That would have been a landing to see: Malcolm MacLean, skipping and capering down the gangplank, clicking his heels in boyish anticipation of what was to come. He was sidetracked by petty considerations of land-clearing and house-building, but eventually was able to stake his intended vocational claim. He is said to have had the floor joists changed in his house three times before he was satisfied with the springiness of his dancing surface.

Willie Fraser doesn't know the name of the man who appeared to him in a dream over seventy years ago and taught him to dance. Perhaps it was the ghost of Malcolm MacLean, although, when I asked him to tell me the story and happened to use the word "ghost," he protested loudly that it wasn't a ghost at all. It was for real. It was true. And he should know, since he was there. It happened like this.

He was just a little boy, though older than Pierre-Léon had been when *his* life changed, maybe five, maybe six years old. He came down from his room one morning and his father, Simon, who was a terrific fiddler, asked him how he had slept. Willie Francis said fine, just fine, but that there had been this fellow in his room who had told him that he, Willie, was going to be a dancer and that he was there to teach him the steps. He was a good-looking young fellow, the dream man. He was dressed in a blue suit, white shirt, and tie. Willie was not alarmed. He felt no fear or threat. He took this visit in his stride, quite literally. He didn't ask the apparition any questions as to his name or provenance, he just paid attention to the dancing. And in the morning, he told his father all about it.

"Ah," said his pa, no more alarmed than his son had been, "let's see what you can do, then." He picked up his fiddle and he played a reel, and sure enough, the boy had learned his lessons well. It was amazing, the things he could do, and there wasn't just one step, either. The young man returned to him a few more times, and on each visit, he saw to it that Willie had five or six dances added to his repertoire. By the time he stopped appearing, he had laid the foundation for the "close to the floor" style that Willie Fraser still practises.

One day, I suppose, years and years from now, Willie might himself appear to some youngster in a dream. Happily, he's not waiting until he's passed beyond to start teaching. He passes on his learning in the here and now. He has made recent trips to the Hebrides in Scotland, and there he instructs the great-great-great-great-grandchildren of the immigrants who entered Canada with their toes tapping and their fiddles primed to sing. It's an act of repatriation, really, like returning an artifact to its tribe of origin. The lively ghost (if I may say so) of Malcolm MacLean must surely be pleased, for any dancer appreciates the beauty of a circle. Any dancer knows the object of the exercise is somehow to get back home.

Willie Francis Fraser's dancing gifts are heaven-sent. They're wakened when the devil's box is played; when *like a mist the music drifts from the silvery strings.* How that old devil must grit his teeth and swear when he hears what his pride and joy, his marvellous toy, has become. Damn, damn, damn! He should have known better than to give it away. "Old Fort Smith," "The Old Blue Tick," and "Eli Green's Cakewalk." He still plays them when he has a mind to kill some time, but it's just not the same. He'll play "8th of January," "Jennie Put the Kettle On," and "Bummer Reel." The mood he's in these days, he's especially fond of "Bummer Reel."

The devil, who likes to be in charge, doesn't usually take requests from the floor. But I've sent him a note and shot of dark rum and asked that he favour us with just one tune, something that will put us in the right frame of mind for what's to come.

"Fine," he said, knocking back the toddy. "But no more than one."

"Do you mind if we dance?" I asked, and he *began to laugh with that sibilant laugh that resembles the hiss of a serpent.*

"Do your damnedest. You'll never keep up!"

His bow is taut. His strings are tuned. Listen between the lines, and you're sure to hear him play. There it is now. Can you place the tune, make it out through the squawk and rasp of overtones? It's called "The Lightning Hornpipe."

Shock

...when thou walkest through the fire,
thou shalt not be burned; neither shall
the flame kindle upon thee.
— Isaiah 43:2

It was an afternoon late in June, the first really hot day of summer. The year was 1906. An electrical storm was cruising through the supercharged ions of the crackling lower atmosphere. It passed above the newly seeded fields of southwestern Manitoba, passed over the farming communities of Rivers and Brandon, passed over sleepy Minnedosa and the gentle rise of Riding Mountain. It grumbled. It spat. From time to time, it sparked, just small-time delinquency. By the time it got to Souris, which was where the Joyners lived, it was primed for headier mischief. It was ready to rumble.

Mrs. Joyner and her husband had taken rooms on the third floor, above the dry goods store. They moved in there after his threshing accident made farming an impossibility, and town the only available option. Everyone was amazed that they chose to install themselves in a place where he would have to cope with all those stairs. They shook their heads, even though they understood the why of it well enough. It was his way of showing he was still capable, that not so very much had changed, that he was still the man he had always been. Even though he was not. You just had to look at him to see that. It broke your heart, watching his slow and painful progress up and down those three flights. He was stubborn, though. He had always been stubborn. Proud, too.

The day of the electrical storm, the Joyners happened to be at home. Truth be told, home is where they usually were. When they went out, he complained that he was looked at, and that people felt sorry for him. He was right. They did. He couldn't abide their pity, so they kept mostly to themselves. It was hard on them both, though in different ways. They stayed indoors, three floors up, under a flat roof that was a magnet for the heat. Their place tended towards the stuffy, as you can imagine, so from the middle of June till the middle of September, depending on the vagaries of the season, they would leave the windows open. By the open window was where Mrs. Joyner liked to sit. The light was good there, and she felt more connected to the world beyond, less homesick and aware of her losses.

On the afternoon in question, when she was in her accustomed place, a breeze that was almost a gust joined them in the room. It was uncommonly warm and sudden. Mrs. Joyner looked up from her hemming. She was finishing off an apron, a gift for her favourite niece who had moved to Winnipeg just before Christmas and was now engaged to be married. This niece might have been her own daughter, they were that close. She herself had never had children, which was her only regret in life, other than her husband's misery. When she told the story of that afternoon — and she often would — Mrs. Joyner would remember that she noted the curtains fluttering back into place, that she looked beyond them to the darkening complexion of the sky, the deep and angry creases of its brow. It gave her a funny turn. She said as much to Mr. Joyner. He was seated across the room on the settee, his one leg propped up on a footstool, and she told him how she was feeling all queer and apprehensive. These were the first words either of them had uttered since breakfast. They had been married for thirty years, and a silence that was not always comfortable had grown up between them.

Directly she had spoken she wondered if this aberrant restlessness might not be another symptom of the onset of her change of life. She had been troubled latterly by inconvenient sweats and mood swings. It was a nuisance, but she wasn't overly concerned. She knew more or less what to expect, and in a way she was glad. A fat lot of good all that cramping and bleeding had done her, anyway. They'd tried and tried for a baby. In all those years, she had never missed her monthly visit from Nurse Blood. Now, she was drying up. She would have to do her best to be uncomplaining, to set a good example for her niece and the young women at the church. She still went to church. She went by herself most Sundays.

"I do feel queer," she said. "I feel queer all of a sudden. Hot, kind of."

Mr. Joyner raised his eyes from his book. He was reading Dickens, *Bleak House*. He used to read the Bible, but abandoned it after "the incident." That's what he called it. "The incident." He had always been a laconic man, given to understatement. He looked across the room and considered his wife for a moment or two before venturing the opinion that perhaps she felt unsettled because a finger of lightning had just tapped her on the shoulder. And as for feeling warm, well, that would be because she was, in fact, on fire. On June 23, 1906, *The Toronto Daily Star* reported that, by the time the blaze was extinguished, "it had burned a hole six inches in diameter into her clothes, to the flesh, though she herself was not injured and the lightning's work was not visible in any other respect."

And it was so. That night, when Mrs. Joyner sat at her vanity, pulling her brush through her long hair — there was very little grey in it yet, a fact which stirred up in her a pride she knew to be wholly irrational — she observed with some disappointment that she was utterly unchanged in her every aspect. One would think that so striking and nearly fatal an encounter would have left behind a visible souvenir. Scars. Stigmata. A limp to match her husband's. A miracle baby, floating in her shrinking womb. It seemed to her, on reflection, that in that quick and shocking instant, when her awareness had been elsewhere, her one and only life had been blasted up to its pinnacle, its apogee. In the blink of an eye she had gone from being the wife of a defeated, one-legged man to being a woman with her own remarkable, annunciatory tale to tell. She had been singled out by lightning and saved by God. Blessed was she among women. But while legend is fine and dandy, it's not as though you can hold it in your hand. From here on in, it would all be downhill. She was hardly fifty and already knew for a fact what the mourners at her funeral would whisper about among themselves. What kind of prescient certainty was that to haul around all the rest of her days? Was there nothing more to hope for? How could she top the split-second searing of this afternoon?

The only redemptive possibility was that lightning might strike twice. She left her mirror. She made three paces through the room, pussyfooting past her snoring husband. He had gone to bed early, worn out by all the excitement, by so many neighbours coming round to gape and to wonder. Of course, the uninvited company had to be served cold drinks, which meant they had run out of ice, which annoyed him. Worse still was that the ghost of his missing leg had chosen that night for one of its occasional hauntings. It was out there, stomping around the field where he'd left it, pining for its old attachments. How the bereaved stump ached! On top of everything else, he had one of those pollen-induced headaches that plagued him at this time of year. He'd taken one of his special draughts and was asleep within minutes. He didn't stir when Mrs. Joyner heaved up the high window and looked down at the dark and dusty streets of Souris. The air had a promising mugginess about it. She turned back to the bed and left the window open to the world and its infinite possibilities. She slid between the summer sheets, fanned her hair out on the pillow. She inhaled deeply, was rewarded by a faint whiff of lavender. She always kept a sachet in with her linens as she found the scent calming. She crossed her hands over her breasts and assumed a look of deep satisfaction. This was how she would like to be found. It was best to be ready. She thought of how upset her mother would have been had she known when she went to bed in her stained old nightgown that she would be dead in the morning, and it would be left to that pedlar to find her and raise the alarm. By the time she, Mrs. Joyner, heard about it and hurried over, half the town had been by to have a gander. As everyone knows, you can never tell what might happen when you're asleep or simply looking the other way. You can just never tell.

I was reminded of Mrs. Joyner on board the ferry for Prince Edward Island. I'd boarded at Cape Tormentine, New Brunswick, and there was nothing about my circumstances to suggest that she should surface in my meditations. It was a clear day in the middle of January. I had been listening to the radio, and the news was innocent of malevolent omens. True, hogs were having a hard time of it. A livestock report leaked word that things were gridlocked at the abbatoir. Porcine executions were running an hour behind schedule. As well, I learned that a card party in Tignish had been cancelled because one of the regular players had passed away, of natural causes, and that two lost dogs were found wandering in the vicinity of Summerside. Sad news, all this, but the world is a sad, sad place. Nothing I heard on the radio seemed so very much out of the ordinary as to contraindicate a voyage over water. Certainly there was no danger of lightning. So, whence came Mrs. Joyner? I'm ashamed to say it must have been eavesdropping that fired the synapses which caused her to breech and gulp for air.

"Where you headed?" one trucker asked another in the little ship's cafeteria. They were both eating ham sandwiches and I couldn't keep from wondering how long the pigs had lingered in the holding pen.

"Just up to Charlottetown. You?"

"Just out to Souris."

Aha! Souris! Hence the Joyner connection. I had never before been to P.E.I., and I was thrilled at the prospect of adding flesh to the bones of places about which I'd heard or read, of seeing if their reality measured up to my imagining. It was disappointing to hear these seasoned travellers shrug off their destinations so casually, demonstrating the indifference, if not the contempt, that is bred by familiarity.

"Just up to Charlatan. You?"

"Just out to Surrey."

That trucker said "Surrey" with such indifference that you knew for a fact he'd never thought about it with a fringe on the top. Still, I was glad to know something about the local inflection, glad to know that on P.E.I. Souris = Surrey. I should have hated to have stopped at a service station and spoiled one of those testosterone-scented under-the-hood discussions by manfully grunting, "Sure, top up the oil, and by the way is this the road to Souris?" pronouncing it as I might the French word for "mouse," tossing it off with that Continental flare for which I am celebrated near and far.

In Manitoba, where I grew up, they anglicize "Souris" even more tellingly. There, it is rendered as "Surris." When the reporter from *The Toronto Daily Star* contacted Mrs. Joyner for a horse's mouth rendering of the story of her miraculous escape, "Surris" would have been where she told him it had all transpired. Yes, she told him, that was right. It was in "Surris" that she lived and it was in "Surris" that she very nearly died. Wasn't that something? Didn't that just about beat all?

The peculiarity of regional vernacular must be well known to Mr. Eddy R. Souris, whom I happened to meet quite by chance one day in a downtown Toronto office lobby. He was a man of indeterminate age, sixty something I would say, pleasantly enough turned out, but unremarkable of stature or mien. He was clutching a manila envelope to his heart. He approached me, inquired after my name, then — seemingly satisfied, God knows why — reached into his envelope and drew forth a single-page brochure. In bold print at the top were the words "Mousing Around." I gathered straight away that this was something he had prepared and printed and with which he wanted to present me. It was a completely unsolicited show of largesse, which is a rare-enough occurrence these days. I thanked him for the proferred sheet, which I accepted. We exchanged a few words and then he walked away. He disappeared through the revolving doors and onto Front Street, leaving me to wonder whether everyone who crosses his path receives such a gift, or whether he spotted me across a crowded room and intuited that I might be interested in owning such a publication. Which, of course, I was. I have it before me now.

Under the "MOUSING AROUND" headline are drawings of two heraldic crests, one French, one Dutch. Each incorporates three mice into its symbology. "Mr. Eddy R. Souris, of Toronto, is fascinated by his surname," the text of his document begins. It goes on to explain that, through explorations both genealogic and geographic, he has pursued the name in all its forms: the German, Maus; the Dutch, Muis or Muys; and the Danish, Muus. The name can be traced back as far as 1462, when the lordship of Lavoud, in Limousin, was held by a French family called — you guessed it — Souris. Eddy "has personally visited twenty-seven localities named Souris. Three are towns, one each in P.E.I., Manitoba, and North Dakota. Others are rivers, or features such as valleys, parks, or hills. They are found in France, Belgium, Madagascar, the Seychelles, and in both North America and the Indian Ocean. Research has brought him knowledge of almost sixty places called Mouse, such as Mouse Creek, Alaska and five lakes of the name in Ontario alone."

I tried, without success and many times, to contact Mr. Souris after this one fated and all too brief encounter. I am sorry for this failure, because I would have liked to have looked more searchingly under the rock of his reasons. I would have liked to have visited his house, to see if his passion extends to home decoration. Would there be novelty door bells, toilet roll covers, wall clocks? Would he have china cabinets burgeoning with rank on rank of Beatrix Potter, Mother Goose, and Walt Disney figurines? What would be on his book shelves? *Of Mice and Men*? *The Mouse and His Child*? Might he keep pets? If so, how many? As it is, I can only reflect on the rarity of his character. How many of us carry our names around with us as thoughtlessly as we do our noses or chins, using them when they are required, regretting sometimes that they don't seem to suit us, but content for the most part to take them for granted? That

Eddy R. Souris, of Toronto, is so smitten with his own family name that he will make the effort to travel as far as Madagascar, just to deepen his connection with it, sets him apart. Whether or not he reaches a destination and thinks about it analytically, forms opinions about his whereabouts, compiles a check-list of pros and cons, takes pictures, and gathers up anecdotes to spin back home, I cannot tell you. I wouldn't be surprised to learn that it is enough for him to arrive, scent the air, confirm that such-and-such a place exists, read the road signs and maps that connect it to the idea of the mouse and therefore, by extension, to him, and then go right back to Toronto. It pleased me to think of Eddy, and the possibility that he might have been a passenger on this self-same ferry, the *Abegweit*, while he made his pilgrimage to Prince Edward Island to take a quick squinny at Souris.

Eddy R. Souris! I wanted more than anything to speak of him, and of Mrs. Joyner too, to the ham-eating truck drivers, but there was something about the serpentine tattoos of the one and the bristling tool belt of the other that made me feel all shy and marshmallowy inside. Sometimes, a shackling timidity comes upon me and I clam right up. Who can say why? It's always been thus with me. That's just the kind of boy I am. I kept my counsel, left them to their cruel lunch, and stepped onto the deck of the *Abegweit*. I stood there alone and stared out at the ice-caked water of the Northumberland Strait. It was very, very cold.

Abegweit, as any tourist brochure will tell you, was the name given to the island by the Mi'kmaq. It means "cradled on the waves," which is prettier and less irritatingly proprietary than "Prince Edward Island," or even "Ile St. Jean," which is what the French called it when they settled in. Abegweit was also a promising contender as a name for the fixed-link bridge which now connects P.E.I. to New Brunswick. That "Confederation" won out is not so surprising. It is a duller but certainly a safer choice; it is far from inappropriate as it is not without historical resonance; and Lord knows it's easy to remember.

One wonders if there might have been a survey that suggested some tourists would be reluctant to trust their families and vehicles to a miles-long bridge the name of which they couldn't reliably pronounce. There was a kind of pathos to be distilled from plying the waves on this January ferry to Borden, chugging along in plain view of the span that was soon to put such a brave little boat out of business. Poor old *Abegweit*! It sluiced blithely through the icy channel, coursing along towards superfluity, towards its own oblivion.

The fixed link is a faint and steely echo of the once-upon-a-time land bridge that connected the two provinces. Thousands of years ago, the assiduous tides managed to wear it away. When officials first raised the prospect of summoning forth the genie of engineering to redraft that old connection, there were countless arguments for and against the venture. Of course there were! How could it have been otherwise?

Predictably, these arguments were based on concerns that were aesthetic, environmental, or socio-economic. The pro-bridge faction said its completion would herald the dawning of a bright day for business on the island. Tourists, who have been flocking to the place for years in any case, would be even more inclined to make the trek if they didn't have to take a boat. The no-bridge contingent peered into the dark side of the crystal. They countered with the theory that local businesses would actually suffer. Islanders, they feared, would give in to the mercantile temptations of Moncton, whose malls and doughnut shops would become shockingly accessible. Worst of all, though, was the sense of threat best expressed in a bumper sticker: "Real islands don't have bridges." This most pervasive fear was the hardest to articulate, as it could be neither proved nor quantified. What if the link should rob the place of its essential "islandness"? What if P.E.I. should lose everything that its relative isolation (a word which is joined at the etymological hip with "island") has made possible?; if it sacrificed its gem-of-the-sea, rural, down-home, red-earthed, potato-cultivating, fiddle-playing, Anne-of-Green-Gables folksiness on the seductive but tarnished altar of cosmopolitanism and financial gain? Good-bye God, hello Mammon. The anti-bridge lobby wanted to see preserved the sentiments celebrated in that turn-of-the-century ditty "My Old Island Home."

Far away to the north lies a dear little island
A Garden 'tis called in the lap of the sea.
'Tis the home of the Pine tree, the Birch and the Maple,
A Garden of promise, a land fair to see.

"Oh yes, everyone has something to say about the bridge," an Island friend told me one Saturday morning as we walked about the lively Charlottetown farmers' market. "Even the bee-keepers are upset. They think it'll now be easier for swarms of killer bees to find their way here."

I confess that I snickered. This seemed so far-fetched, so desperate a reaching. Paranoid, even. In the moment, a vision swam up before me of secretive cells of these singularly anti-social insects stowing away in camper vans with Ontario plates. I saw scheming, stinging cabals concealed in the luggage of Japanese tourists. I imagined how they had all been coached to choreograph themselves at the moment of landing into swarms that were as hard as mailed fists, that they would take to the air, and throw down the gauntlet before the gatekeepers of every local hive, and then proceed to pound the shit right out of them. But further reflection brought back the memory of St. Modom-noc. The useful didacticism of his story is too often overlooked or forgotten, no doubt because his feast day falls one day before St. Valentine's, who has received a disproportionate amount of press over the years. Modomnoc was an Irish holy man of the sixth century, probably of royal lineage. He travelled to Pem-brokeshire, where he studied at Menevia, in the monastery headed up by David: the very David who went on to become patron saint of Wales. One of Modomnoc's duties among this clan Davidian was to serve them as bee wrangler. He would have become well acquainted with such curious and ancient apiary customs and beliefs as the one which posits that, when bees remove themselves from a hive, it is a sign that their owner is not long for this world. If a keeper died in Modomnoc's time, and his bees were still in place, the hive was draped in mourning, and a piece of funeral cake placed before its opening. As well, when a cadaver was removed from the house, the hives were turned away so that the bees would not witness the removal of the body. This tradition persisted well into the eighteenth century. Hazlitt quotes a story that appeared in the London newspaper *Argus*, September 13, 1790. It tells of the aftermath of the collapse of a rich old farmer who died and "just as the corpse was placed in the herse [*sic*], and the horsemen, to a large number, were drawn up in order for the procession of the funeral, a person called out, 'Turn the bees,' when a servant who had no knowledge of such a custom, instead of turning the hives about, lifted them up, and then laid them down on their sides. The bees, thus hastily invaded, instantly attacked and fastened on the horses and their riders. It was in vain they galloped off, the bees as precipitately followed, and left their stings as marks of their indignation. A general confusion took place, attended with loss of hats, wigs, &c., and the corpse during the conflict was left unattended; nor was it till after a considerable time that the funeral attendants could be rallied, in order to proceed to the interment of their deceased friend."

Modomnoc, having established a connection with his bees, and knowing what he knew about the hardiness of such relationships, could hardly have been surprised that they decided to share in his leave-taking when his studies were done, and he was dispatched back to Ireland. After he had bade the monks a fond farewell, and had hopped into his barque, he heard the familiar buzz of a pleasing, harmonious chorus. He looked up and, lo and behold, there were his bees, settling themselves around his single mast. There they clustered and there they remained, all the way over the sparkling Irish Sea. So it was that Modomnoc brought apiculture to Ireland. The moral of the story is that if bees are willing not only to accept a transfer, but to endure the rigours of so uncertain a voyage at their own expense, they would surely be happy to hitch a ride on faster and more reliable transport. If I were a bee-keeper on Prince Edward Island, I would make sure that certain pertinent clauses were added to my insurance policy.

"I have an opinion about the bridge," says Fred Sauer, who is a watchman by night, an inventor by day, and one of the best friends electricity has ever known. We are standing around in his Charlottetown kitchen, which looks nothing like any other kitchen I've ever seen. It is a circus of circuitry, a jungle thickly hung with brightly coloured wires, a canopy of vivid liana. We are standing because there is really no place to sit, other than on the well-loved La-Z-Boy rocker which is the throne from which Fred rules this, his wondrous, high-voltage kingdom. From time to time, a light flashes to indicate that something is going on elsewhere in the house. Perhaps the sump pump in the basement has kicked into action, for instance, or it may be that one of Fred's two dogs, a gallumphing big mutt called Marmaduke, has retired for a nap. "Big Dukie's in Bed" reads the masking-tape label stuck under one of a panel of eight red lights arranged along one wall. Big Dukie's bed is upstairs next to Fred's bed. Fred has a water-bed, likewise his dog. The canine version is an inner tube filled with water and covered with a blanket. As soon as Big Dukie — a good-natured, shepherd–Dobermann cross with a white muzzle and floppy, comical ears — takes his ponderous weight off his feet and stretches out on his little couch for a kip, the water rises through a tube and makes a circuit. Electricity takes over. Hot, sharp impulses fly along the intestinal twist of wires that are stretched and coiled behind the drywall, passing a baton from hand to electronic hand. The last runner hits the finish line and the light illumines. "Big Dukie's in Bed" is the message it broadcasts.

It might seem an invention of limited utility, but it's perfect for Fred, who has an eye for detail, and likes to keep close track of just about everything that's trackable. For instance, he has a digital counter he can look at to ascertain how many times Big Dukie and Twister — that's Marmaduke's companion pooch — use their doggie door. He has devised a way to determine how much heat his tenant uses, proportionate to overall energy consumption, which has not as much to do with sharing utility costs as with Fred's being able to do it. It's the kind of thing he likes to know, just as he likes to keep the half-dozen clocks in the house synchronized to the second. Similarly, there is no good reason to be sure that Big Dukie's in Bed, other than if bed is where he is, it means he isn't out roaming the neighbourhood, and Fred knows there's no need to activate his electronic dog whistle, which is another of his inventions.

"For the most part I approve of the bridge," says Fred, lighting his pipe from a furnace transformer he's mounted on the workbench near his rocker. A crazy line of sparks crackles between its two delicate prongs, and Fred assures me that they are the trusted agents for 10,000 volts. "That bridge is going to bring more tourist business, that's for sure. This summer will be a dandy if the weather is nice and people don't have to fool around with the boat. But at the same time as it'll bring business, you can bet that it'll bring more thieves. They won't have to wait around for an early morning boat, so they'll be able to come over, rob someone's shop, and get off the island in the middle of the night."

Since Fred is both a watchman and an inventor, he has, of course, been figuring out prophylactic measures businesses and warehouses could take to safeguard against an anticipated criminal invasion. He has come up with a robotic alarm system made up of a wild conglomeration of parts, including copper tubing and a spray of water and something along the lines of his furnace generator that would add 10,000 volts to the mix. It would be activated when someone broke through a window with malice aforethought. Not only would the feisty partnership of water and electricity stop him in his tracks, it would send him reeling back into a collage of spikes and shards and leave him begging for prison.

I ask if a receiving line with a 10,000-volt grip wouldn't effectively eliminate the need for the sharp objects, but Fred assures me that it is not so powerful a charge if handled correctly. Fred is a connoisseur of shocks. They are part of his quotidian experience, and he knows just how much the human body can withstand before it is dragged across damage's jagged threshold. He wonders if I'd like to feel a moderate jolt, just so I know what he's talking about. I decline.

P.E.I. looks so sleepy and docile in the wintertime as to make the presence of a criminal element seem incongruous. However, it has often been said, because it is self-evident and true, that history is repetitive. There is much to be learned about the perils of the present from studying the past. Charlottetown, for all its here-and-now placidity, has seen its share of unsavoury activity. In fact, the hotel where I put up was built on the site of the old gallows. A plaque in the lobby gives an abbreviated account of the city's last public hanging. It took place in 1869. George Dowie (also spelled Dowey) was the star of the show. He was born in Montreal and went to sea as a lad. He wound up as a steward on the *Clara Novello*. One of his shipmates was a man named Cullen, from Limerick. Late in November 1868, while on shore-leave in Charlottetown, they were embroiled in a midnight quarrel over a woman named Miss McQuarry. They fought it out in an alley-way. It came to a calamitous end when Dowie drew a knife and stabbed it into Cullen's heart.

Dr. Beer's coroner's jury rendered a verdict of "wilful murder." The matter went to the Supreme Court, where it was an open-and-shut case. The judge came down fast and he came down hard. This kind of heinous act would not be tolerated in his jurisdiction. The scroll containing the written verdict is available for viewing in the provincial archives in Charlottetown, and it makes for fascinating reading. The many ink blots suggest that the clerk of the Court couldn't wait to wade through the tedious prose of jurisprudence to get to the punchline, the glorious capper which condemns the dagger-happy Dowie to be "taken from hence to the place from whence you came and that from hence you be taken to Pownal Square in Charlottetown on Tuesday, the thirtieth day of March next, between the hours of six o'clock in the morning and six o'clock in the afternoon, where you are to be hanged by the neck till you are dead and may God almighty have mercy upon your soul."

Between the passing of sentence and the actual hanging, the newspaper *The Islander* was chock-a-block with disgruntled letters and editorials. While no one disputed Dowie's guilt, there was a bluster of discontent about the severity of the penalty and about the public nature of his intended earthly demissioning. Surely there was nothing to be gained from so macabre and gruesome an exercise! There were appeals, and stays of execution, and various delays. Finally, on April 6, when every route to clemency had been tried and found blocked, Dowie's sentence ended with a gory period.

By half-past noon, a crowd of 1,500 had gathered for the show. The volunteer militia was present, armed and ready. There had been rumours that Dowie's more radical sympathizers might try something rash. The tension hung in the air *like a swift eagle in the morning glare breasting the whirlwind with impetuous flight*. Every shoulder tensed as the prisoner was led from the jail. He blinked at the midday light, and held his manacled hands up to his eyes. He climbed the stairs to the platform and turned to acknowledge his audience. He looked emaciated, unshaven. There was a welling of pity in every heart. Poor lost soul! Wasn't he some mother's son? Some woman's husband? How had he come to this sorry end? The man he had killed was trash, no one would dispute that. The world was none the worse off for the loss of him, no one would dispute that. As for the woman who'd led him astray — well, she wasn't spoken of in polite society. It didn't seem right, it surely wasn't fair, it was enough to make you choke, and yet, and yet, and yet it was all so irresistible!

The throng pressed in, sucked towards the delicious vortex of punishment, vying for position, eager for proximity until they saw the twenty militiamen lift their rifles, saw the glint of the bayonets, and they all fell back, *hushed as a breathless lyre.* Then they caught sight of something curious, some activity in the wings. Who was that? Only a stage-hand. But what was he carrying? Why, a chair! He held it above his head. He hefted it with as much ceremony and dignity as he could muster, right up the gallows stairs. He set it down stage centre, in front of the drop, and motioned for Dowie to sit. The crowd muttered. This was most unusual. "Down in front," called latecomers, as they craned and scrambled for a better view. They saw the sheriff remove the manacles, saw him hand his prisoner a sheaf of paper. Dowie nodded his thanks and cleared his throat. He took a swig of water from a glass passed him by a prison official. He began to speak. No one had ever heard anything like it. They were held in thrall by the power of his oratory. Scant minutes before he was scheduled to swing, Dowie delivered himself of a stunning sermon. He spoke in a clarion voice that could be heard at the back of the stalls, heard clearly over the squalling of the babies and the bellowing of the chestnut-sellers. It was hard-hitting, no-holds-barred, confessional, cautionary stuff.

"During all my voyages and when I was in port, there was no sin of which I was not guilty....Thousands there are in the world whose record is as black and as heinous as mine — whose lives are as wild and as reckless — who never think of their God as their last end....Seafaring men! I would caution you to avoid such streets as Park Lane in London; Barrack Street in Liverpool; North Street in Boston; Baker Street in New York; Empire Street in New Orleans."

He went on in this vein for a very long time, speaking, related *The Islander*, "with wonderful fortitude and distinctness, only pausing occasionally to take a mouthful of cold water." Who wouldn't wax windy in such adverse circumstances? He knew what lay ahead. Every declamation delayed damnation. Dowie took his time. He thanked those who needed to be thanked (the constables who had been so attentive to his needs while incarcerated, his attorneys who had done their best), and forgave those who needed to be forgiven (the judge, the jury, the hangman). Once again, he advised young men to abandon vicious behaviour, and most especially drink. Then, by way of a peroration, and perhaps most remarkably of all, he launched into a poem of unsurpassingly tearful sentimentality. It was said afterwards that he wrote the whole opus himself, unaided and unencouraged, on the very eve of his execution. The whole opus runs to seventeen stanzas. Here are an illustrative few:

> Weep my dear old mother weep
> Let tears fall fast and free,
> They will help ease your troubled heart
> Of woe and agony....

> Farewell, my mother, sad farewell,
> Likewise my loving wife
> I leave you poor and desolate
> Within this world of strife....

> And from each Christian heart then doth
> A tearful prayer ascend
> That Christ will take me to his home
> Where Sabbaths never end.

He rose from his chair. The hangman turned his hand to his grisly work.

He is buried, I was told, in the Elm Street Cemetery on University Avenue. It's directly across from a laundromat and adjacent to a radiator repair shop. Look up from reading the stony register of the dead and you're struck by a billboard that says "Rust check." I had no luck turning over any trace of Dowie, but did note the prominent marker of Francis Longworth. Longworth was the sheriff who presided over the execution, and it was Longworth who bore the brunt of the blame for what was widely regarded as a badly handled job. In *The Islander* of April

16, 1869, he was given a chance to tell his side of the story, and the archly defensive tone of his writing leaves no doubt that he was feeling a great deal of heat. Little wonder. Public sympathy, in this case, was not with the law. Dowie had moved the people to fits of near rapture. If he was owed anything, it was surely the courtesy of a proper climax. But things went awry. Almost everything that could go wrong with a hanging did. There was no quick dispatch. It lasted for over an hour, a cruel, prolonged, hideous death. Word of the travesty spread, fanning the fires of community outrage. The officials were vilified. The Attorney General demanded an explanation. Sheriff Longworth's exhaustive account is a masterpiece of evasiveness.

It should be stressed at the outset, wrote Longworth, that there was nothing amiss with the gallows themselves. They were in tiptop shape, and all the requisite personnel had been lined up to do their dirty but necessary jobs. He had worked hard to find someone who could fill "the dreaded and unenviable post of hangman. The rope, which the day before I had procured, after searching Charlottetown from one end to the other, was apparently the best and most secure I could find." It must have been an aggravation to him, after all that time devoted to rope shopping, to see the twine break and the intended tumble fifteen feet to the earth below. The Sheriff admits that, while this did happen, there is no truth to the story that Dowie broke both his legs when he fell. He was shaken up, nothing more. He had a contusion on the side of his neck, and a minor case of rope burn. He was returned to his cell to regroup, and then they tried again. Dowie remounted the gallows without a fuss. He did not make a reprise of his speech. Once again the killing lever was thrown. From this point forward, says Longworth, the stories making the rounds are just bald lies, falsehoods from beginning to end. It was true that on the second try Dowie's feet touched the ground, and it was true that, strictly speaking, this might be a breach of hanging etiquette, but there was no doubt that he was dead at the moment of impact. His neck had been dislocated and he was beyond feeling pain. The reason he was then raised up and left to measure the blowing of the breeze for the next forty-five minutes had nothing to do with torturing the man or completing the process of strangulation. It was just done on the doctor's orders, and was strictly routine in such cases. And that, he says, is all there is to report. That, he hopes, will put minds to rest.

Fred Sauer lives just a block or two from where Longworth lies and Dowie is said to rest. When I read the story of that botched hanging, I thought how different it might have been, how much more humane, had someone with Fred's technical expertise been on hand. It would have gone off without a hitch. Fred, I imagined, would even have found a way of automating the procedure. He might even have stood on the other side of the square and worked the drop by way of remote control.

In Fred's house, doors swing and appliances leap into action as if by magic. He activates most everything with a garage-door opener he carries around in his shirt pocket. He can sit in his kitchen rocker and turn on the faucet at the sink, or open any one of the several cabinets he has built and installed around the room. Their doors swivel and lift noiselessly, mysteriously, as if they possess independence of will, to reveal the computers or television contained within. These, too, are coaxed into life with his all-purpose clicker. He can use it to open the under-the-sink cupboard where the garbage lives, or open and close the window. He can use it to start his lathe. The lathe is in a corner of the kitchen, which is not a usual place to find such a tool, but it looks very much at home there. Just about the only thing for which Fred does not use the garage-door opener is to open the garage door. There is no garage.

Fred lives on a little street that has a name but no sign. Save for the tractor parked in the driveway, his two-storey, wood-frame house is unremarkable from the outside. His father bought the tractor for $1,600 in 1955, which was also the year Fred was born. He came into the world on New Year's Eve. He grew up in Savage Harbour, where his parents, German immigrants, ran a hog operation. It was observing the pigs that led Fred to one of his opinions, which has to do with diet.

"One of the things about staying healthy is keeping your weight consistent. Even putting on a pound or two is already screwing up balances in various mechanisms. That's what your body is, a mechanism, and if you treat it like one it'll respond like one. We're always told to eat a cross-section of all these different foods in order to be healthy, but I think you should eat one, high-quality food substance every day. When we were raising pigs — and we were dealing with four or five hundred at a time — they ate the same food, all of them. It was good quality, and there was enough of it, not too much. We never overfed them. They grew fast. They were all healthy. And it clicked. The reason they use pigs for experiments is because their chemistry is similar to ours. It doesn't hurt a human not to eat a wide range of everything from the grocery store. We can get by on just a few things."

Fred, who is lithe and thin and sports a handsome goatee, sustains himself on hamburger, macaroni, and coffee. Especially coffee. He drinks lots and lots of coffee. He likes to add almond flavouring to the brew, and to this end he's recycled a soap dispenser from a dishwasher to squirt out a precisely measured amount of syrup into his cup. As well, he has devised a way to signal the coffee to start brewing downstairs in the kitchen while he is upstairs in the bedroom. Ask Fred why he doesn't avail himself of the timing device that is already built into most automatic coffee makers and he will explain, patiently, that his way gives him more control. He can get up when he feels like it and start the java bubbling, rather than feeling compelled to rise at, say, 7.20 because the coffee maker was set to kick into action at 7.30. It takes him, on average, ten minutes to get dressed. He used to be faster, but he has had to spend more time taking care of such pedestrian business since he lost his left arm.

It happened on May 11, 1977, in Ottawa. Fred had moved there to take a good job in a motorcycle repair shop. He was on his way to work, driving his Kawasaki 900, when he was broadsided by a taxi. The insurance adjusters apportioned the fault equally, but the weight of injury fell entirely on Fred. The impact damaged the brachial plexus nerves of the left arm, leaving it limp "like a big spaghetti hanging there. I woke up in the hospital about ten or eleven days after the accident."

He went back to Savage Harbour to convalesce. When he had adjusted somewhat to his loss, he found work as a mechanic, fixing lawnmowers in the summer and snowmobiles in the winter. In the spring of 1982, he had the arm amputated.

"I'd been talking to doctors about it for five years. I couldn't find any treatment to improve it or to do anything about the pain. I'd hoped amputation might improve that, but it hasn't changed much. That's the worst part of an amputation, the pain. It's like it's burning on fire all the time. The weather influences it, too. When the weather is miserable the pain is miserable."

Fred's arm is gone, but he carries the sensory memory of it. It's very detailed. He shows me with his right arm how he can feel his left arm angled in front of him. The hand really hurts, he says. Oddly, the thumb does not. He shows me where the thumb juts, comfortable and invisible, parallel to his lower ribs. Then he pulls the right arm away, creating a glum vacancy. He has a prosthesis, but says it's useless to him. "Let's just say it's not something the Terminator would use. I've thought of trying to design some kind of a hand, but it would cost hundreds of dollars a month just for the cables. You'd wear them out. God made the human body to repair itself all its life. But cables wear, so how long would it be useful?"

"When did you start inventing stuff?"

"I'd say I got serious about it after I stopped drinking."

"You drank a lot?"

"Yes. That started after the accident."

"Were you alcoholic?"

"I guess so, but it wasn't like I was out making trouble all the time. I'd drink with friends, or I'd drink alone. I preferred to drink alone. I'd sit here and listen to music and drink. Then, ten years later, the day came when I realized that I was going to lose my job if I kept it up. I stopped on St. Paddy's Day, 1987. I didn't need anyone to help me. My opinion is that if you want to do it right, you have to do it by yourself. And you have to find something to replace the booze. You have to do something else with the time."

Fred had always been good with his hands. Now, with that clarity of purpose that so often settles on people who are getting over drinking problems, he determined that he would find ways to be just as good with his hand. He would redirect the obsessive energy he'd put into boozing into finding ways to make life easier for himself. Perhaps he would also find ways to help others with his or a similar disability.

There is no doubt that Fred can lay claim to a particular brilliance. His gift, in addition to pure indomitability, is that he can strip away the limitations of form and function we place on commonplace objects, and see in them possibilities of usage that are obscure to most of us. No talent comes without a price, and Fred has had to pay for his by developing a high tolerance for clutter. Step into the foyer of his house and the first thing that meets the eye is a workbench piled high with a Babel of foundling mechanical bits, lying dormant and still, attending the day that Fred finds a way to reanimate them as part of some unlikely kinetic contrivance. If you were to turn to the left, and walk past the aquarium with the homespun feeding system, you would come to what I think is meant to be the living room, but which is completely inaccessible for anything like conventional living. It is piled chest deep with old turntables, toasters, blenders, kettles, coffee makers, and other such odds and sods: kitchen appliances that have seen better days, but are motherlodes of nifty bits Fred will be able to cannibalize for his inventions, such as the whatnot now under construction, which at this point consists of a pole with a bleach bottle on the top, and what I think is the motor from a tape deck. The basement of the house presents the kind of scene that must rise like a miasma in a fire marshal's nightmare. It is a rat's nest of wires, a tangle of mechanical dross, an accumulation of bags and papers. I wonder out loud if this garish weaving is entirely safe, but Fred shrugs off my concern. He has it under control. Unlike most people, he says, he understands electricity. He is close to it. He knows it's not some wild thing lurking out there, licking its lips, and waiting to pounce. He has it tamed. He knows precisely how it works.

Back in the kitchen he launders his mug before filling it up with more coffee. How do you wash your dishes at the sink when you have just one arm? Fred met the challenge with a motor from an old cash register and a dish-scrubbing brush he attached near the spiggot. When he turns on the water — this time he uses a foot pedal, rather than the aforementioned garage-door opener — the brush whirls around, doing the sinister work that would once have fallen to his missing arm. I notice that the kitchen cabinets are marked with stick-on numbers, one through five, and mention it in passing.

"What do those mean?" I am sure they must have some Kabbalistic significance in Fred's eccentric universe.

"What? The numbers? They're just numbers. Somebody gave them to me and I thought I should use them."

John Valerius was a German of the Upper Palatinate, born without arms in 1667. He developed uncommonly agile feet and he more than got by. There was nothing he couldn't do. With his feet and his toes he could play cards, throw dice, shave himself, fence with a rapier. He became a popular salon figure in London and on the Continent. He does not seem to have wanted for friends or social contacts. Like Valerius, Fred Sauer is a man of enormous talent and psychic reserve. Unlike Valerius, he has not found widespread acceptance for the work he has taken on in response to his disability. He has not been able to coax anyone who might make a difference to the wider dissemination of his inventions into taking them seriously, or even into coming by for a long chat and a good hard look at what he has to offer. It may be that his gadgets are just too particular to his own needs and situation. Certainly, they are unusual. They are every bit as idiosyncratic as the man who made them, as Fred, who could never be accused of feeling sorry for himself, but who has had, by any objective measure, a rough row to hoe in his life, and who freely admits to being lonely.

"I don't understand it. I'll invite people to come around and see the gadgets, I'll invite them four or five times, but no one wants to come near the place. I don't know if they're afraid of it, or of the dogs, or of me. I just don't know. I mean, no one comes to the door, the phone doesn't ring."

We spent just four hours together, over two days. Fred talked fluently and steadily that whole time, but of course there was much that was left unsaid. Two weeks would hardly have been sufficient, there was that much more that he wanted to tell me about his life, his philosophy, his work, his opinions. There were many other inventions, or adaptations, that he wanted to show me. There was so much more for me to learn about his oblique and useful way of looking at the world, about the way his right hand understood what his left hand longed to do. I've shown you just a tiny piece of his valiant, crazy heart.

Disgusting weather was blowing in off the Atlantic when I walked to my hotel. The wind howled *like the fierce fiend of a distempered dream* as I turned my steps back to my own temporary bed, which was made on the spot where the gallows once stood. What pinched face might I see peering down at me when I woke with a start in the thick of the night? The rain streamed down on the unfinished bridge. It thickened and turned to sleet in town. It swarmed. It stung. It fell fast on the pavements, and there became ice, and walking was tough on the Charlatan streets.

Ark

I have been thinking of the difference between
water and the waves on it.
— Kabir

Good old Noah. He was a just man, and perfect in his generations. The Bible tells us so. He was reliable, a paragon of
dependability. It was ever thus with him. "Noah is a careful boy
who follows instructions well." That was what his teachers
would chisel on his report cards. He was the kind of pupil they
liked. He was no trouble at all, and they could forget his name
the minute school dismissed for the summer. He didn't show
much of a predilection for the more academic subjects, so a
vocational counsellor suggested he should be channelled into
the technical stream. That was fine with his parents. They had
a studious daughter who looked to have all the makings of a
doctor or a lawyer and on whom they could heap their white-
collar expectations. It was fine with Noah, too. He was happiest
in the shop. He felt right at home there. It was where his particular intelligence flourished, where he felt most himself. He
understood instinctively the process of materials assemblage.
He always knew what had to be done and when. He never
fussed. He was slow, he was steady, he got the job done. It was
never innovative or visionary, but you knew for a fact that whatever he built was not going to come unseamed after a single use.
Nothing much seemed to worry or rile him. His blood pressure
was consistent, his bowels functioned like clockwork, he slept
eight hours a night, he never once thought about suicide. He

was obviously someone who would never succumb to a stress-related illness.

Noah grew up. He went out into the world. He continued along his measured, circumspect path. He got married right out of high school to a young woman who was the daughter of long-time friends of the family. They only ever quarrelled once, and that was after the birth of their third son. They couldn't agree on a name. She favoured Japheth. He wanted to call the boy Tom. He liked names of one syllable, and thought that Tom would work well with Shem and Ham, who were the baby's older brothers. He imagined them walking down the road, singing "Shem, Ham, Tom" to the tune of "Three Blind Mice." Japheth, he said, was too lispy. It was a name the lad might have to defend with his fists on the playground. The missus held firm. She had had a favourite uncle called Japheth who had died when she was young after being gored by an ox. Noah and his wife exchanged heated words. Finally, he gave in. The tears were too much to bear. All the same, he continued to think of Japheth as Tom, to call him that in the privacy of his own thoughts. He would call him Tom on his deathbed, although he would not lie there for a long, long time. That would not be until all the days of Noah tallied 950 years. The Bible tells us so.

Noah never had a job, exactly. It wasn't for want of trying, it was just that he didn't present well at interviews. He still managed. He kept his family fed, kept body and soul together by working on small contracts and making himself available to his neighbours as a handyman. Everyone knew you could count on Noah. He had all the right tools for all the right jobs. He knew a cubit from a ploughshare, and there was no one who could touch him when it came to working with gopher wood. He knew about pitch, too, knew how to get the really good stuff at a reasonable price, knew how to slather it on for maximum impermeability. There was no need to fret over the possibility of leakage when Noah was around. He had never been known to leave a chink or crevice unplugged.

"Must be a mid-life crisis," everyone said when they noticed him cupping his ear in the direction of the heavens, when he commenced nailing together his three-storey ark. "Do you spell that with a 'c' or a 'k'?" asked the reporter from the local rag who came by hoping for a "lighter side of the news" story he could use as filler. "And do you mind telling me your age?"

"Six hundred," answered the obliging Noah, but his mouth was full of nails, and the reporter understood him to say "fuck off." He left in a huff. He wrote a denunciatory rant and ran it as the lead story in the paper that was published the day before the long rains kicked in; before the waters began to prevail upon the earth. The neighbours read it and shook their heads. Poor Noah, he'd gone off the rails. It's always the quiet ones who surprise you. They turned to the weather forecast on page three. It was for "sunny skies, above-average temperatures." A few planned picnics.

The last thing Noah thought to make was a cribbage board. He was hesitant at first, because it hadn't been mentioned by the Lord as a piece of necessary equipment. However, by the time his precipitation-measuring device was showing an accumulated rainfall of fifteen cubits, and by the time even the mountain peaks were completely submerged, he was glad of this recreational foresight. So was his family. A spirited round or two offered them all a much-needed break from the tedium of shovelling manure. It was a way to kill time when there was no longer any need to beat down the poor drowning buggers who were trying to cling to the side of the ark. Noah had always thought of Japheth's wife as a flighty creature without a practical bone in her body, but it was she who thought to bring along earplugs to block out their screams, and for that he blessed her.

"When you have your sons," he said to her, "it might be nice if you called the first-born Tom."

She smiled, but noncommittally. She hadn't yet told him, had only begun to suspect herself, that there was a wiggling newt in the pond. She didn't want to heap still more trouble on the old fellow's plate by telling him she had already decided her baby would go by Gomer.

Noah stood the midnight watch, so he did his dreaming at noon. He would wake at two, flushed and troubled. He didn't even care to eat the lunch his wife kept covered and waiting in the warming oven. He was having disconcerting dreams about betrayal, about sabotage. Noah had lived long enough to know when to trust his dreams, and there was no question that this was one of great import. He saw that this floating refuge of all that was good and salvageable in the world had somehow come to harbour an agent of evil. How was this possible? The devil must have made his way onto the ark as part of the two-by-two procession, slipping past security in one of his many disguises. Noah would rise from his pallet and stride through the stalls and aviaries, stride among the things that walk and stalk and creep and leap, would study the features of various creatures, would look deep into the eyes of the goats, and the stoats, and the chattering apes, the hens, and the wrens and the slithering snakes. "Is it you?" he would whisper. "Is it you?" But of course, there was never any answer other than a seasick bleating, or a bone-weary whine.

For forty days and forty nights they bobbed around, until "every living substance was destroyed which was upon the face of the ground, both man and cattle, and the creeping things, and the fowl of the heaven." And another 150 days passed after that, while the winds blew and the waters were somewhat assuaged. Eventually, the favoured eight found themselves teetering on the tip of Ararat. At this point, Noah decided enough was enough. They couldn't go on like this for ever. He would have to strike a reconaissance mission, dispatch some trusty agent into the field to see if there was in fact any sign of a field. But who? To whom could he entrust so vital an assignment? He could not be too careful, especially given the opprobrious infiltration of which he had been warned in his dreams.

Now, Noah knew as well as you or I that there are only two animals whose shape is inimitable by Satan. One is the dove.

The other is the lamb. The only way he could be sure of side-stepping a potential snare would be to send one of them out in search of land. Which was it to be? The sweet little dove, all pale and frail, could never endure so arduous a charge, besides which he would miss her gentle cooing. The lamb was another story. The lamb was full of beans, bumptious, and always kicking up a fuss. He had energy to burn. Yes. He would be the one. It would be best to do it fast. Noah picked the fleecy thing up and carried him to the upper deck. He held him under his arm and galloped, nearly tripping on the hem of his robe as he took the stairs two at a time. There was no time to lose and he could not run the risk of reflection, lest he question the mettle of his intuition and stay his hand. If he did that, they would all be lost. He ran past the amazed Mrs. Japheth, who was stroking her swelling belly, ran past Shem and Ham, who were checking each other over for fleas, which had multiplied, and ran past his own wife, who was combing the angora rabbits to within an inch of their lives. (It was Noah's birthday coming up, and she had some mittens in mind.) He ran to the deck railing and hurled the struggling lamb into the green and churning sea. It cried and cried and swam around the ark, its four little hoofs churning up a froth the colour of ewe's milk. Noah had to hurl stones to drive it away. "Get out! Get going! God bless your journey! Come back with news!" he shouted as it paddled off, dragging its tail behind it, struggling to keep afloat against the relentless roll of the waves, and the heavy ballast of its sodden woolly coat.

God looked down from His Heaven and wept. Noah, His trusted simpleton, His old, industrious fool, His chosen one, had got it all wrong. The lamb, the lamb, the pretty little lamb! What a waste. He could not watch it suffering. He pointed a finger and smote it from on high. Only Mrs. Ham saw a slight puff of smoke rise up from the horizon. "Mirage," she said out loud, not knowing whence the word had come. It was the first time anyone had spoken it since the beginning of time. "Mirage," she said again, pleased with her own cunning coining. It would be a fine name for a daughter. She would have told her ship-mates all about this minor epiphany, but her attention was diverted by a raucous blast, half trumpet, half wheeze, from the bottom deck. It was the elephant, who inhabited the stall adjacent to the departed lamb. He sounded for all the world as if he were laughing. God heard him, too, and felt something like suspicion catch in His infinite craw. He peered down through the clouds, directed His X-ray vision through the floorboards of the vessel. He located the source of the sound. His unassailable gaze travelled the length of that snake of a trunk. He looked into the great beast's eye, and saw soon enough what Noah had missed.

"Aha," said the Lord. "It's you. I ought to have guessed. Do you have any idea what you've done? Because of you I had to smite my sweet little pet, my precious doll, my favourite among all my creatures. Well, laugh this off, you coal-eyed dung machine! This is the way it will be with you and with all your children and with your children's children's children, from hence forward, all the days of their lives. This diaspora will not end for you when the waves are worn out and the waters have relinquished their hold on the land. Oh, no, my hearty. You will be hunted, and captured, and killed. Your bodies will be torn asunder and your parts dispersed the world around. And some of you will die in cages. And some will die by water. On this I set my seal!" And He took the blood of the wasted lamb and smeared it all across the western sky.

"Nice sunset," said Ham to his wife.

"Hmmm," she said, although she wasn't really listening. She was trying to remember her marvellous word. That night, as Ham lay on top of her, she whispered strange sounds into the dark. Collage. Triage. Steerage. None of them was right. None of them would do. Oh, well. You couldn't force these things. Perhaps it would come back to her in that no man's land between waking and sleeping. It had worked for her before. Only last month she'd remembered the whereabouts of a button hook that had been missing for weeks. What was it, what was it? Peerage? Marriage? Marriage was close. Ham, who always loved the little games she thought of to play in bed, traced her ear with his tongue and answered her with nonsense sounds, with nursery-rhyme syllables, before shouting out his own private, joyous word. He shuddered, collapsed, and rolled away. He was asleep within seconds. His chest heaved like the slow tumble of the waves. She closed her eyes, pulled the blanket up around her neck, and began to count sheep. Soon she was gone. Everyone slept except Noah. He was down in the cote, talking softly to the white-breasted dove, explaining what would happen next.

And God, as always, kept His word. Thus it was that the psalmist was able to write of ivory palaces. Thus it was that Solomon's throne was made of the stuff. Every three years Solomon's navy pulled into port, the ships spilling over with gold, silver, peacocks, apes, and tusks. "What shall we do with these?" his artisans would ask, holding up the vast elephantine scythes. "Oh, make me up another throne for the summer palace," Solomon would answer, hardly looking up from his writing. "Thy lips," he wrote, "O my spouse, drop as the honeycomb: honey and milk are under thy tongue; and the smell of thy garments is like the smell of Lebanon.... Awake O north wind; and come, thou south; blow upon my garden, that the spices thereof may flow out. Let my beloved come into his garden, and eat his pleasant fruits" (Song of Solomon 4:11, 16).

God never forgets. He's got a memory like — well, let's just say that He never forgets. Yea, verily, unto the present day you can see the working-out of His vengeful promise in cameo brooches, in key chains, in any number of carved trinkets: angels, monkeys, little Buddhas. You can see it in the delicate inlay work on furniture or guitars. You can see it in the eighty-eight keys strung across the thousands of pianos that in the nineteenth century were hauled across the Atlantic or around the Cape, all the way to Canada, where they were manoeuvred overland and hefted into the parlours of homesick immigrants: their link to all they had left behind, their link to more than they knew or imagined. Were it not for the incursions of the devil, none of this would have happened and the elephant Mogul would have lived a blissful life on the Serengeti plain, showering himself with dust, bellowing sweet hymns to the ponderous moon, servicing his harem. Were it not for the incursions of the devil, the elephant Mogul would never have found himself striking out across the Atlantic, paddling to distance himself from a burning ship, his cavernous sinuses clogged with smoke, his heart pounding with an urgency and a hope that had never before inhabited an elephant heart — namely, that he would find the strength to make it to the shores of New Brunswick.

I love a good pachyderm tale, and this one was brought to my attention in Yarmouth, Nova Scotia. Mogul has become part of local lore because Yarmouth was among the last towns to host him in all his magnificence. He fell victim to the family curse not long after leaving that South Shore port on board the good ship *Royal Tar*. That was in October 1836. He was part of a floating menagerie that was operated under the auspices of the Zoological Institute of Boston.

The story of the bizarre fate that befell that circus ship would be a fascinating digression, and a less disciplined writer than I would give in to the urge to tell it, right here and now. However, I had no more gone to Yarmouth to learn about the *Royal Tar* or about Mogul than I had gone there to learn about Mr. Bean. I mean Merit Bean, of course, not Samuel Bean. They are two quite separate stories. Samuel Bean, who claimed to have read the Bible sixty-five times, and who was a physician before he became a preacher, was born in Wilmot Township, Ontario, in 1842. As near as I know, he was never in Yarmouth, although he might have passed through *en route* to Cuba, where he drowned in 1904. Merit Bean is of much more recent vintage and had better luck with water, although just barely. He made a conspicuous entrance into Yarmouth shortly before Christmas in 1975. That was when he barged his house 200 miles across the Bay of Fundy from Cundy's Harbor, Maine. It was a very nice house, and Mr. Bean was attached to it, which is why he didn't want to just leave it behind when he started having set-tos with the Cundy's Harbor fishing co-operative about their wharf. It was a very nice wharf, too. The timbers they used were the best around, a hundred years old, and they blended in beautifully with the Howard Johnson's semi-trailer rig which was one of the principal components of the construction. The wharf measured ninety feet, and Mr. Bean's angry contention was that it had been positioned in such a way as to interfere with his view. "I never would have paid a nickel for this lot had the pier been here," he fumed to *The Bath Brunswick Times Record*. At this, the fishermen scoffed. "We could be two hundred feet longer before we would bother his view," one of them told *The Boston Globe*. "Two hundred feet longer!" he said, gesturing with his scaling knife at the contentious shoreline and derisively stamping his gumboots.

Merit Bean was described by locals as a bit of a mystery man. It was generally understood that he had done well for himself back in New Hampshire with his dealings in real estate and the lumber industry. God only knew why he had come to Cundy's Harbor or what contentment he hoped to find there. He bought some land on Quahog Bay and built a replica of a French farmhouse, seven rooms contained in a yellow frame. The roof was flared, curving up at the eaves. It had a stone front, and three gabled dormers, and was panelled inside with pumpkin-coloured pine. No wonder he didn't want to just pull up stakes and move on. No wonder he thought it worthwhile to run the place through with twin steel I-beams, heft it onto a barge he was renting for $3,000 a day, and steer it through the quarter-mile of ledges and wharves that stood between him and the open waters of the Bay of Fundy, with its uncertain winds and its punishing tides. On the other side lay the twenty-five acres he had bought in Markland, across the harbour from the town of Yarmouth. Mr. Bean had selected it after flying around in his private plane, up and down the Atlantic coast, surveying the scene from above like a dove, scouting about in the hope of finding an appropriate parcel of land. Nova Scotians, he was sure, would give him a warmer welcome than he had received in Maine. The talk around Cundy's Harbor was that he could have built a new and comparable home on those twenty-five Canadian acres for a third of what it was going to cost him to lift and float his treasured French farmhouse. There was great speculation as to whether or not he would ever get it as far as the Bay, the squeeze would be so tight. "He's different than any-body on this earth," the assistant co-op manager told the man from the *Globe*. "A lot of people are really going to be sorry when he goes."

And perhaps it was a sadness for them to say goodbye to Mr. Bean, to see the receding back of his house as the ocean-going tug — newly painted in Germany — hauled it and him away from them for ever. What would they have to talk about now? What would they have to gaze at from their ninety-foot wharf? Just an empty lot. Mr. Bean, for his part, was Lot-like and never looked back. What was done was done. He was fifty-three years old when he said goodbye to Maine and sailed for the north. He was fifty-three years old, which made him 547 years younger than Noah was when he set out on his journey of a lifetime.

Nathaniel Hawthorne was only eleven when he went to Maine. His sea-captain father had died of yellow fever, and his widowed mother was deeply mired in grief. They took a house deep in the woods and led a reclusive, sequestered life. Mrs. Hawthorne rarely stirred from her room. Nathaniel's own activ-ity was restricted because of a foot injury, and so he acquired the habits of reading and solitude. He went on to college and then returned to Salem, where he had been born, a place that for him was full of ghosts. Here, his founding-family ancestors had ordered Quakers to be whipped and had sat in judgment at the witchcraft trials. He wrote to his mother, "I do not want to be a doctor to live by men's diseases, nor a minister to live by their sins, nor a lawyer to live by their quarrels. So I don't see there is anything left for me but to be an author." He continued to live hermetically while he studied the writer's trade. In the very year that Mogul the elephant swam panting, struggling against the downward tug of the cold Atlantic currents, Hawthorne was locked away, setting down the stories he would publish in 1837 as *Twice-Told Tales*. One of them, "Chippings With a Chisel," has to do with visits paid to the workshop of a Martha's Vineyard gravestone carver, "an elderly man, a descendant of the old Puritan family of Wigglesworth." He's an uncluttered character, but not by any stretch simple-minded. He has acquired a certain salty wisdom through his years of dealing with the recently bereaved, of chipping into marble slabs the names of the newly dead. The narrator spends time with Mr. Wigglesworth, observing the various comings and goings of his customers. "None of the applicants, I think, affected me more disagreeably than an old man who came, with his fourth wife hanging on his arm, to bespeak grave-stones for the three former occupants of his marriage-bed. I watched with some anxiety to see whether his remembrance of either were more affectionate than of the other two, but could discover no symptom of the kind....I shuddered at the gray polygamist, who had so utterly lost the holy sense of individuality in wedlock, that methought he was fain to reckon upon his fingers how many women who had once slept by his side were now sleeping in their graves. There was even — if I wrong him it is no great matter — a glance side-long at his living spouse, as if he were inclined to drive a thriftier bargain by bespeaking four grave-stones in a lot."

Physician–preacher Samuel Bean, who drowned thousands of leagues to the south of where Mogul fought his pitched and valiant battle against both the sea and divine will, and who was born five years after the publication of *Twice-Told Tales*, might have been labouring under the influence of "Chippings" when he commissioned the single stone that marks the grave of his first two wives, Henrietta Furry and Susanna Clegg. (Some sources say they were sisters.) His first marriage lasted only seven months. He took Susanna to wife shortly after Henrietta's death. Alas, she also found the strains of married life too much to bear — those doctors and their long hours — and proved herself to be just as eager as Henrietta to turn out the lights. In fact, the second Mrs. Bean died nineteen months to the day after the first. Henrietta and Susanna are buried side by each in the Rushes Cemetery, which is south of Crosshill, which is near Wellesley, Ontario, which is near Kitchener. Their marker has been much observed and admired. It has weathered badly, however, and in recent years a duplicate stone has been planted next to the original. The local carver — the Crosshill equivalent of Hawthorne's Mr. Wigglesworth — decorated it with a common funerary symbol of the day: a clenched hand, the index finger extended and pointing upwards. The text, however, is anything but common.

We deal individually with grief, as we need and must. Some weep, some sleep, some put the crypt back in cryptogram. Dr. Bean knew how to heal his broken heart. He sat down with a piece of paper and a quill and he got right to work on a puzzle, fifteen characters across and fifteen characters down. He was a peculiar chap, with a turn of mind that was both mischievous and mystic. He was two times a widower, and still he had the wherewithal to smile as he imagined future graveyard visitors doing a double take as they passed by his crafty arrangement of numbers and letters. This was a bone they could worry at for years and years to come!

Of course, he made sure the number seven figured prominently in the solution. He knew about the power of seven. He had grown up hearing that a sick man could be made whole if his shirt were dipped seven times in south-flowing water. He was well acquainted with the powers ascribed to the seventh son, or better yet, the seventh son of a seventh son: that his touch could cure scrofula, or that warts would vanish if you washed them in his baptismal water. As a Bible scholar, he knew that Elijah, atop Carmel, sent out his servant seven times to look for rain, knew that Elisha sent Naaman to wash in the river Jordan seven times, knew that when Jericho was taken they compassed the city seven times. Seven, then, gives you the key. Start at the top left-hand corner, and count seven letters in. Then, count seven letters down. Then, read from the centre in a zigzag counter-clockwise spiral.

In memoriam Henrietta, 1st wife of S. Bean M.D. who died 27 Sep 1865 aged 23 years 2 months & 17 days & Susanna his 2nd wife who died 27th April 1867 aged 26 years 10 months & 15 days. 2 better wives 1 man never had. They were gifts from God but are now in Heaven. May God help me so to meet them there.

Dr. Bean's neighbours weren't so very surprised when they saw the stone. They had been more or less prepared for it by

Henrietta's memorial service. Then, they were presented with a black-edged funeral card on which was inscribed a similarly crafted brain teaser. Hardly anyone paid any attention to the eulogy, they were all so intent on deciphering the message.

In memoream Henriettah Furry Bean born in Penn. Married in Philadelphia to Samuel Bean M.D. & went with him to Canada leaving all her friends behind — died in Linwood the 27th of Sep. 1865 after an illness of 11 weeks aged 23 years 2 months & 17 days she was a model wife 1 of 1000 — Much regretted by her sorrowing husband & all who knew her — Was married 7 months & 10 days — Lived a godly life for 5 years & died happy in the Lord — Peace be to her ashes — So mote it be.

What did the townfolk think? Were they in any way suspicious about his short back-to-back marriages, about the truncated lives of the two has-Beans? Was it just bad luck, or did medicine play a part? A few of the locals must surely have wondered. He was plenty unusual, that Dr. Bean; he had all that easy access to poisons, and he would know just how to use them. In the end, they shelved such fruitless musings. They led precisely nowhere, and were convincingly invalidated by the evidence of his third marriage to Annie Wankmiller, which went on for thirty-four years. Happily, happily were they wed. Happily, happily did they live, in New York and in Iowa. And then he went to Cuba for his old-man-and-the-sea routine.

Dr. Sam divided public opinion, but there was no neighbourly equivocation about Merit of Maine. They couldn't abide him in Cundy's Harbor and he wasn't quick to endear himself to Yarmouthians, either, after he quite literally barged into their lives. The crew made good time getting from Cundy over Fundy on a Monday. The house was towed through the treacherous shoals and into the bay that evening, and by Tuesday midnight the tug's pilot could see the several unextinguished lights of Yarmouth, which is an early-to-bed kind of town. The barge drew near to the wharf, and that was the end of the smooth sailing. The wind picked up and dislodged the chimney, which crashed through the roof with its pagoda-style eaves, and sullied with plaster dust the pumpkin-hued panelling. There was a problem establishing an equitable relationship between the moorings and the tide, and when the tug of one met the too-taut resistance of the other, the enterprise was nearly pulled asunder. The cranes that were to actually hoist the building onto its new foundation site were delayed. A nasty gale blew up, the barge slipped its moorings and scuttled across the harbour, by which time a corner of the house had been split open, leaving the interior exposed to the lashings of the freezing, salty spray. The cranes arrived but got mired in the mud on the public access road to Bean's twenty-five acres, and when they were finally removed, the road was so badly chewed up as to be impassable, which vexed the new arrival's neighbours who were counting on being able to use the thoroughfare to get to and from their home, especially with Christmas coming on and whatnot. Not only had the cranes damaged their road and their property, Bean had been seen tampering with their lobster traps, shoving them out of his way, in strict violation of an unwritten code of maritime etiquette. Ask any Easterner to complete the sentence "Thou shalt not" and he or she will invariably respond with "dislodge another man's lobster traps." Strong words were bandied. The neighbours, who were not about to forgive him his trespassing, summoned the Mounties. Lawyers were soon on the scene. Writs were issued. Merit Bean had arrived in Canada.

That's just the way of it when you live in a harbour town. You get out of bed in the morning, step onto the porch to pick up the paper, and you're like as not to find yourself staring at some damn thing or other that wasn't there when you retired, something that started out in a distant elsewhere, and that the waves piggybacked to your door, overnight express. Sometimes it's a note in a cerulean bottle, or a bit of driftwood sculpted by the acid wash of the sea to look like the holy rood. Sometimes, it's a house on a barge and a cantankerous American. You just never know from one day to the next, and isn't that one of the reasons you live there? The shores around Yarmouth have seen their share of flotsam and jetsam, both the mundane and the obscure: ships' masts and timbers, tea chests, harp frames, glass floats, beaded evening gloves, monogrammed cigarette cases, horseshoes, a lamb skull of great antiquity, men with their legs amputated at the knees. Oh, yes. Even that. Among the citizens who were aghast at the antics of Mr. Bean were several who remembered the death in 1912 of Jerome, a transplant to nearby Meteghan. His obituary appeared in *The Yarmouth Herald* on April 23.

DEATH OF JEROME

This well-known but mysterious man of Meteghan died on Friday last. With his passing away disappears a most remarkable character in the Province, if not in the world. Although for upwards of half a century (we think since 1854) he has been living in Meteghan no one knows his name, his nationality, nor any particulars of his relatives. The family who took care of him have [sic] been receiving from the local Government the sum of $104 annually for his care. He was found on the shore by two men early one morning without legs, with his palate cut, moaning piteously. He was taken care of, and as he could not speak, his identity remains a mystery up to the present. He had apparently been an officer of some warship, as his garments led to this belief. He was then about 24 years old, so that he was about 82 years when he died.

There he lay, languishing on the beach, all of a morning early, legless, mute, a sack of damp biscuits and a jug of water nearby, a scene that might have been cooked up by Edgar Allan Poe while channelling the spirit of Omar Khayyám. He had only one sound in his repertoire, and his rescuers took it as a given that he was telling them his name. "Jerome, Jerome," is what they understood him to mumble, forcing the sounds out over his damaged palate. What? His name? Come now! Let us summon empathy to the fore, something the slack-jawed Meteghanians were excusably too stunned to manage. Let's put ourselves in the castaway's shoes, never minding for the moment that he had no need of them. Consider. If you had spent hours and hours, possibly even days, sprawled out on the sand and unable to walk or speak, defenceless against the crueller ministrations of the sun, the wind, the rain, would your name necessarily be the first piece of intelligence you would hasten to impart to the passers-by who were your only chance for worldly salvation? Or would you be more inclined to ask for something that would be truly useful?

"Cologne! Cologne!"

"A tome! A tome!"

How long it had been since he'd had a bath or something decent to read? But no. "Jerome, Jerome" was the consensus they reached that morning, standing over him while he wheezed on the sand, or so the story is told.

Who's to say, who's to say? It is, in film-business parlance, a story "with legs." It has stumped along smartly over the years, and there's no need to probe too deeply to understand why this might be so. You need only hear the story in its barest outline, as I first did — "and then there was Jerome who was washed up legless on the shore" — to willingly pick up the hook, lance your own lip, and beg to be reeled in. "Washed up legless on the shore." What could be more evocative? You'd have to be as senseless as granite to hear those words and not conjure an image of the beached half-man; not to see him there by day, stunned by the sun, crumpled where *the surf was like the advancing lines of an unknown enemy flinging itself upon the shore*; not to see him there at night, prone Jerome alone among the stones, when *the stars lay on the lapis-lazuli sky like white flower petals on still deep water*. It is a story that is magnificent for its sparseness, that begs for individual investiture. How and why did he? Who and where was he? It's because of everything we don't know that Jerome has become a twice-told, thrice-told, oft-told tale: oft-told, at least, in and around that part of the world where he spent more than half of his peculiar life. It is the absence of fact that lends Jerome his strength. It is because there is so little about him that is concrete that he floats. It's because he is a mystery that he became a legend. Leg end.

Jerome is a juicy bit of gossip, a chuckle in the endless dialogue between the land and the sea. The same could be said of Mogul, the circus elephant who went down with the ship, and whose last battle was in all ways elemental. The same could be said of Merit Bean, who turned up like a tortoise with his house on his back, and who didn't last long in Yarmouth; who went elsewhere to find whatever it was he was looking for, and who left behind the rumour that his strangeness was due to a brain tumour; who left behind his squabbled-over French farmhouse; who made like a pigeon and flew the coop.

Pigeons. Yes. Now I remember. Pigeons are the reason I'm telling you all this. It was because of those scruffy and ubiquitous birds that I went to Yarmouth in the first place. An explorer in search of a totem or an emblem to stitch on his standard could do worse than to settle on the pigeon. It would be a mistake to call these intrepid navigators "fly by night," as they are among those sensible birds that prefer to migrate during the day and orient their compasses to the sun. They are capable, if required, of finding their way after dark. Pigeon trainers with the U.S. Army were able to convince them to do just that during the First World War, thus increasing their chances of avoiding capture by taloned and enemy raptors.

One would think that their directional genius alone would be reason enough for us to venerate these motley birds. Unfortunately for pigeons, we have never been much inclined to value them just because they can distinguish one isthmus from another from a height of 6,000 feet. We shoo them from pedestals, rather than placing them there, not caring in the slightest that they are able to discern the subtle vibrations of even the slightest of ley lines and use them to find their way home. If ever an avian order stood to benefit from the interventions of a good publicist, it would be the columbidae. Those among their number who can get away with being called "doves" have an easier time of it, of course. Symbol of peace, of the Holy Ghost, a convenient rhyme for "love": all this dictates that we respond to the soft syllable "dove" with a kind of warm fuzziness and generosity of spirit. When we read that doves were a favourite sacrifice on Old Testament altars, we wince. But the news that their more maladroit cousins, the garden-variety columba, were every bit as agreeable an offering elicits nothing but plain indifference, or possibly even a tiny twinge of gladness.

"And if the burnt sacrifice for his offering to the Lord be of fowls, then he shall bring his offering of turtledoves, or of young pigeons. And the priest shall bring it unto the altar, and wring off his head, and burn it on the altar; and the blood thereof shall be wrung out at the side of the altar: And he shall pluck away his crop with his feathers, and cast it beside the altar on the east part, by the place of the ashes: And he shall cleave it with the wings thereof, but shall not divide it asunder: and the priest shall burn it upon the altar, upon the wood that is upon the fire: it is a burnt sacrifice, an offering made by fire, of a sweet savour unto the Lord" (Leviticus 1:14–17).

In my hotel room in Yarmouth, I turned on the TV and caught the end of a newscast about how the city of Moncton had just introduced an ordinance making it illegal to feed pigeons in public places. None of the council's reasons for enacting this prohibition was startling, unusual, or particularly unreasonable. The birds were a nuisance. They were a health hazard. They were fouling public walkways. The population was growing out of control. I watched and listened as the reporter read through the predictable inventory of columbaceous crimes, knowing with sibylline certainty what was to come next. And sure enough, the sequence cut to a park. There was a man in a park and also in a parka. He was tossing corn, a snowbound Demeter, and he was surrounded by a hundred beating wings, spinning away from him like Catherine-wheel sparks. He was the local pigeon man and when the camera cut to a close-up, his face filled the screen. His knitted toque. His sad eyes behind smudged glasses. His nose, threatening to run. He was vowing defiance. The law was an ass, he would continue to feed his birds, it was winter, it was cold, they relied on him and on others with tender hearts and bags of grain, what would they do, what would they do, and what real harm was it, anyway? What harm?

I once lived down the street from a vacant lot in the west end of Vancouver. Every morning, an old woman came and stood by the sign that specifically forbade feeding the pigeons, and gleefully fed the pigeons. They would wait for her to come, this hungry feathered legion, in their dunnish coats with their greasy collars, with their ringed and snapping eyes, with their flawless sense of direction, all of them lined up, polite after a fashion, respecting an order of their own devising, kind of like rock fans camped out and lolling on the sidewalk in front of the box office on the night before tickets go on sale for a Stones concert. They perched on the rooftops of the nearby church, the apartment buildings, and houses, waiting and prating, cooing and pooing. Oh, how they loved to poo! It lay thick on the paving bricks, it marred the cars, they let it fly on the passers-by. It was terribly unpleasant. They had worked out a routine. It never varied. A posted sentry would send out word when their renegade benefactor turned the corner, and they would rise like a well-trained choir from their loft, and flutter down around her. She had bags of feed she bought at the pet-food store, and she talked to her soup-kitchen hangers-on as she doled out the grub. "Pigeons," I heard her say once, with a commendable sense of understatement, "yes, yes, my pigeons." It was irritating as all get-out, of course. Feelings ran high against her. There was no one in the neighbourhood who couldn't be relied upon to spell "psittacosis," that unfortunate chlamydial disorder activated by inhaling the microbial nastiness that thrives among pigeon (or parrot) feathers and droppings. It can bring on bouts of pneumonia, and in severe cases patients may require artificial ventilation. Pigeons can also play a role in transmitting aspergillosis, candidiasis, coccidiosis, cryptococcosis, encephalitis, erysipelas, histoplasmosis, Newcastle disease, salmonellosis, toxoplasmosis, tuberculosis, yersiniosis, helminths, ectoparasites, and that's not all. You'd want to think twice about accepting a blood transfusion if you knew a pigeon had been the donor. (Anyone who feels a need to plumb the subject should refer to Walter J. Weber's seminal work, *Health Hazards from Pigeons, Starlings, and English Sparrows*. It is an enlivening text, full of conversational ice-breakers. One's cocktail-party chatter is hugely enriched by the knowledge that Manson's eyeworm is a common parasite among pigeons, and that they often pick it up from chowing down on cockroaches.)

The old girl who came out every morning and fed the pigeons in contravention of the posted bylaw didn't give a hoot for toxicology. While it might have been galling to watch her give succour to these half-wit plague incubators, it was impossible not to admire her pluck. She had determination to burn, she had the strength of her convictions, and she simply didn't care about the parochial priorities of civic authorities. She certainly had the undivided attention of a great many pigeons. I'm not sure I would go so far as to say she had their love, but I don't doubt for a second that they had hers. I don't doubt for a second that she nourished them because she loved them. It was that simple, and that rich. She loved them, they were an outlet for her love, and perhaps she was able to believe, feeling the beat of their wings, that they loved her back.

"Well, they were like family. It was a relationship. You've got to have an emotional connection to something," says Arthur Thurston, explaining why he kept pigeons, and not just a few either. Mr. Thurston, who is a historian, author, and columnist, is well known in Yarmouth. He has often been in the papers and often for reasons other than his column, in which he describes events of historical interest in the area. In this regard, he has a rich vein to mine. Stories of shipwrecks alone could keep his engines stoked for years at a stretch. He is a prolific writer. He thinks that at this point in his career — he is nearly seventy

— he has written more than three million words. On the day I visited, he had just fired off a new batch of writing, including a piece about two Yarmouth boys who rode with Custer. There is no end to the stories you can find if you're willing to dig for them.

Arthur Thurston lives kitty corner to a funeral home, and next door to the synagogue. The synagogue is a handsome structure, built in 1906. These days, it is little used. The numbers in the congregation have dwindled, which is a familiar-enough scenario in small-town churches and temples the country over. It is still maintained, however, and stands as a reminder that Yarmouth, not so very long ago, was a cosmopolitan burg, a thriving mercantile centre, the second-largest shipping port in the country. While this is not to say that the present-day town is hanging on the precipice of ruin, it does seem very much the kind of place that is a monument to an earlier heyday. Having said that, I would add that it looks to be a very well-preserved monument, and that preservation of a noteable past seems to me a perfectly adequate *raison d'être* in the present moment. There are not many places of a similar size with so impressive a stock of heritage buildings. It is a pleasure, even in winter, with the wind whipping off the harbour, to stroll the streets and take in the houses, with their abundance of gingerbread and their elegant façades. Look to the rooftops and you will see a regular widow's cruse of widow's walks. Every block is a showcase of architectural fashion, Italianate, Second Empire, Georgian, as well as the various styles of revival: Greek, Gothic and Queen Anne. You can easily imagine how sea captains, returning from their far-flung travels, might have wanted to build a dwelling that would be, in effect, a souvenir, a home base that would capture something of the fancy of far away. They built their houses to withstand the insistent pressure of their own nostalgia, and they continue to bear up well under the weight of ours.

Arthur Thurston's family has been in Yarmouth for generations. He lives on a street that was laid out by and named for his great-uncle. The house in which he grew up and lived for sixty-one years stood on the same lot occupied by his present home, which is new and cottage-like. Its construction was organized by a consortium of concerned citizens who banded together to help him out after the family home was demolished in 1990. There's a cheerful, hand-lettered sign in the window — you can see it plainly from across the street — that says "Welcome Home Mr. Thurston." It seems to have been there for some time, which lends it an air of stubborn defiance. The window is also decorated with a Confederate flag. He likes to ask visitors if they are bothered by it. One of his abiding interests is the American Civil War, which he has often written about, in articles and in his books, such as *Tallahassee Skipper*. He has named his house "Tallahassee."

"I don't know why you want to see me," Mr. Thurston had told me on the phone when I'd called to see about an appointment and explained my little project. "I'm not eccentric at all. I can't think why anyone would say so! But you can come around if you wish. You know that I'm on oxygen?"

I'd heard that was the case, heard that he suffers from chronic asthma. But what I'd mostly heard about was pigeons. For all his three million words, for all his research, for all his hard and valuable work to keep local history a part of the continuum, it is with pigeons that his wider celebrity lies. Toss out Arthur Thurston's name to just about anybody in Yarmouth and they will say, pigeons, pigeons, Arthur and his pigeons. He kept them, you know, kept them for years, lots and lots of them, so many, many pigeons. They had the run of his house. They were everywhere. After a while, well, you can imagine. It was two and a half storeys, that house, and the upper window was always open, so in and out they flew. In and out. It had been different when his mother was alive; she was a bit of a neat freak, really. When she was alive she kept things in line. But after she was gone, the pigeons took over. It just got to be too much.

At first a few people complained, then more people complained. And it wasn't just the mess. It was Arthur, living like that. It wasn't just that they were angry about the birds, they were concerned for him. It couldn't go on. Something had to be done. So it was that the pigeons came to roost at the epicentre of a decade-long battle that was played out in the town-council chambers, in the papers, in the courts. Pigeons feathered a fracas in which just about everyone took part and took sides.

It seemed that the one person who couldn't say pigeons and problem in the same breath was Arthur Thurston. Arthur Thurston thought then what Arthur Thurston thinks now, which is that there wasn't any problem. There were only pigeons, and he was quite happy to have them living there, in his house, and living there in their hundreds. "Hundreds" is what everyone remembers. "Hundreds" is what the papers reported. He says there were considerably fewer. Dozens, perhaps. Anyway, what did it matter to anyone else? It was nobody's business but his own. But of course, it was. Finally, it fell to the Supreme Court of Nova Scotia to issue an ultimatum. Mr. Thurston was found guilty of housing-standards violations. On Hallowe'en day, 1989, the court declared that, unless he was able to clean his place up, unless he was able to bring it up to scratch within ninety days, the corporation would be within its rights to take possession and deal with the problem as the town elders saw fit. They could bulldoze, if they wanted to. They wanted to. The house in which Arthur Thurston was raised was razed ninety-four days later, on February 2, 1990.

So much attention was focused that day on Mr. Thurston's forced removal from his premises, and the demolition of his house, that hardly anyone thought to remark that it just happened to be the fourteenth anniversary of the great Ground Hog's Day storm, which was the worst recorded meteorological contretemps in the history of south-shore Nova Scotia. Boats and buildings were battered, insurance companies wept, streets became rivers on which people rowed. It was as though the flood had come again: not the flood of Genesis, mind, but the flood that is spoken of in Mi'kmaq legend. In that story, after a long and cleansing rain, a pigeon is dispatched from a boat that is the last remaining outpost of virtue. The bird flies and flies and finally finds not just any old piece of land, but the country we now call Canada. He lands, scouts around, scoops up a blueberry leaf as proof of his discovery (not, note, a maple leaf), and wings his way back to the vessel, where the holy people rejoice at this sign that drier days are near to hand. Then the pigeon perches on the prow, and guides them to that distant shore.

Three of that antediluvial navigator's descendants now live in Arthur Thurston's living room. They are caged, and look to be carefully attended. His cosy house (eight metres long and seven metres wide) is likewise well looked-after, cluttered but clean. It is redolent of bird, that sour, somewhat fecal smell, but it's an odour you adjust to. Mr. Thurston has not been well in recent years. His asthma has taken its toll, and he must be hooked up to a cumbersome oxygen-feeding system, which means that he's pretty much a shut-in. There's a hospital bed in the corner of the room, and various medications round about. He takes fifteen different pills as part of his daily regimen. A "meals on wheels" volunteer turns up with his lunch. For all these signs of invalidism, he's lively of mind; he continues to research and to clack out his column on his typewriter, and his famous memory is as prodigious as ever. He can rhyme off names and dates in Yarmouth history with Gatling-gun efficiency, his speech patterns punctuated by occasional pauses while the oxygen makes its way from tank to lungs. While I am there, a student phones asking for help with a history assignment. Mr. Thurston was for many years a high-school teacher, and is the very soul of consideration with his caller, suggesting this and that source or tack she might take, telling her tidbits about her own family's role in recent Yarmouth history.

"I know too much," he says with a chuckle, when he puts down the phone, "and I think that scares some people. I have all the dirt, you see. I know about who did what when and to whom, know about which wife from which respectable family had an affair with a boy scout. That makes them nervous. Did you say you're a writer? I am, too. My interests are history, especially of Yarmouth; the Civil War; guns and swords; and capital punishment. Have you read my books?"

I was sorry to say I had not, although it was not for want of trying. They are hard to come by, and even the Yarmouth bookstore didn't stock any of his nineteen titles. Arthur Thurston is proud, and justifiably so, of these fruits of his historical research. He has written about Nova Scotia flying aces, in *Bluenose Spitfires*. He has written about some of the Yarmouth County First World War dead, in *A Monument Speaks*. He is especially fascinated by the role Yarmouth played in the Civil War, when Yarmouth fast boats operated out of Saint John as Union blockade runners, ferrying supplies to the Confederate army in Wilmington and Charleston. Mr. Thurston is very happy to talk about his writing, as well as about his collection of vintage swords and pistols. Each of them has a distinguished pedigree. He has a sabre that was brandished in the Charge of the Light Brigade, and a sword that was worn by a Governor General of Bermuda. He has a handgun that was presented by Robert E. Lee to his son.

"How did you begin collecting guns and swords?"

"There was a sheriff here. A son of a bitch, a real prick. He had a big gun collection, and I wanted to outshine him. So I started collecting with a vengeance. I have one that belonged to Cornelius William Van Horne who built the CPR. He was presented with it a year after the railway was finished. It's very rare, a first of that calibre."

"Aren't you worried about security? These are valuable pieces."

"No. Anyone who came in here and tried to rob me would get a sabre through the butt, and not a very clean sabre, either."

"And how did you get interested in pigeons?"

"I thought you said you were a writer."

"I am. Well, I'm a sort of a writer. I'm more of a story gatherer."

"If you're a writer, why are you asking me about pigeons? Why aren't you asking me about writing?"

"Because of everything people have told me about you. I'm collecting stories about eccentrics, and you kept all those pigeons. That's not exactly usual, is it?"

"I'm not eccentric. I can't help it if people say so. They get nervous around me because I know so much more than they do."

"But the house. Didn't they tear down the house because of the pigeons?"

Silence. Then, "You must have seen my book *Tallahassee Skipper*. If you look under those papers you'll find a copy."

This was a conversation that made me feel profoundly uncomfortable. Cannibalistic. What was I doing here? Trying to trick him in some way? What was I expecting of this bright-eyed, white-tufted, intelligent, housebound man who didn't know me from Mogul, the sanctity of whose home I had invaded with my little notebook and my prying questions? How big a piece of him was I after? Oh come on, Arthur! Tell me how the pigeon shit was three feet deep in some places, that there were fifty to sixty dead birds around the house when it was finally demolished; tell me about the three oil heaters that were teetering on various chairs, about the blanket on the droppings-covered floor. Tell me, was that where you slept? That's what the provincial inspector for the Nova Scotia Society for the Prevention of Cruelty to Animals suggested in a letter to *The Chronicle-Herald*. It was published on February 28, 1990, a month after the demolition, and when the heated controversy about your ousting was still making the news around the province.

The house came down on a Friday. "'They're killing my pigeons,' he said as he watched his home fall." That was the sub-headline for an article that appeared in section B of Saturday's Halifax paper. It painted a piteous picture. A small group gathered to watch the demolition of the 120-year-old house. It took just a few minutes to effect its transformation to rubble. Some said that not all the birds, which were to have been removed and put in the care of the SPCA, were clear of the structure before the power shovels came in with their jaws wide open. Arthur Thurston watched from a police cruiser, powerless to stop the carnage. "How much blood do they want? How much blood is there in one human being?" Those are the Shylockian words he is reported to have cried out, buckling under the weight of his persecution. Some children brought him a pigeon whose leg had been mangled. He wrapped it in a handkerchief and held it close.

His first pigeon had also been hurt. It was given to him by Cecil Mangue, a golf pro at the course where Arthur used to play. (He was once an avid golfer, and still pays sufficient attention to the game to know that one of his pigeons, Brownie, died on the day golf wizard Tiger Woods was born: December 30, 1975.) He named it Cephas, as in: "And he brought him to Jesus. And when Jesus beheld him, he said, Thou art Simon the son of Jona: thou shalt be called Cephas, which is by interpretation, A stone" (John 1:42). This much about his troubled life as a pigeon fancier Arthur Thurston told me. It was an ironic choice of names, given that it was the beginning of an obsession that led finally to the casting of the stones that brought his life crashing down around him.

The handling of the pigeon man of Yarmouth divided public opinion. There were those who said he had been given ample warning, time and again, that he had been advised of the possible consequences of purposefully and wilfully ignoring instructions to bring his house in line with standards clearly spelled out in city bylaws. He had been so careless about its maintenance that it was structurally unsound as well as unsanitary, and there was nothing for it but to call in the wreckers. Others thought the town-sanctioned action was unnecessarily severe, that the public-nuisance factor of the pigeons had been grossly exaggerated, that their guardian was a man who had chosen to follow a different path, and it was for that more than anything else that he was being punished. Among the Thurston supporters was, and is, Sheriff Basil Pero. "People," he told me, "live their own lives in their own way, and if they're not hurting anyone they should be left alone." He was one of the prime movers in arranging a mortgage for "Tallahassee." Sheriff Pero feels that the RCMP, who had the responsibility for removing Mr. Thurston from his natal home, were heavy-handed in the extreme. Fred Hatfield, on the other hand, who is the editor of the venerable *Yarmouth Vanguard*, for which paper Mr. Thurston writes his column, and who was also there on the eventful day, says that the officers did an unpleasant job with considerable compassion. It's a question of hermeneutics, of interpretation. Stories change as they travel, which is how a legend grows.

Arthur Thurston, for all his expressed reluctance to talk about the pigeons of the past, still harbours so much anger about the events of February 2 that he can't hold back from a now-and-again need to vent. He can't help himself. It just comes up in conversation. He says that he owes his bad health to a small stroke he suffered when he was forcibly removed from the house. He talks of the various lawsuits he has launched or is planning to launch against the town. He still reports — as he did in the days following the demolition, when he was being pestered for comments — that some of his personal possessions, such as various papers and academic certificates, were stolen or hauled off to the dump with the detritus that was once his home. And that's not all. He knows more than he's saying. He can name names.

When the house was gone, Arthur Thurston lived in rented rooms and did a stint or two in hospital. He moved into his new digs at the end of March 1994. He's comfortable there. It looks like home. There's a calendar from Ernie's Bar & Grill tacked to the wall, as well as a few newspaper clippings, some of them about other pigeon lovers elsewhere in the country who have run afoul of authority. And there's a photograph of Arthur himself, taken by Fred Hatfield. He's standing outside the house that is no more, surrounded by his one-time flock.

After the old place came down, the birds remained in the neighbourhood. Of course. It was what they knew. Deprived of their habitual haunt, they sought out other nearby roosts. They clung to the eaves of the synagogue, heedless of the cruelties dealt them by the rabbis of yore. They swarmed all over the

Arthur Thurston.

neighbours' rooftops. They were more of a nuisance than ever before. Once again, the town elders gnashed their teeth. Solutions were considered, including hiring a Pied Piper to lure the winged vermin to some out-of-sight, out-of-mind, Never-Never Land. New Brunswick was mentioned as a possibility. Eventually, the birds agreed to disperse, seemingly of their own accord, and migrated to the waterfront. Mr. Thurston continued to see to the maintenance of the flock, paying for the feed which his supporters would distribute twice a week: six to eight forty-kilogram sacks of whole corn would be spread out on a grassy location. "I love them," Arthur Thurston said once, by way of explaining his devotion, "they're like little people. They've been my only life. Other than my writing, they're really all I have."

It is said that Noah first released his sweet dove into the sky above the endless sea on April 1. Poor old fool! The joke was on him, as the elephant knew very well. Perhaps he allowed himself a covert snicker when he heard the bird had come back, hungry and empty-beaked, her white breast heaving, so tuckered from her exertions that she could hardly keep to her perch with her little red feet. It was not until her second foray that she was able to find the tell-tale olive branch, and the reluctant mariners could finally count on bidding "ta ra ra" to Ararat. And the elephant might have laughed even then, knowing full well that all the purging had been for naught. They'd get back on dry land, they'd go forth and multiply, as directed, and things would go from bad to worse. It was human nature. God would be helpless to turn on the faucet again. He had set His rainbow in the sky as a sign of His dry-land covenant. So, har-de-har-har on all of them, and a plague on all their houses. Oh, that elephant, that rogue! Would he have been so careless, so conceited, if he could have imagined or in any way anticipated the fate of his great-, great-, umpteen-times-great-grandson; if he could have foreseen the agonies of Mogul, whose time has finally come?

Let us return to the *Royal Tar* and its unusual cargo, the Boston menagerie, that had just been exhibited at Yarmouth, had made another stop or two in Nova Scotia, and had boarded the ship at Saint John. It consisted of *a rare collection of Animals and Birds, many of which (taken at great hazard and expense by the Company's Hunters in India and Africa) have never been exhibited in this Province, among which are the Gnu, or horned horse, a rare specimen of nature's handiwork; — the Zebra, Pelican, Angola Goat, &c., &c., a very large Elephant, with a splendid Eastern 'Saddle,' Lions, Tigers, Monkeys, Hyenas, Dromedaries, &c., &c....The exercises of the highly trained Elephant Mogul — the leading of the wild beasts — the entering of the Lion's Cage; and the performances in the ring of the Monkey and Pony — form a truly astonishing and interesting exhibition.* Also berthed on the *Tar* were an anaconda, two golden pheasants, several species of talking parrots, and two Comic Negro Singers of celebrity.

Captain Reed was in command. She was a new ship, scarcely six months old. What's more, she was sturdy and fast, built to make the run between Saint John, New Brunswick, and New York City in just two and a half days, with all scheduled stops taken into account. The *Tar* weighed 400 tons, and no expense was spared in her outfitting. There were seventy-two passengers on board, and twenty-one crew members. They must have been looking forward to reaching their destination, and telling their families about how they had travelled with this menagerie. They required a lot of room, Mogul especially, and two of the lifeboats had been removed to enable their passage. Between them, and in a pinch, those boats could accommodate thirty passengers. But what were the chances of needing them? Perhaps it was this same optimism that obviated in the minds of the ship's owners any need for the prudent measure of insuring their $10,000 ship.

It was late October, and the weather had been rough. Captain Reed, facing a gale, and with the wind blowing hard from the northwest, thought it best to shelter behind Fox Island on Penobscot Bay. He asked that the boiler be filled, but through some carelessness on the part of the engineer, this order was never obeyed. Thus did the worm enter the bud. Before long, that boiler ran dry. Before long, it was red hot. Here is part of Captain Reed's own statement, as it appeared in *The Yarmouth Herald*, on November 4, 1836:

"The steam being down, after we had been at anchor about half an hour, the Boat was discovered to be on fire immediately over the boiler, under the deck; the cable was slipped instantly and the fire engine began to work, but in five minutes the men could not stand at the pump, which was below; the smoke nearly suffocating them; at this awful juncture, there was a rush for the boats, there being only two; sixteen of the passengers and crew took the largest boat, and went away before the wind, which blew so hard that they were afraid to bring her to. I got possession of the Jolly Boat, with two men; Mr. Sherwood, Mr. Fowler and a man from the Caravan jumped overboard and we picked them up."

Luckily, the U.S. revenue cutter *Veto* was in the same waters and was able to offer assistance to the distressed ship. The *Royal Tar* was in "a sheet of flame" by the time Captain Dyer was able to steer his vessel close enough to rescue forty passengers who would otherwise surely have perished, augmenting the final death toll of thirty-two: twenty-nine passengers and three crew. Among those who wound up as wave fodder was one of the animal keepers, who went down carrying $500 in coin. The fortunate ones made their way to Isle of Haut, nine miles distant, and there were taken in by Esquire Kimball. Mr. Stinson Patten, of Saint John, was among those who were sufficiently quick and devoted to self-preservation to be able to find a place in one of the two lifeboats. He offered this eye-witness account:

"We lost all our baggage and goods. A temporary raft was made of ladders and planks, on which some of the suffering people took refuge, but it was of little avail, as most of those who trusted to such a frail machine were precipitated into the sea and sank to rise no more. Many who had been driven overboard by the fire sustained themselves on parts of the wreck which had fallen overboard, but the violence of the sea and the cold soon terminated their earthly career. The horrors of the scene were truly appalling; the women threw their children overboard and jumped after them. The screams of these poor creatures at that time, added to the roaring of the two vexed elements, combined to produce a scene that beggars description and can only be conceived by those who have witnessed such scenes of horror. When the fire first burst through the deck such was its rapidity that the caravans immediately ignited, and so overpowering was the smoke and fire that the animals in their cages met an instantaneous death, as not a sound was heard from any one of them. The horses and camels were backed overboard, in hopes that they might reach the shore, but neither force nor any other means could induce the elephant to follow, and he remained, poor fellow, viewing the devastation, until the fire scorching him, he sprang over the side, and was seen striking out lustily for the shore with his trunk held high in the air."

For weeks after the *Tar* went down, the papers were full of follow-up stories and recriminations. How could such a travesty and tragedy have insinuated its way into the annals of seafaring? Who was responsible? Who would pay? And most of all, whatever happened to the elephant, Mogul, last seen striking out across the Atlantic — bravely, hopelessly — his trunk held high? In a way, it was because of Mogul that the fire was such an unmitigated disaster. It was feared that the deck would not be sturdy enough to support him. Wooden wedges had been driven in between the boiler and the deck, in order to bolster its carrying capacity. It was these wedges that first caught fire. Some sources reported that it was Mogul, when he crashed through the deck railing and flung his scorched hide into the sea, who took out the jerry-built raft made of ladders and timbers. What a magnificent image! Every person with vision who leaves this vale of tears must look on one earthly object and know that it is the last thing he or she will ever see. How grand it must have been to look up, to be captivated by the sight of a tumbling elephant, and then to see no more! Mogul swam off and left a wake that was frothy with hearsay. It was rumoured that he made it to shore, in the company of a pony. It was said that he had made his way to a grazing pasture, where he alarmed a herd of dairy cows. Someone heard he was safe and sound and had taken shelter in a farmer's barn.

The story of the burning *Tar* got wide play in Boston, a city where the zoological gardens would be the poorer for the losses incurred on a Canadian ship. *The Boston Transcript* even ran a long and elegaic poem of extraordinary quality. Alas, the name of the author has not survived the onslaught of the intervening years. The title, however, has come down to us. It is the *Royal Tar*. The last stanza reads as follows:

All — all had sunk in that wild sea
    Had human aid alone
Been left to combat with the breeze
    Of terror round them thrown;
But in the hour of deepest need
    A refuge was supplied,
And God his saving hand displayed
    Upon the whelming tide.

"And God his saving hand displayed upon the whelming tide." Did He? Well, perhaps. Perhaps for some. Not for Mogul, though. At least, I'd wager not. Not for Mogul who leapt from the fire and smashed through a raft and into the cold and sucking currents of the sea; who struck out for shore, his trunk held high, trumpeting useless defiance; Mogul, with his enormous feet reaching, reaching, reaching dumbly, hopelessly, reaching for something hard, for something warm, reaching for something like the plains of home, reaching, reaching, and trying so hard to remember them, all those hot, tall grasses, how they tickled his wrinkled knees, reaching and trying to remember the comfortable winds, his great wise mother, the smell of the herd, the colour of that impossible sun, half amber, half blood. Reaching. Reaching. He died reaching. If there was a pitiful or even a forgetful God above, his dying would have been eased by one final glimpse, one guttering memory of that paradise on earth. But all he saw was a filthy cage, and all he felt was the dash of the waves, and all he heard was a terrible laugh, completely foreign yet shocking in its familiarity, and then he heard no more. And he was no more seen, until he washed up on the shores of an island. Brimstone Island, as it happens. Oh, yes. It was Brimstone Island that received the bloated corpse, the stinking remains of all that was Mogul. A flock of doves fought over who would get to eat his eyes. The gulls and the crows lived for weeks on what the pigeons left behind. A high tide came and claimed the bones. And then, Mogul was utterly done. God would have chuckled, if He'd thought it was worth the effort of shaking His belly.

You wonder — how much is he making up?

I say — not much.

You wonder — how can I know what is true?

I say — there is one sure way.

You say — yes?

I say — Reader, meet us in Heaven.

Chapter Eight

Food for the Phoenix

...Behold, how great a matter a little fire kindleth!
And the tongue is a fire...
— James 3:5–6

In memoriam Keith Pelton, burned to death at age 13,
Yarmouth, Nova Scotia, August 15, 1898

He died before his time, they always say. They always say, he died too young. When the brakes fail, when the rope frays, when the gun goes off while it's being cleaned, when the mezzanine collapses under the weight of the Christmas shoppers, they say, too young, and they say, too soon. He had his whole life before him, they always say, which wakens something niggling within me, which makes me want to beg to differ, which makes me want to say, no no no, the fact is his whole life was behind him. Whatever life he had was over and done. One dies when and as one dies. That's all there is to it. Nothing is as impartial or as disregarding of the calendar as the forces of termination.

Of course, I understand perfectly well that the reason we fall back on such smooth-edged platitudes is that they usher us into a comfort zone. When death comes and we hum, too young; when life ends and we croon, too soon, we are only making the gentle noises of assuagement, just as a mother might whisper lullay, lully to her baby. We mourn our own diminishing. With every loss, we are lessened. We are left to look wistfully into the west and say, "Oh, but we hardly knew ye."

Keith died in the morning, just before sunrise. He slipped away as the foolish birds of August were tuning their pipes, deked out once again by that thin glimmer in the east, by false dawn, their morning chorus a mourning chorus. By 8 a.m., the first of the neighbours knew, and the words "too young, too soon" began their door-to-door and over-the-fence passage. By noontime, the undertaker had visited and Keith's mother was on a mission of recovery. She went through the house, carrying the trug she used when picking flowers. She combed the place from top to bottom, went from room to room, gathering pieces and remnants of her son, *memento mori* for the reliquary she had in mind. In the kitchen, on the counter, she found a crust of bread, and a knife, sticky with raspberry jam. She had to shoo away a pair of wasps before she could pick it up. From the piano lectern she removed the sheet music for a song by Cecile Chaminade, "Les Fleurs Jetées." He had been at the piano that morning, had been practising when they left for their picnic. He had chosen to stay at home. There were many details that required his attention before his play premièred that night. He was mounting this new opus in honour of his brother and his brother's new bride, just arrived from California. "Hope the ants leave you be!" he called over his shoulder as they trooped out the door. Those were his last words, he with whom the ants and worms would soon have their way.

In the parlour, she found her son's illustrated copy of *Cinderella*. She picked it up gingerly, as though it might combust, and studied the picture of the transformed ash girl, radiant in a gossamer gown, in a candlelit ballroom, no present danger, not so much as a drop of wax on her gauzy, white raiment. There was a costume sketch between two of the leaves, Keith's work. She tucked it back into the book, being careful not to crease or tear its edges, and placed the book in her basket.

She went upstairs, counting the steps — one, two, three — gripping the banister with her right hand, holding her basket in the crook of her opposite elbow, trailing the left hand over the singe marks on the wallpaper. On the landing she found the slipper he had lost while he was tearing down the stairs. Eleven, twelve, thirteen, she summoned all her nerve as she reached the hallway, as she came to Keith's room. Here was his bed, with its precisely turned corners, his shirt and breeches folded on the comforter, the steamer trunk where he kept the makings of his costumes, the lid propped open, his little desk, the notebook in which he wrote his poems, the sun on the wall and the curtains, now scorched and ragged. Ash on the carpet. A tiara still on the dresser, and her face paint. The curling-iron on the floor, the hardwood scarred by the burn mark it left when it fell from the gas fire, a blemish that would never lift.

She set down her trug. She knelt to pick up the iron, testing it first, to see if it retained any of its killing warmth. It was cold, of course. Cold as a dagger. If only! She held it before her, a samurai sword, and liberated from her throat the hell-freezing howl that had been welling all morning, then sprawled on the floor, crying, crying, Keith, oh Keith, my own dear son, oh Keith, I hardly knew you.

I know him. I think I do. Keith Pelton, who was different from the other boys. All his short life he had been an animating force, leading the other children in games of dress-up, organizing the plays in which he would invariably take the lead. Everyone in the neighbourhood knew his name. Keith Pelton, who overnight would become "Poor Keith." Keith Pelton, who was burned to a crisp while dressed as Cinderella, who came to grief at four o'clock on an August afternoon. August: when the shimmering mid-month light breeds chimera; when the heat becomes so heavy it melts away sense and breeds unhealthy sensibility. Everything gets overripe. This was the season Keith's brother chose to come from California, with his new bride in tow. She was so lovely. He was so handsome. They were junior gods, newly come down from their warm Olympus. A celebration was called for! Keith would stage one of his famous spectacles. It would be *Cinderella*. What better way to honour this princess and her consort than with a fable about the transformative powers of love?

Keith massed his forces. It didn't take him more than an hour or two to find the ugly half-sisters, the cruel stepmother, the fairy godmother, the palace courtiers, the others. No one had to ask who would play Cinderella herself. He toiled late into the night, worked deftly and secretively on his sets and costumes. The *pièce de résistance*, the ball gown, heavy with seed pearls, thick with tulle, he saved till the end, knowing as he did that such a monumental robe would tax his every resource. His mother remarked on the bags under his eyes at breakfast that morning, told him that he should really think about getting some beauty rest if he wanted to win the heart of Prince Charming. That made them all laugh, Keith and his seven brothers and his new sister-in-law, too. They all chuckled at the pleasantry, all except his father, Stipendiary Sandford H. Pelton, who was beginning to wonder if Keith might not benefit from a year or two at a military academy.

Keith stayed at the piano for an hour after his family had left on their picnic. The Chaminade was transcendent music. It helped him forget he was stuck in Yarmouth, a town whose charms he had long since outgrown. Sometimes, he would go to the shore and stare into the east, wishing away the curve of the earth, imagining that he could see all the way to France. One day, and before too long, he would get out. He would be the toast of Paris. Yes, sooner rather than later, he would be the toast.

He went into the pantry, found a loaf of bread, cut off a thick slice, spread it generously with raspberry jam. The housemaid, who was polishing the silver, asked Master Keith how his play was coming along. She had secretly hoped he might have assigned her a part, something minor, a church mouse perhaps, something suitable for a country girl with no education but plenty of goodwill. She expected nothing more. She was thirty-three years old. She had always slept alone. She could not point to one moment of what she would call "glory" in her life.

Keith heard the word "play" and snapped out of his reverie. Goodness! He still had work to do. He hurried upstairs. He opened his trunk and took out his princess gown. He had come by it in a way that was not entirely above reproach. It had started out as a wedding dress, and it was meant for Alice Walcott. She had been engaged to the scion of a wealthy shipping family. It was tragic that she should have succumbed to meningitis just a few days before the wedding. She had just turned eighteen. Her mother became quite unhinged. She took the yards and yards of fabric that had been cut and shaped to her daughter's dimensions, but had not been fully seamed and were still pinned to the mannequin, down to the cemetery. She placed the dummy bride at the head of the grave, put it right where the marker would be planted. There the mannequin stood, its gorgeous flags blowing in the wind, a riveted ghost, an improbable scarecrow. No one knew quite what to do about it. It was sheer lunacy to sacrifice such beautiful stuff to the gnawing predations of the sun and the rain. At the same time, it didn't seem right to violate a mother's mourning by removing the totem. It was spooky, though. You had to admit it was spooky, and there was a tacit sense of relief when one morning word got round that the dress had disappeared.

Keith tried not to think of Alice in Heaven, looking down at him as he stripped off his own clothes and laid them neatly on the bed. He studied his body in the mirror. He liked what he saw. His chest was taking on some shape. His nipples were coming into their own. It would be worth paying the price of their present tenderness. The new tufts under his arms and down below were growing in nicely. He was happy with his hair, too. It was quite long, it was thick, and it had a healthy sheen to it. He was confident that he wouldn't go bald before his time, as his father had done. If only his locks had more curl to them! He sighed, but took some consolation in knowing that God did everything for a reason and that one could rely on art to assist nature in matters such as these. To this end, he had borrowed his mother's curling-iron. He hadn't exactly asked if he might help himself to this tool, nor had he received her approval for the loan of her rouge, her lipstick, or her kohl. He was certain she wouldn't mind. She would understand that no self-respecting

Cinderella could look anything but her best for the ball. He ignited the fire, placed the curling-iron to warm, and turned his attention to the dress.

Too young, they say. They say, too soon. He had his whole life before him, we hardly knew him. But I'm telling you, I do. I know exactly who he was, and I know just how it happened. He picked up the dress, held it before his naked body, studied the effect, this way, that way, in the mirror. He stepped into it, reminding himself that he would have to engage someone, maybe his new sister-in-law, to be his dresser, to help him with the hook-and-eye fastenings. It would be a bonding moment between them. Perhaps they would become good friends. He could tell already that she liked him. He imagined that one day she might share with him some of the more intimate details of her wedding night. Had his brother unfastened her dress, his hands moving slowly, deliberately down her back? Or had he torn it away, unseamed it in his eagerness? Keith giggled at the thought. He closed his eyes. He moved his hands over his chest, pressed himself under the lace. His imaginings shifted, and now he became the servant girl who rose up from the ashes. She had come to the ball. She had dazzled the prince. The slipper had fit. She had passed every test. There had been a big wedding feast. Now, at last, they were alone. His hands were at her back. Keith shivered at his touch. He knew just what to do. He mouthed the word "bride," then turned to offer up his lips. He opened his eyes then, and found himself staring into the face of Apollo. Apollo! He was the most beautiful thing Keith had ever seen. God of music, god of poetry, everything that was lovely and manly, all trussed up together in this one divine package! Apollo! Keith threw open his arms in wonder, in welcome, to draw in the god of fire, and it was in that moment of fitful exuberance that a fold of his dress brushed over the curling-iron and passed into the flame.

"It happened so fast, he burned so fast!" That was all the maid could say to the family when they came home from their picnic. She told them how he had come screaming down the stairs, told them how he ran right through the parlour, where she was buffing the monogrammed teapot. She grabbed a rug, chased him out the door, caught up with him on the walk, but by the time she was able to extinguish the flames, there was nothing to be done but to kneel beside him, kneel in his cinders. She was sorry. She was sorry.

Of course, she couldn't stay on. She just couldn't bear the thought of it, nor could she bear the idea of severing her connection with this family, how could she, they were bound for ever. Finally, it was decided that she would return to California with Keith's brother and his bride. Their house was so big! "Like a castle," she wrote in a letter home. She had never imagined that she would live in a castle. The day did not go by that she didn't think of Keith, or tell his story, to herself mostly, but sometimes to others. The nurses in the old folks' home, to which they sent her when she could no longer tend to her own needs, learned to stop listening when they heard her say "Keith." As her time drew near and her own light faded, she forgot his name. She died remembering not so much the burning boy himself, but the brilliant fire and the hot fury of his final flight. She died without ever having heard the word "apotheosis." The attending physician said he had never seen a corpse with eyes so bright. They were as bright as the pennies he pressed to her lids when finally those eyes were closed.

The Offending Hand

As though Pharoah should set the Israelites
to make a pin instead of a pyramid.
— Grenville Kleiser, *Fifteen Thousand Useful Phrases*

I have always been a late bloomer. Always. When I was thirteen, for instance, I knew nothing about anything. Absolutely nothing at all. The first clue I had that something was up was when I attended a special band workshop led by a Miss Perkins. I was enthusiastic about learning to play the flute. Miss Perkins, it was widely known, had been disappointed in love. She had been engaged once, to a soldier. Unfortunately, her fiancé had stopped a German bullet with his skull, at Dieppe or some such place, and she had never recovered from the loss. From that day forward, she harboured a deep resentment against all things Teutonic. One manifestation of this lingering aversion was that she refused to make any effort whatsoever to pronounce German words when they arose. As you can imagine, this was something of a liability for a music teacher. On the day in question, which was the day I realized I had some catching-up to do, she presented us with a sight reading exercise, a transcription of a movement from the Bach cantata No. 140, "Wachet auf."

"All right, everyone," she said, "get out your instruments and we'll all play 'Whack it off.'"

It was an offhand remark that precipitated a profoundly adolescent moment. There was a charged silence in the room, akin to the one that always settled in after a teacher said "frigate," or else solemnly intoned "The curse is come upon me!" when reading aloud from Tennyson's "The Lady of Shallot." "Whack it off" echoed from the bells of the euphoniums, bounced off the taut skin of the snare drums. There was a snicker. Then the assembly collapsed into a wholesale guffaw. It took Miss Perkins several minutes of baton rapping before she was able to restore order. I was canny enough to know that something of import had taken place, and canny enough to make a show of snickering along with everyone else. But the truth was, I didn't get it at all.

I attribute my naivety in this regard to the fact that I was a solitary child, and out of the information loop. Whack it off. What could it mean? Other boys of my age had learned about their body's new and amazing tricks from cooperative older brothers, or from experienced cousins visiting from out of town, or at scout camp, where they were tutored under canvas. Night after night, they would lie in their beds and practise their new five-finger exercises, all the while imagining private conjugation lessons with Mademoiselle Dubois, our French instructor, who was dishy and young and newly arrived from Rimouski.

It wasn't that I didn't have a fantasy life. I did, but it was hugely deficient and unproductive. I invented dreamy romances that were based on B-movie plots. I would play them out in geometry class, or between the covers while I waited for sleep to come. There being no women available through the casting agency of my imagination, I had to take the role of the heroine myself. I had two favourite leading men. One was Tony Curtis. The other was Robert Goulet. All the stories followed pretty much the same scenario, with only slight variations to accommodate shifts in location. For example:

I have been captured by a band of Wild West brigands. They have bound me hand and foot and tied me to a stake. They are threatening to cut off my ear unless my father, a fabulously wealthy rancher, pays an enormous ransom. For some reason, he is reluctant to do so. I can't imagine why. The banditos are at the end of their tether. They have waited long enough. Death to the gringo scum! They are coming at me with a knife, they are just about to make good on their terrible promise, when who should come riding over the crest of a hill, the sun at his back — straddling with his muscular thighs a lightning-quick white charger — with fire in his eyes and wearing a white stetson, too, but Tony Curtis. He fires his six-gun into the air, bang! bang! bang! and the outlaws all scatter, terrified. *Carumba!* The handsome rustler, the one who had been nice to me when the others weren't paying attention, jumps over a cactus as he makes his escape. He rips his trousers, and I can see a patch of his exposed flesh as he flees into the night. I feel a slight, incongruous pang of affection and loss, the well-documented hostage syndrome. Tony Curtis jumps down off his charger. He rushes over and unties me. He is so very solicitous of my well-being. He picks me up and places me before him on his saddle. He encircles me with his arms, so strong, and away we ride. And ride. And ride. And ride and ride and ride and ride and ride. And then I fall asleep.

Or, I am on the roof of a burning skyscraper. Someone, I don't know who, and I can't say why, has bound me hand and foot and tied me to an air shaft and left me there to die a terrible, excruciating death. The smoke is thick. The flames are near. The building is high. It's not looking good. Just then, who should appear out of nowhere, wearing a hard hat and a very tattered shirt, and smelling all of sweat and good intentions, but Robert Goulet! He sings "If Ever I Would Leave You" while he gnaws through the ropes with his immaculate white teeth, then scoops me up in his arms. He holds me tight to his torso; I can see myself reflected in his hard hat. I look so vulnerable and grateful and, happily, my hair is still in place, and with all the careless grace of a mighty stag, and carrying me as if I weighed nothing more than a cream puff, he leaps across the gaping chasm to the next building, then leaps to the next. And the next. And the next. And the next and the next and the next and the next. And then I fall asleep.

I always had the feeling that something else should happen, but I was never quite sure what that might be. Then came the fateful night I went off to bed with the ovens of desire stoked to bursting by a glorious evening of television watching. Not only had I thrilled to Robert Goulet on "The Ed Sullivan Show" — he had performed, I believe, "My Cup Runneth Over" — but I had seen Tony Curtis in a Sunday-night movie presentation of *Some Like It Hot.* I spread my legs on the cool sheets. I closed my eyes.

I have been captured by pygmy cannibals. They have stripped me and bound me hand and foot — what else? — and placed me in a pot of water. It's a steamy jungle scene, with the tom-toms going mad. The savages are dancing up a storm. The bones in their noses quiver as they hop, and they shake their spears at me in a way that bodes nothing but ill. They are just about to light the wood that will make the fire that will heat the water that will boil me alive, when the air is rent by a tremendous roar. The pygmies look up, astonished, alarmed, and who should they see crashing through the jungle but Robert Goulet, wearing a loin cloth, and riding atop an elephant. Holy doodle! Then there is another heart-stopping bellow, and all their heads swivel comically in the opposite direction. Look! If it isn't Tony Curtis, also wearing a loin cloth, and swinging through the trees on a vine, hollering like Tarzan. Well! This *is* my lucky day! Tony and Robert (as I know I can call them) arrive simultaneously and terrifyingly at the centre of the camp, and my captors scamper off into the forest, issuing little shrieks of alarm. The elephant, understanding that we want to be left alone, exits gracefully, stage right. Together, my heroes lift me out of the pot. I stand before them, naked and unashamed. This is paradise. I hardly know what to say to express my gratitude, my surprise, my deep affection for them both. Happily, emergency steps in and obviates the need for speech. A sickening wind, hot and sweet, has blown up out of nowhere. A ferocious tropical storm is brewing, and we're in terrible danger! But wait! Tony knows of a cave nearby where we could take shelter, but we can get there only by swinging through the trees. We'll have to share a vine! Fine with me, I say, let's go! The men hold me between them, they hold my naked body, I am the meat in their sandwich, and we are in the air, we are as one, we are swinging from vine to vine, up and down, up and down, and on my back I feel the press of Robert Goulet's marmoreal chest, his muscles chiselled by Bernini, and on my chest is the press of Tony Curtis's back, the intricate ladder of his spine, up and down, up and down, the wind is howling, and Robert, to make us all feel better, decides to offer the comfort of song, decides it is time to sing "The Impossible Dream," and we are swinging up and down, up and down, and when a torrid blast blows away their loin cloths, up and down, they say, oh well, that's the way it goes, up and down, that's the way it goes, I say, and now it isn't just Robert singing a capella, but a whole orchestra is playing along, soaring strings, and Robert's chest is rumbling, and my whole being vibrates with his baritone strains as he chants that he will follow his star, even if it's hopeless, and oh but it is hot, and oh but my body is slick with their sweat, and theirs with mine, and I decide that as long as there is an orchestra I might as well conduct, and I seem to have a baton in my hand, up and down, up and down, who can say where it came from, the baton I mean, it's as if I have waited my whole life just to wield this stick, and in the distance I can hear — what? no! yes! — the rumble of a volcano, oh my God, well, there is nothing to be done, we are on a charted course with destiny, we are swinging up and down towards the fiery crater, its perilous hissing is drowning out everything except the unquenchable Robert, who holds on tight to me, while my one unengaged hand is around Tony's waist, and with the other I coax the orchestra to greater and greater heights, up and down, up and down, it is all too much, I feel as though my DNA is uncurling, I feel as though I am replicating Tony's and Robert's cells, and nothing can stop what is going to happen now, whatever it is, we are on top of the volcano, we are passing right over it, and just as Robert bellows out that the unreachable star is nigh, it erupts and I can feel its molten lava spewing and then everything shudders and everything goes black. And that is the way it stayed until the sun rose on a new day in a new world that would never be quite the same again.

"In order to make strong babies," says the inventor Jean St-Germain, tugging at the magnificent shrubbery of his beard, "ejaculation must be preceded by at least one hour of physical affection. At least one hour." We are sitting in his sparsely furnished office, which is adjacent to his pyramid, which is at St-Simon-de-Bagot, which is not far from St-Hyacinthe, which is some sixty kilometres to the east of Montreal. You will see it if you are driving by. It is the only pyramid in St-Simon-de-Bagot. A large sign proclaims "Pyramids Are the Solution," an assertion that might provoke the Gertrude Steinian riposte, "Then what is the question?" The pyramid is part of a compound that also includes a restaurant (closed) in the shape of a flying saucer. The service, I gather, was provided robotically. Also advertised are a parachute school and facilities for something called Astro Golf. Even though it's all rather sad and deserted-looking in the winter — in the summer I'm sure it's a regular hive — I was delighted by what I found. I anticipated nothing more than a garden-variety pyramid. Certainly I'd never thought of a UFO, and never did it occur to me to expect a discussion of ejaculation, and in French, *en plus*! As M. St-Germain and I talk, it dawns on me that I have just said "ejaculation" in French for the first time, ever, in my life. I am amazed at the way it feels in my mouth, and at the way it makes me feel deeply, deeply homesick.

"At least one hour of physical affection is necessary to prepare the spermatozoa. Otherwise they will be weak. It is also helpful to eat many green vegetables."

"My! How do you know all this?"

"I have received this information from they who make human beings."

"Oh."

If anyone has earned a right to claim inside knowledge on how best to make durable infants, I suppose it would be Jean St-Germain. By the time he was thirty-six, he was the father of a dozen children. His starter fluid must have been adequately primed for the production of feisty babies, at least if we are to judge by the career path of one of his daughters. He tells me that she has recently enlisted with the RCMP and is part of an élite corps whose members serve as bodyguards to Prime Minister Jean Chrétien. I remark that she must be the sort of girl who can look after herself, and he agrees that this is so. The remaining eleven offspring are also launched and are forging successful lives for themselves out in the world.

Twelve children! Holy Dinah! This kind of fervent spawning was not at all uncommon among Québécois of an earlier, more Catholic generation. In our present and secular age, when the province's birth rate is at an all-time low and continues to decline, and when generally reliable birth control is easy to obtain, such prolificacy has become rare, anachronistic. *Ancien régime*, even. Of course, none of this clan building would have been possible without the cooperation of Mme. St-Germain, Adrienne, whom I did not meet, but of whom I read in Jean's autobiography. He wrote it in three weeks, in Florida, and published it himself in 1979 under the inspirational title *Lâche pas y'a toujours un moyen: Mes aventure, mes inventions*. It's a paean to his own perseverance, and I think he wrote it mostly as a way of dealing with people such as I, who come to ask questions like the ones I'm bent on asking. He tells of how he met Adrienne when he was a young skydiver, and how she used to hang around after his precipitous descents and help him fold up his parachute, and when he asked her to marry him he told her frankly what she could expect of him, which wasn't much, since he was broke, had no immediate prospects for earning any money, was overly fond of travel, wanted to be free, and in addition to all that had a notebook which contained the salient details (dates, places, names) of the 276 women with whom he had made love from the time he was seventeen until he was twenty-two. He showed it to her. You have to hand it to him. He wanted everything to be on the up-and-up. She digested all this.

"And you're choosing me among all of them?" she asked.

"Yes."

"Then I'm very happy."

From earliest childhood, Jean St-Germain demonstrated the inclinations that have been manifest throughout his developing career: an aversion to authority, a love of flying, a passion for risk taking, and a burning desire to invent stuff. An indifferent scholar from the get-go, he was forever skipping school to work on his own inspired projects. The community did not necessarily see these creative forays as benign. He ran afoul of the neighbours by pressing their pet cats into service as test pilots for his parachute contraptions. He would damage passing cars when his enormous kites fell prey to gravity. He would inflict injuries on pedestrians by running them down with hot-rods he'd hammered together out of whatever spare parts happened to be around. The police would be summoned. His parents despaired. Things went from bad to worse. He began to run away. He quit high school. Somewhere along the line, he took up the accordion. It looked like he would never amount to anything.

When he was sixteen, Jean St-Germain had his first near brush with big-time success. He was staying with one of his brothers and a sister-in-law. They bottle-fed their baby, and the poor mite was colicky and gassy because of the amount of air he ingested along with his milk. Ti-Jean, as his family called him, considered the problem for a few moments and had an inspiration. All that was required to make the baby comfortable during his meal was to eliminate the air problem. *Façile à faire*! He purchased some condoms, scrubbed them up, inserted one in a feeding bottle, filled the improvised balloon with formula, and gave it to the baby. When the child sucked up the liquid, the condom collapsed behind it, creating a seal. *Résultat:* no more air to trouble the heir. Thus did a high-school drop-out devise the prototype of the disposable baby bottle. All told, it took about three hours from conception through execution. "You have some genius in that head of yours," exclaimed an early appreciator of his brainchild. He knew he had a concept that was marketable, but couldn't quite figure what to do with it, which is a pity, since the disposable baby bottle was exactly the kind of modern aid the mothers of baby boomers craved, occupying as it does the same aesthetic rung as TV dinners, or Pampers. By rights, he should have made a fortune. At sixteen, though, what do you know? At sixteen, when you're in debt to your parents and you're carrying the burden of their disappointment besides, you won't necessarily hold out for the best deal. At sixteen, you'll take the money and run. Eventually, some sharp-eyed entrepreneur talked him into selling the patent for a thousand dollars. Eventually, it fell to Playtex to finally manufacture and market a bottle based on his design. They cleared considerably more than a thousand dollars.

If one were writing Jean St-Germain's life as a novel, this would be the moment one would have to choose a fictive fork to follow. Would he spend the rest of his life boring drunks in bars with the story of what might have been? Would he channel his bitterness into something warped and sociopathic, such as sneaking into pharmacies and lacing formula with strychnine? Would he collapse into weeping every time he saw a happy, swilling, gas-free baby? The truth, as is usually the case, is more pedestrian than fiction. The truth is that he happily took the thousand dollars, didn't look back, and simply trundled on. He joined the army, went to Europe, did a stint as a paratrooper, met the lovely Adrienne, and the two of them commenced having babies. Jean continued jimmying with this gizmo and that gizmo, inventing motor components, developing light aircraft and safety handles for snowmobiles, coming up with innovative milk jugs and children's toys, consolidating his reputation as an inventor and patent taker. Now and then he made some money. Now and then he took a bath. There were adversaries along the way. As he tells his story in *Lâche pas*, he was constantly doing battle with the banks, with various lawyers and politicians and safety inspectors and civic or aviation officials who simply couldn't see with his clarity of vision. He never lost faith in his own ability or sight of his own path.

Family life was important, too. Several of the St-Germain children were featured in an article that appeared in *National Geographic World*, in February 1982. Four of them — Daniel, Pierre, François, and Nathalie — appear on the cover. Daniel, wearing a vivid green flying-suit, a helmet and goggles, hovers in mid-air. He looks like a comic-book superhero, preparing to descend and lash out at a baddy. The other three, swathed in yellow, stand about the perimeter of what might be a brightly coloured circus tent and watch him fly. In fact, they were photographed while demonstrating the Aérodium, another of their father's inventions, which he designed and opened to the public in 1980. The Aérodium is a wind-tunnel affair where the emphasis is placed on vertical rather than horizontal thrust. St-Germain's first thought was that it would be useful to teach sky-divers how to handle themselves in a simulated free fall, but saw that it had a broader public application as an amusement-park attraction. After all, who hasn't dreamed of flying, free as a bird, spirit-like, without the shackling confines of a plane? The aspiring aviator gets decked out in an oversized Day-Glo flying-suit in a primary colour, as well as all kinds of protective padding. Then, she throws herself onto an upward draft created — at least in the prototype — by a propeller from a DC-3, and is hoisted aloft on a lusty column of air. Experienced flyers ride the upward current like happy swallows. First-timers are chucked around the room like poker chips, smashing into the walls until they get the hang of this windy levitation.

By the time of the advent of the Aérodium, Jean St-Germain was considerably more experienced in the rough-and-tumble legalistic world of rights, patents, and distribution. He sold the franchising rights to the Aérodium concept for a tidy sum. Rich as Pharaoh, and hardly over the threshold of middle age, Jean St-Germain turned his attention towards the construction of a pyramid.

Middle age. It is dangerous terrain. I often think there is little more pathetic than a man in mid-life, no matter how happy and well adjusted he seems. You can never tell, nor can he, what psychic malaise will come crashing, comet-like, through his window and damage him in his sleep. One day he wakes up, looks around, and realizes that the life he is living is both dreadful and real, that it has no sound, no fury, only nothingness, and that death or divorce is his only real prospect for change. How he longs for that distant season when *he radiated vigor and abundance like a happy child.* The dreams of his youth have *fallen like dead leaves on the highway.* Before long, he will grow *weak, like a shrunk cedar white with the hoar-frost.* He will be *wrinkled and scored like a dried apple.*

It's a grim time, there's no denying it, and it comes with its nutty, reactive pathology in tow. The biology of middle age prescribes that men fly off in one of two directions. Some will hunger after the world. They will gallop after the things of youth, thumbing their nose at mortality by buying absurdly flashy cars, having their love handles suctioned or their eyelids bolstered, and dallying with women half their age. Others — those who are inclined by nature to go more gentle into that good and relentless night — will seek hermitage. They will retire to basement workshops to sort endlessly through their accumulation of washers and screws, or they will construct little outbuildings in their backyards, slightly more vaunted versions of the clubhouses of their school days, those shacks hung with signs that warned "No Girls Allowed." I remember, while I was growing up, how a contemporary of my father's did this very thing. Night after night he hammered and sawed, building for himself what eventually evolved into an almost alarmingly pretty cottage, with a delicately painted trim, dainty shutters, and flouncy curtains. Night after night, once his project was done, this fellow — who must have been then my present age — would leave his house and whatever domestic strains might have been beating their wings around its rafters, and revel in the solitude of his little sanctuary. We could walk by and look at him there, could see him through the sheer drapes. It was like looking at a ghost, or a zoo exhibit: *homo sapiens in media vita.* He never appeared to do anything, not even to read. He just sat by himself, with a small lamp burning, and the evening settling around him. None of us children, I feel sure, saw him as a prophet of things to come.

As Jean St-Germain grew into middle age, his physical aspect became more and more prophet-like. With his long hair, and his burning bush of a beard, he was reminiscent of an illustration from a child's Old Testament. He was — still is — the very picture of a craggy desert Elijah or Jeremiah. It's a look he wears well, a look he has in some measure earned, since he once underwent a kind of John the Baptist stint in the wilderness. He took to the desert to keep a promise he made to God. One day, the story goes, he was testing out a light aircraft, a gyrocopter. Everthing went wrong. All systems were failing. It seemed hopeless. He was surely going to crash. He asked for assistance from on high. Get me out of this pickle, Jean prayed to God, and I promise that I'll come to Israel and visit You in the desert. ("*Si Tu me sors de ce pétrin, je promets d'aller te rendre visite dans le désert en Israel.*") Sure enough, a deep calm descended on him, and he knew exactly what he needed to do to bring his wonky craft safely back to earth. He did not forget. He was a man of his word. Shortly afterwards, he told Adrienne that she would have to look after things for a while. He had pressing business elsewhere. When she asked why he was going to Israel, he answered that he would tell her later, that for the time being she shouldn't ask questions.

His account of his journey across the sands from Beersheba to the Dead Sea presents the reader with a fascinating mélange of spirituality and sensuality. Not only does he dialogue directly with God, and learn the reason why there are such huge disparities between the rich and the poor, why the stars are at such a great remove from the earth, learn the truth about life after death, and the mystery of free will; he also spends the night in a Bedouin tent and makes love with two young girls, and winds up his voyage in a hotel room back in Beersheba with eight beautiful and bisexual women with whom he spends "une nuit sexuelle indescriptible." (I confess that when I read this I felt a wee pang of sympathy for Adrienne, back at home with who knows how many children and another bun in the oven. Readers of like sensibility might be relieved to learn, as I was, that, at a later juncture, Jean is able to converse directly with Jesus. When he asks the Saviour if it is wrong to make love to a woman other than one's own wife, he is assured that all is relative, and that he, Jean, is the only one who can pass judgment on himself. Since he not only recorded this tale of extravagant infidelity as part of a public record of his life, but did so in a book in which his wife is credited as "recherchiste," we can take it that Adrienne was at least as tolerant of his philandering as was Jesus.)

Given that he had not once, but twice, been privileged to sniff the rich breath of Divinity; and given that the success of his inventions, particularly the Aérodium, had made him a man of financial substance; and given that middle age and its "acting out" prerogatives were upon him, it is not so surprising that M. St-Germain would choose to build a temple expressive of his spiritual and fiscal achievements Why should it not take the form of a half-a-millon-dollar, 2.3-million-pound marble and granite pyramid? After all, these were the eighties, a period of great ecumenism, as well as a time when everyone was discovering that pyramids — albeit tiny ones — could sharpen razor blades, enhance the growth of house plants, effect the erasure of tumours, and bring the individual in closer touch with the cosmos. After the handsome *nouveau-égyptien* edifice was finished in 1982, and opened to the public as the first major installation in what was anticipated to be a kind of New Age Disneyland, St-Germain made personal weekly visits of about five minutes each to its inner chamber. There he would clear his mind, and enjoy the benefits of so concentrated a dose of magnetic energy. Early in 1983, to demonstrate its power as a high-frequency meditation chamber, he spent all night inside, and emerged with 2,000 written sequences of numbers between one and thirty-six to play on the roulette wheel of the Tropicana Hotel and Casino in Las Vegas. Thus armed, and with a thousand dollars in his pocket, he made another trip to another desert. It was his intention to see the thousand transformed into a million. At one point he was up by a hundred thousand dollars. However, by the evening's end, he had lost all but his original stake, a failure he attributed to being overtired after choosing the first thousand numbers.

I would recommend to anyone a visit to the dark inner sanctum of the St-Germain pyramid. It may not lead to an immediate lottery win, but it is a restful and pleasantly weird way to drop twenty-five bucks. An assistant will show you into a preparatory anteroom where you will remove your shoes and any metal objects you might be carrying or wearing: bracelets, belts, change, and the like. Metal interferes with the magnetic principle on which the whole thing operates and which I freely confess not to understand. Once you have sat for a calming few minutes, listening to environmental music (brooks, birds, quiet strings), with your feet resting upon a footstool that I think is meant to have a grounding effect, you will be ushered down a long and echoing candlelit corridor — stooping, because the ceiling is very low — until you emerge under the pointed dome of the pyramid itself. Here too, there is an evocative, flickering illumination that comes from many, many candles. It's terrifically pretty, it really is. The assistant will orient you, then leave you to stand or sit and receive the beneficial vibrations for fifteen minutes, at which point a gong will sound to let you know your time is up. The room is acoustically resonant, and she will tell you that you may sing, if you wish. I listened to the receding pit-a-pat of her footfalls as she padded away down the tunnel. When I was sure she was gone, I hummed a few trial notes. My voice rang pleasingly all around me. I tried and tried to think of an appropriate song, which I can never do when required. The only tunes that came to mind were "What I Did for Love" and "Lulu's Back in Town." I sang a quick chorus or two of each, made my way through as many verses of "Blowin' in the Wind" as I could remember, then sat quietly and waited for the gong.

Jean St-Germain eats lunch most days at a crowded strip-mall restaurant in St-Hyacinthe. It's full of folks on hour-long lunch breaks, many of whom are regulars, and many of whom greet him as he walks to his table. He's been coming here for years. They all have. I tag along with him, at his kind invitation, and when the waitress takes our order, he asks if she wouldn't mind bringing him an egg, not a cooked one, just an egg from the fridge, brown or white, it doesn't matter. There is a trick he wants to show me that will impart a clear and present tangible proof of his powers of mind. I don't much feel the need of such a demonstration, as I don't doubt for one second that he is a man of huge energy and varied accomplishment. The record speaks for itself. He has been incredibly fecund, with dozens more patents than he has children registered in his name, and he has made enormous whacks of cash over the years. By way of proving his solvency, he had earlier flashed before my eyes a letter from someone at Revenue Canada, an official with whom I gather he has been in fairly regular correspondence over the years. The bureaucrat was inquiring as to whether or not something might be done about paying off some of the interest that has been accruing on the St-Germain tax account. The amount mentioned — and this is interest, mind — was tens of thousands of dollars in excess of what most Canadians would consider a comfortable middle-class income. When I asked M. St-Germain if he was not concerned about the tax people, he chuckled. He has been playing a cat-and-mouse game with them for years now. Eventually, he'll render something unto Caesar, but he doesn't like to make it too easy. He believes inventors should be exempt from tax collection since they plough the money they earn right back into their creative enterprise.

"So you see," he said, "I am not really eccentric. My feet are solidly on the ground. I don't think an eccentric can owe that much in taxes!"

Though our acquaintance was short, and though he wasn't so very interested in answering my questions ("Vous verrez ça dans le livre"), and though much of what I have garnered about his life and thinking has come from his autobiography and from the magazine and newspaper pieces that have been published about him, I would still presume to say, on the basis of this slight evidence, that Jean St-Germain inhabits an ethical universe with parentheses wide and elastic enough to accommodate both a rooted Catholicism and such New Age philosophies as pyramid power. His chummy accord with Jesus lives alongside a *laissez-faire* attitude towards marital fidelity. He can take pride in his daughter who guards the physical person of the prime minister and at the same time revel in his sporting fondness for baiting her boss's cash collectors. The pyramid builder of St-Simon has a received philosophy about leading a good life that enables him to shelter such seeming contradictions under one roof; a code of conduct which has come his way via the same source that made manifest the business about an taking an hour for physical affection before giving in to ejaculation. The gist of his broader remarks, which I am both paraphrasing and translating, is that we are all the holders of moral bank accounts. We can fill them or deplete them as we wish, while we go about the business of whittling down the stump of our days. It does not matter if we give in to such base desires as the urge to smoke or to masturbate. (He was very specific about masturbation and smoking.) We won't be judged harshly for such laxness. However, we need to understand that, when we abuse ourselves in these ways, we demonstrate a lack of respect for the stuff of life. When we refrain from smoking, or from enjoying auto-erotic stimulation, and do so as a deliberate show of respect for the life with which we have been entrusted, then our moral bank accounts are topped up all over again. It is this awareness and this respect that are the keys to right living — at least, so I understood him to say. It is the kind of speculative moralizing that makes me feel a vice is being tightened around my temples.

The waitress brings an egg, as requested. She hands it to St-Germain.

"Qu'est-ce qu'il va faire?" she asks, and laughs. One senses there's not much he could do that would surprise her. He sets the *oeuf* down on the table on one of its elliptical ends, then tries to coax it into balancing, like a top.

"You are not supposed to be able to do this," he says, "but it is possible. You just need to be able to concentrate, to focus the mind. You just need to find the right point..."

And for the next ten minutes, while his soup cools, he gives the ovum the whole of his attention. He blots out the chatter and the clatter of a hundred other lunchers, and concentrates on making the egg stand at attention. I sit there quietly, hoping my expression betrays only rapt interest, even though I am mostly regretting the absence of placemats you can read.

Lâche pas is Jean St-Germain's motto. Don't give up. It's a dictum he applies to this kind of parlour trick, and to more momentous tasks, such as building the Aérodium or a pyramid. The present pyramid of St-Simon, splendid and useful though it may be, is not the pyramid of his grandest dreams. Several years ago, he announced his intentions to erect, right in his own back-yard, "la plus grande pyramide du monde." Yes, the biggest in the world, larger even than the great monument created by Cheops more than 4,000 years ago in the Egyptian sands. It would also be more inclusive. Cheops built his pyrmaid as a tomb for himself and a few of his closest friends. The St-Germain pyramid, which would measure about 1,000 feet at the base, and 500 feet in height, would accommodate, post-mortem, most of the present population of Canada on thirty-three of its forty-two levels. His plan was to have space for 22 million memorial urns. They would be arrayed, along with iden-tifying plaques, along the many corridors, and would be sold for fees ranging from $1,000 and $9,250. High rollers would be assigned to the upper levels of the structure, the view suites, I guess. Sales would be arranged through a non-profit organiza-tion called Citadelle de la Paix, and the money raised would underwrite the projected $750-million price tag attached to the concrete structure, as well as give a much-needed surge to the province's economy. As he explained to *La Presse*, in August 1988, "my great funerary pyramid I see as a source of life for future generations. Such a project shouldn't have a financial objective: it should be useful for all Québécois in such fields as health, education, ecology, and humanitarian work." Not the least-attractive feature of the pyramid would be a forty-two-ton prism that would be installed at the apex, and would project into the atmosphere, by way of skylights, a rainbow of luminous lights that would be very pretty indeed. Within, the ambience would be one of calm, peace, and serenity.

How can one help but admire this man for his tenacity and independence of spirit? Whatever else one might think about his philosophies, one has to commend his refusal to abandon, in spite of the drubbings meted out by age and experience, his passion for dreaming big. In his 1909 text *Ten Thousand Dreams Interpreted* — which reference source is nearly as necessary to my happiness and sense of well-being as *Fifteen Thousand Useful Phrases* — Gustavus Hindman Miller says that to dream of pyramids "denotes that many changes will come to you. If you scale them, you will journey along before you find the gratification of your desires." Whether Jean St-Germain received such warning prognosticatory signs, I can't tell you. However, it is a fact that construction of *la grande pyramide de St-Simon*, which he intended to go up right beside the Trans-Canada Highway halfway between Montreal and Quebec City, has been stalled, and for almost ten years now, by the conservationist truculence of the Agricultural Land Reserve (L'Office de Protection du Territoire Agricole). There is no sign that the long-standing dispute over land use is going to be solved any time soon. Ask him if he still plans to build his pyramid, and Jean St-Germain will tell you, quietly, almost shruggingly, yes. However, as it is a project that can't be realized in the short term, it has taken a back-burner position to his current undertaking, the erection of a 128-foot concrete cross in which he will house displays that will tell the story of religion. It's a relief to know that he has a channel for his energies. He is the kind of man who needs a project, a mission. He is now what he has always been: a man with his own sense of enigmatic purpose.

"I know why we are here," he tells me, as the waitress brings our cheque, "and I know where we are going. When the time is right, I will be able to say all I know."

"When will that be?"

"Maybe two months. Maybe two years. When the time is right to say, I will know."

It seems so long to wait! So much could be helped and planned if only one knew. Is it worthwhile having that dental work done? Is there any point in renegotiating the mortgage? Oh, well. Garrulous old Time, in tandem with Jean, will one day deign to tell. In the meantime, by way of a stopgap, by way of a promise, there is the egg, unassisted, holding its balance beside the ashtray, white and blameless as a dancer *en pointe*.

Jean has an appointment to keep. I want to get back to Montreal before a forecast snowstorm settles in. I head west, to the city of many restaurants, none of which looks even remotely like a flying saucer. He heads east, back to his parcel of land that could be made prettier only by the presence of the world's biggest pyramid. I turn on the radio, hoping for the weather. Instead, I get the news. In Albania, the announcer says, there is civil unrest in the wake of the collapse of a pyramid scheme. Civil unrest? Go figure! Here, at least, in this vicintiy, the disappointing dissolution of a pyramid doesn't disrupt the peace. I smile when I think of that. It makes me feel optimistic. It makes me feel that I am in Canada, after all.

● ● ●

Let a bear robbed of her whelps meet a man,
rather than a fool in his folly.
— Proverbs 17:12

In *The Canadian Boy Scout* (1911), Robert Baden-Powell enjoined his disciples from smoking, telling dirty stories, reading trashy books, and looking at lewd pictures. Such indulgences are, he said, "very apt to lead a thoughtless boy into the temptation of self-abuse. This is a most dangerous thing for him, for should it become a habit it quickly destroys both health and spirits; he becomes feeble in body and mind, and often ends in a lunatic asylum."

He does not add "with hair on his palms," but might just as well have done so. In that same edition of his gospel, B.-P. warned that "many a tenderfoot has got lost on the prairie or the forest, and has never been seen again, through not having learned a little scouting, or what is called 'eye of the country,' when a boy."

"Eye of the country" is something I utterly failed to acquire during the long and terrible years I spent as a beret-wearing Powellian anchorite. Nor was I otherwise accomplished. My only badges were for my expertise in such womanly arts as housekeeping, singing, and reading. I may have been awarded one for philately, I'm not sure. I did my duty to God and the Queen, and tried to adhere to the most ringing of the many tenets, the one that demanded we Be Prepared. That was the total sum of my accomplishments. Knotting was an impossibility, as was campfire lighting, and the pivotal scouting skill of pathfinding eluded me altogether. It was neither within my reach or grasp. I had — I have — no innate sense of direction, and since every location-finding technique our leaders thought to teach us had to do with grasping for north, I felt no incentive to learn. North? What was the point in all that compass-reading, star-watching, moss-measuring, and sun-squinting if north was all it would net you? What was so all-fired great about north, anyway? What was there? An Arctic waste. A walrus or two. The Inuit, who have no word for love, which was all I craved. I could have cared less about north. It was the south that interested me. South was glamour, beaches, Hollywood, tans, bullfights, orange groves, hula dancers, torrid nights of romance. It was everything your little frozen heart could desire. During the Winnipeg winters, when south winds blew, I would face them head on, would welcome them, sniff them, longing for the scent of frangipani, of magnolia. Of otherness. Of elsewhere. For the most part, those winds were vicious and smelled like North

Dakota. But over time, if you managed to harden yourself against their full-frontal onslaught, you could learn to suss out a certain softness hidden deep beneath the bluster. At the cold south wind's remotest edges was the promise of something sweeter to come.

It was in such a southerly gale that I drove the fifty-four miles from my parents' home in the city to the pretty little town of Portage la Prairie. I went there to meet with Nick Kolansky. Nick owns a camping and fishing lodge in the Whiteshell. For years before that, he ran a popular family restaurant in Portage. Before that he was in the air force. And before that, when he was still a kid, he worked with his brother, Alex. Alex was a trapper for almost forty years. Finding out about Alex was why I went to Portage. It's an easy trip, even for someone as directionally challenged and tender-footed as I. You simply point your car in the general direction of Vancouver and step on the gas. You scarcely need to steer as you speed along the Trans-Canada. Early on a Sunday morning in February, there's no traffic to hold you up. The Sunday I went, there was only the gusting south wind, exercising its decorator prerogative, shoving the dry snow from one field to another, mindless of the highway that divides them. It's an amazing sight, all that snow blowing. It's the polar equivalent of a sandstorm, and in that geography, driving across the magnificent stretch of farm-friendly flatness, you can't help but think of tumbling topsoil, of the dust bowls of the last great Depression. Alex was born in Sundown, Manitoba, in 1914, but it's in the Depression that his story really starts.

Nick Kolansky and his wife, Evelyn, live in a comfortable bungalow on a quiet, sheltered street a few blocks from the railway line. Nick's many stories about his remarkable brother are well-loved party pieces, but Nick has the knack of making them fresh. He is a terrific storyteller, and as generous and gregarious a host as you could ever hope to find.

"When he started out, Alex lived the hard life. Everybody did, back then. The thirties. It was just the times. Alex would get a job in the fields at harvest; he'd get paid a dollar a day for twelve hours' worth of work. And then he'd ride the rails. He'd hop freights out of Winnipeg. He'd ride in a boxcar, or strap himself to the top. Three days he'd be up there, sometimes, going to B.C., to get a job in a lumber camp. Those trains would sometimes have a hard time getting through the tunnel. They'd be pouring out smoke. Alex told me about how he'd almost suffocate up there, there'd be nothing to breathe. He went into the bush in 1939. He liked that backwoods country. He applied for and got trapline number five. It ran for about 200 square miles in what is still the deepest part of that wilderness. It wasn't so much beaver he trapped back then, but lynx, weasels, fox, timber wolf, squirrels even. They were legholds, sure. It was a cruel way to make a living. But one thing about Alex is that even though he needed to take the animals, he never took any who lived around his own lake. No, they were his friends."

Talk to anyone who remembers Alex Kolansky, and you will be told this: that he was a man of extraordinary gentleness, of deep spirituality. He loved children. He forged a strong link with the land on which he lived, deep bush country, miles and miles from the nearest habitation. In his early years on the trapline, he'd go for months at a stretch without seeing or talking to another living soul. Animals were his society, and he got to know them well.

"The squirrel would come and have dinner with him every day," Nick remembered. "The wasps decided to build a nest in his cabin. He didn't bother them. They didn't bother him. And there was a bear that had a cave, about 200 yards from his cabin. Alex would go over to visit the bear. He'd go over in the winter and wake him up, and they'd just visit. Once, when he'd been away from the cabin for a few days, there'd been a forest fire. He got back and found these three little bear cubs, crying. The mother had been killed. So Alex made them some bannock with honey and milk and fed it to them and they stayed with him. He'd get in the canoe and they'd get in the canoe. He'd walk to the next lake and they'd follow him along, like puppies.

He slept with them in the camp, they kept him awake rolling on the floor and swatting each other. He lived with them all summer, and in the fall he found an old bear den and took them over there. He sealed them up and bid them farewell. This was, maybe, 1968. On the day before Christmas, I went down to visit him on the Skidoo. I told him I was taking him to Green Lake for Christmas dinner. He said, I'm not going to no Christmas dinner. I'm going to have Christmas dinner with the bears! And that's just what he did. He made up some bannock, honey, and milk. He went over to their cave. He woke them up. And he had Christmas dinner with the bears.

"And one time I remember, he'd finally managed to save around $500. He put it in a tin can, it was a baking-powder tin, and closed the lid. He buried it in the garbage pile. I had the restaurant by then, and Alex would sometimes come in the summers to help me out. He stayed with me for a couple of months. When he got back to his camp, he found the groundhog had decided to make a home where the can was, and he'd thrown it out. The bear came along and he wanted to know what was in the can and he chewed at it and the lid popped off and the south wind took all the money into the bush. All bills — fives, tens, twenties — all in the bush. Every time the wind came, it would blow it a little further into the bush. Alex went into the bush and started looking and he found everything but twenty or thirty dollars. Took him two weeks to find all his money."

Alex was a resourceful man. He made his own skis, out of birch planks, with soup tins for the tips. He made his own saw-mill and cut up the lumber to make his various shacks. He made a kind of waterwheel thingy, and an automatic washing machine. He was a religious man, too. He never worked on Sundays, and would close his traps on Saturday night. He smoked for a while, but gave it up. He never drank. He never, ever swore, and didn't appreciate hearing it from others. Nick remembers how his brother would clam up when they were out on the trapline together and Nick would use salty language.

Alex was never without a Bible, not even when he was riding the rails. He'd read it cover to cover several times. He was a compact man, just five-feet tall, 130 pounds, all muscle. Even after he lost his hand, he could heave his canoe up onto his shoulder, with one arm, like there was nothing to it. Even after he lost his hand, he would paddle his canoe, would gather wild rice, would operate his chainsaw. He ran his line and lived happily in the bush for thirty years after he lost his hand.

Alex Kolansky's story is fascinating by any measure, but it was the loss of the hand that cemented his legend, and earned him the nickname "The Mad Trapper of the Whiteshell." Different people to whom I've spoken have told me different stories. Some said he'd had an accident while chopping ice. Some had a darker tale to tell. Nick, who was the first person to see him after it happened, says this is the authoritative version:

"Alex, see, he was deeply religious. And when you're alone, and you read the Bible, you only have the one opinion that you yourself construct when you read a verse or chapter. Alex was carried away by the theory that if an eye offends you, pluck it out. If a hand offends you, cut it off. And of course, living alone, and being alone, and never seeing anyone, and only coming out once or twice a year, he never had anyone to set him right or contradict him. And his hand offended him. Well, he was playing with himself and he figured that wasn't right, so he read the Bible again and that's what it told him to do. On December 17, 1948, it was thirty-three below. I saw his calendar, he was marking down the temperatures. He was living at Cave Lake then. At thirty-three below, he tied a rope around the wrist to stop the blood circulation. He tied it tight, then he walked that way to the next lake. By the time he got back, he told me, he could put a knife through his hand anywhere. He had one of those big ice chisels — he used to chisel ice with it — and it weighed about nine pounds, maybe. He just put his hand on a block of wood and dropped the chisel down and the hand came right off. He shoved his arm in the fire to sear it. He had this big fire going.

"Eventually, someone heard about it, and they got hold of me, and in the spring of '49 I went down to see him. I finally made it to the camp with this pack-sack of food, and I found him skinning a beaver. He had a knife tied to the stub, and he was skinning a beaver. Well, I was tired and I didn't really know what had happened, didn't know what to expect. He was just so happy to see me! He jumped up and ran over and wanted to throw his arms around me and I looked at that knife and I thought he was going to kill me there and then. I thought, well, let him kill me, I haven't got any more strength left anyway. He untied his knife and I made supper and he wanted to talk, and I was so tired I was falling asleep, and he got a hold of the fiddle and he strapped on the bow, right on the stump, and he played for me. He could still play the guitar, too.

"That hand healed up. When I was there that time, I watched him take a knife and flick off the last piece of bone. He never saw anyone for it. He had a pack of those paper serviettes, and that's what he used for a dressing. He told me how he suffered. He told me I didn't know what pain was. He ran out of food. For a month he lived on prunes and wild rice. But he never regretted it. He was so deeply religious, so loyal to his thoughts. And he was completely rid of whatever had bothered him. He was at peace with the world. And after that, he started coming out more often."

A hard, holy story. Impossible not to try to fill in the blanks. Impossible not to imagine the sound in the forest.

Alex died in 1978. They found him in his cabin on Bernard Lake. The cause of death is uncertain. They think he may have choked on some bannock. He'd never seen a doctor once, not for any reason, and had never been sick a day in his life. Nick and a few friends cleaned out the cabin. They found a box full of receipts. He'd given five dollars a year to the Salvation Army. They found fifty dollars rolled up in the bread box, rainy-day money. They removed anything of importance, and burned the cabin down. A few years ago, a ski trail south of Big Whiteshell Lake was named the Kolansky Trail.

By the time I left Nick's and headed back to Winnipeg, the south wind had dropped any pretense of chumminess. It was howling over the Trans-Canada, and the snow was blinding. White-out. It was like driving home through the eye of the country, and all there was to fill it, all it could hope to see was every howling ghost that ever bothered to linger on the round and troubled earth.

Past Forgetting

Leave to the imagination the endless vista of possibilities.
— Grenville Kleiser, *Fifteen Thousand Useful Phrases*

Rumour is Death's dependable sidekick, the dogger of his steps. Strange, since they are such misbegotten companions. Magnetic opposites, really. Yin and yang. Death is light of foot, discreet. Rumour is a noisy batman. Death does his efficient work and hits the road. Rumour hangs around to sit shiva. His acrid waft lingers and lingers in the room. It's ever been thus. Even before the dear departed one has given himself over to the rigours of rigor, passing from *in extremis* to *in paradisum*; even before his insubstantial shade has peeled itself from the sucking exigencies of the flesh, his sad survivors have begun to expropriate his story, to turn it to their own purposes. Directly upon dispersal of the soul's properties, he becomes the sole property of the living, a sequence of dots they can connect in any old way they choose to make whatever picture they long to see. Well, what do the dead care, anyway? Not a thing! And we value them for their needlessness and pliability. Through them, we are made whole, wholer than we really are. Through them, we can magnify our own possibilities and foibles. We do this by turning them into legends. We make them our enduring delights.

I went to Englehart, Ontario, hoping to grasp a few tattered shreds of the ghost of the legendary Nellee Reid. To get to Englehart from Ottawa, you drive about 560 kilometres to the west and north along gouged and icy roads where the wind eggs the snow into capering, lane-obscuring *feux follets*. You drive along Highway 148, drive parallel to the Quebec border, pass through Cobden, and drive along the margins of Muskrat Lake, in whose unplumbed depths a serpentine monster is said to have set up house, and on whose shores the careless Champlain pitched his tent, leaving behind his astrolab when he decamped. For more than 300 years the instrument lay buried in the iron-rich earth, inhabited the whole time by its hankering for all that is north. It was hereabouts that the feisty Margaret McDonald engaged in a defiant act of self-defence which attracted the attention of the tabloid *The National Enquirer*, and will certainly earn her a place in the pantheon of Canadian school-book Amazons, alongside such stalwarts as daring Laura Secord, who famously used her cow as camouflage and almost single-handedly won the War of 1812; and the plucky Madeleine de Verchères, who, with her brother, Pierre, held off an Iroquois attack.

In the summer of 1996, Mrs. Margaret McDonald — who was then fifty-four and who is, according to *The National Enquirer*, a retired cook and a divorced mother of four — was making her way home after a peaceable night of bingo at the community hall. It was round about 10 p.m., a respectable time of the night for law-abiding souls to be out in the world, an hour of a summer night when, especially in the North, there is still enough light that no one need fear stumbling into harm's way. Margaret walked along contentedly enough. She was turning over in her mind the small triumphs and disappointments of the evening just gone, when her attention was drawn to a rustling in the bushes that lined the road. She paused to see what might be hiding in the greenery, stopped to peer into the darkening tangle of the branches, and it was then that she was set upon by a snapping and hissing muskrat: one of the sharp-toothed mammals for whom the lake is named. It all happened very quickly. There was no time to consider flight. In a trice, the varmint was upon her. Margaret swung at it with her purse, but missed. The muskrat must have felt the jet stream as it passed in front of its snout. It went straight for her ankle and lit in, causing Margaret to yelp with pain, panic, and drop her handbag.

Who knows how it all might have ended had she not been armed with a back-up weapon, a nylon bag containing six bingo dabbers, which are the implements used to mark the numbers on your card of record, and are each about the size and heft of a good-sized felt-tip marker?

"GRANNY FIGHTS OFF CRAZED MUSKRAT WITH BAG OF BINGO MARKERS" was the headline in the *Enquirer*. They ran two photographs, too, one of a muskrat and its gaping, menacing maw, and another of Margaret herself. She is shown in the high grass, squatting in a kind of sumo-wrestler pose, her hands on her thighs. Her face is set in a look of "so's your old man" bravado, as if she might be challenging any of the muskrat's kin to come at her and try the same trick. Every curve of her features, as Grenville Kleiser would say, *seems to express a fine arrogant acrimony and harsh truculence.* In her right hand, she holds a bag appliquéd with the slogan "I ♥ Bingo." This is the weapon she used to flail "the muskrat mugger" to death. She stunned him with her first whack, and then kept on swinging, blow after punishing blow, until there was hardly enough of him left to make one of those tacky steering-wheel mufflers. She comported herself with remarkable courage and aplomb throughout the entire ordeal, which left her *flushed with a suffusion that crimsoned her whole countenance.* "I was so worked up I had an angina attack that night and ended up in the hospital for three days. The bite didn't require stitches and, fortunately, the muskrat didn't have rabies." An ending which has about it the sanctity of happily-ever-after.

To get to Englehart from Cobden and dangerous Muskrat Lake, you drive through Pembroke, Deep River, and Chalk River, through Petawawa, through Mattawa, through any number of places whose names and mineral output or industrial *raison d'être* you memorized in elementary school. At North Bay, you switch your allegiance to Highway 11, trying not to be too unnerved by the jackknifed transport trucks, or by news reports of two fatalities on this very stretch of pavement in the last week. Turn off the radio. Choose a tape. Choose Leonard

Cohen. Drive through the pine, the blasted rock, through the snow the snow the snow. Sing. Sing along with Leonard. Sing about the enigmatic Suzanne. Call on the Sisters of Mercy. Drive and drive through Marten River and Temagami, drive through Earlton. Don't bother stopping to look at its zoo, which is closed for the season. Its inmates have been transferred to some warmer resort. A hulking, solitary buffalo statue guards the empty fields and cages, guards the trailer park next door. The buffalo faces east, and its hump, a furry scoliosis, is outlined with delicate fairy lights. When you clear Earlton, you can let yourself gear down. Relax your bison shoulders. You are almost there. Even if you miss the sign that announces it — Englehart, Population 1,700 — you will know you've arrived by the smoke. By day, by night, the waferboard plant — such a cosy, almost tasty name for so bland a commodity — expels into the sky a thick, phantasmic plume made in equal parts of effulgent and prayers: prayers for the health of the construction industry, for its enhanced appetite for waferboard; prayers for the prosperity and good health of the citizens of this shrinking town. Englehart, Englehart. Straight to Heaven go the prayers. To angel hearts, angel hearts.

Ten years ago — in one of those language-fuelled fits of ire that, sadly, have long been routine in our home and native land — Englehart declared itself unilingual. English heart. It is the woman who runs my hotel — and who also sells in the lobby a vast array of health foods, herbal cures, and religious tracts — who tells me so. She remembers how she and her husband, whose name happens to be French, were cold-shouldered when they arrived here, smack dab in the middle of that kerfuffle. She sloughs it off now, it's an old story, but from my outsider's point of view it seems an odd and rather confrontative decision to have made, however fractious the issue. After all, Earlton and New Liskeard to the south are largely French. Kirkland Lake and Timmins to the north both have sizeable Franco-Ontarian populations. And the province of Quebec is just a few scant kilometres to the east. Indeed, a cursory flip through the phone book will reveal that a considerable number of Englehartian surnames are also Gallic in origin: all of which proves nothing, I suppose, save that we humans are a clannish lot, and that sometimes we express our tribalism in ways that don't stand up to scrutiny. Dorothy Dupuis, who grew up in this neighbourhood in the fifties and lives here still, looks a little embarrassed when I ask her about that chapter in the town's recent history, and I'm immediately sorry I even brought it up, especially since I haven't come here to cry "J'accuse" on behalf of national unity. At the same time, it's hard to harmonize such apparent xenophobia with the tolerance this place showed, more than forty years ago, for a character as extravagant as Nellee Jessee Reid.

Dorothy is on the board of the Englehart & Area Historical Museum. Its extensive collection of local artifacts is housed in a handsome old schoolhouse on 6th Avenue. Like the zoo in Earlton, the museum is closed pending the thaw. Even so, Dorothy has kindly agreed to meet me here, the first Saturday morning in February. She has even persuaded her second cousin, Merlin Black, to join us. Dorothy is tiny, very slight. Her kinsman is more portentous of stature, seventy-eight years old, fit, with a powerful grip. Merlin began working at the age of twelve, delivering groceries in a horse-drawn cart. It was often midnight by the time he made his last delivery, and he speaks nostalgically of the town as a thriving mercantile centre, back when he was a boy. As a man, he spent his livelong days working on the railroad. Merlin knows this place as well as anyone alive. As we leaf through one of the museum's photograph albums, the shifting images jump-start his keen recall. A portrait of some once-upon-a-time town fathers moves him to sow wild oaths. "Look at them. Bunch of goddam Conservative parasites. That's what they were, sucking this town dry, sucking the blood right out of it. Bunch of goddam Conservative parasites."

There's a picture of John Price, taken on the occasion of his 100th birthday. He is playing the accordion. John was a wart charmer of local renown. Merlin sought his advice because he had a hand that was fairly taken over with the things. They were so bad and so populous he wore gloves to conceal the offending paw whenever he went out in public. John told him to take a census of the colonizers and record his findings on a slip of paper. Merlin counted them up and wrote 119. John placed the paper on a warming shelf above his stove.

"I thought there'd be a little more to it," says Merlin now, looking at the unblemished hand that betrays the story's ending, "but that was it. He sent me on my way. And the next day, when I took off my glove..."

There were many other remedies to which Merlin might have turned to clear his hand, although most are more cumbersome than John Price's efficacious conjuring. He might have found pins enough to stick in every wart, and then he would have had to put the pins in his pocket and carry them around until the wayward lumps disappeared. He could have taken a piece of meat — pork is preferred, though some will tell you any meat is fine, so long as it is rotten — and rubbed his blemishes with it while looking at the moon and saying "moony, moony"; then buried the meat, and his warts would have vanished commensurate with its decomposition. He might have rubbed the warts with a wedding ring, or with chalk, or with a penny, on which he would then have spat, and which he would then have buried. Rubbing them thoroughly with an onion, while invoking biblical names might have worked, as might have burning them one by one with a lighted match. He could have given away his warts by buffing them with a piece of flannel until they bled. Then, if he'd thrown away the cloth, the warts would have been passed on to whoever picked it up. There are also those who would have prescribed burning a cobweb over the wart, but best of all is to find a charmer such as Mr. Price. Charmers have different ways of working. Some will just look at the warts and wish them away; others rely on tokens, such as Mr. Price's required piece of paper.

I was fascinated by this story, as I have myself been troubled for years by plantar warts on my left foot. I have consulted several doctors and dermatologists for their best advice on how to rid myself of the things, but their prescriptions for removal have always struck me as so dire and crippling and invasive that I have preferred to tolerate their rooted presence. While passing through Garden Cove, Newfoundland, I happened to hear of a wart charmer named Don. Don had a good track record, I was told, and what's more he was able to charm warts over the phone. I wasted no time in calling him up. I had been warned that, for the magic to work, I must be sure not to offer him payment for his services, and I must be careful not to thank him. Talk of money or signs of gratitude would jinx the process.

"Hello, is this Don?"

"Yep."

"Don, my name is Bill. I understand you charm warts."

"Yep."

"Well, I have these plantar warts and I wondered if you might, well, you know, like, charm them?"

"How many?"

"Fourteen."

"Okay."

"Okay?"

"Okay."

"That's it?"

"Yep."

"Oh."

"I'll tell my sister."

"Your sister?"

"She charms 'em too."

"Great! Uh, okay! Bye!"

Click.

Our short chat was innocent of any discussion of money or thanks, and also of time frame. It might be that Don's remedy is very slow-acting. The fact is that as I write this, some six months after our session, there are seventeen plantar warts on my left foot. However, it is also a fact that no more than two days after Don and his sister unleashed the power of their charms in Garden Cove, Newfoundland, a wart that had been troubling my dog back in Vancouver, B.C., mysteriously and precipitously decamped from a toe on her left front foot. Coincidence? Reader, you decide.

We turn over the leaves in that Englehart Museum album until we come to the series of ten snapshots of Nellee Reid. Merlin has brought another picture from home to add to the community cache. Taken in 1942, it shows Nellee standing next to Merlin's brother, Elgin. We see them from the waist up. Elgin is dashing in his airman's uniform. Nellee is wearing a sort of Margaret Rutherford get-up: an Edwardian-style dress, amply ruffled, high collared, many buttoned. Nellee is corsetted, bust prominent, and sports a hat, which looks to be a kind of pelt which has been accessorized with a bone. The chapeau is pulled low on her brow, and Nellee's face beneath it, it must be said, is decidedly simian. There is something gross and excessive around the jaw line, either a case of the mumps or a monstrous overbite.

"Nellee had two sets of teeth," Dorothy remembers, "and that's what gave him that look. He was quite a sight. I was scared of him. His dresses were always covered with buttons, just buttons everywhere. He got around on a bicycle. Whenever I'd see him downtown, I'd hide behind my mother. I knew him a little when he was in the hospital. I was eleven and having my appendix out. Nellee was a patient there by that time. It was just before they sent him to North Bay. He always used to come into the women's ward. He'd come into the women's ward and crawl under the beds and hide there until they took him away. He had a birthday while he was there, and a bunch of the women got together and made him a dress. I remember that dress."

Here is Nellee astride his bicycle. He is in a sensible skirt cut just below the knee, a jacket with a *ceinture*, and a jaunty tam. A purse is slung on his shoulder. His shoes are dusty flats. Here is Nellee in an ankle-length, floral-patterned dress and a beribboned bonnet. He is outside a tarpaper shack, maybe in Tomstown, which is nearby Englehart, and he is feeding a few of his twenty-five cats. (After they removed him from Tomstown to the hospital, it fell to the police to take care of the feline population. They did this so efficiently that they never had to make a return visit.) Here is Nellee with his striking white hair, long skirt, and wide-tired bike, posing outside a general store. A boy in the background stands at attention. He forces his shoulders back. His shirt is unbuttoned and you can see his navel. Neither Dorothy nor Merlin can identify the boy, or the suited gent who appears in another picture. Nellee is shaking the mystery man's hand, looking up at him, smiling. Here you can see clearly how tiny Nellee was. It looks as though he is receiving a prize. Best of show. Miss Congeniality. I remark on how compact a person he was.

Nellee Jessee Reid.

"Oh, Nellee was small, but Nellee was strong," Merlin says. "I knew him from the time I was a boy. He lived at our place for a bit. There was nothing he couldn't do around the farm. He used to labour for everyone around here, baling hay, digging wells, whatever. He worked on the railroad for a time, I know that. He fought in the Boer War. And he was smart. He could talk and talk. He always wore dresses. Always. It didn't matter where he was or what he was doing, a dress was what he wore. I'm not sure where he got them. Maybe women gave their cast-offs to him. He was trained as a millwright and they can make anything, so it wouldn't surprise me to learn that he sewed them up himself. I only ever once saw him in overalls, and that was the day he went to court. He broke into someone's house."

"My mother told me he sometimes stole dresses, too," adds Dorothy. "He'd steal them right off the line. It was for the buttons."

Merlin concurred. "Yes, Nellee loved buttons. He was just covered in buttons. Beads, too. But you know, none of that stealing was malicious. If he broke into someone's house it was just because he needed something to eat. That's what I figure, anyway. It was a hard life he led, living way out in the bush like that. I remember what a relief it was to him when the pension came through, even though it was hardly more than a few dollars a month. I'd see him sometimes, hauling wood on his back. And he was old then, too. He was old when I first met him, when I was still a little boy. My God, when I think of it now! Why did he wear dresses? Well, he used to say that his mother had had five boys and he was the sixth. She simply decided she was going to have a girl, so she dressed him up as one. He said he just never lost the habit; that's the way he was. Everyone knew about Nellee. No one said much about it, not that I recall. It was different, then. People were more accepting. They helped each other. You had to, just to survive. What else? Oh, he was a big tobacco chewer. Must have poisoned his gums, all that juice. I wish I could tell you more. I wish sometimes I could get fifteen minutes with Nellee, just to clear a few things up."

Me, too. I ask a few questions to fill in some of the more conspicuous blanks. How old was Nellee when he died? Close to ninety. When did he die? Must have been in the early sixties. By then, he was in the mental hospital in North Bay. He'd become too much to handle at the local facility. And what about the spelling of his name? On some photos it appears as "Nellie." On others, "Nellee." Similarly, his surname. Reid? Or Read? And what was Nellee called before he was Nellee? Ah. Jack. He was Jack. Any known family? He had a brother who lived nearby, who worked for the sawmill and had a hook for a hand. At least, it was believed he was a brother. The two never saw each other. Merlin went to see this man when Nellee was very sick, before he went into hospital. He asked him if he was the brother of Nellee Reid, and the hook-hand man disavowed all knowledge. Merlin told him that that was too bad, because Nellee was terribly sick and if ever he needed help it was now.

The next day, someone alerted the RCMP to the situation, and they came and took Nellee away, and that was the beginning of his final chapter.

When the town of Englehart celebrated its fiftieth birthday in 1958, a group of archivally-minded citizens got together to compile a pocket history of the place. The book makes mention of several colourful characters of local renown, Nellee Reid among them. Nellee, it says, "was always well-informed about the happenings of the world, and apart from his phobia [*sic*] for wearing women's clothes, he appeared to be quite sensible." The life and times of Percy Legitt, a contemporary of Nellee's, are summed up thus: "Percy Legitt, the hermit from Savard, was well known in Englehart for the way he obtained lodging. His home was a tumble-down shack out in the country, but in order to keep warm during the long, cold winters, Percy would ride his bicycle into Englehart and heave a brick through the nearest store window — usually the liquor store. Since he had no way of paying the inevitable fines, he would spend the winter months as a guest at the crow bar hotel! *We know there are many others who deserve mention, but the time allotted us for this task has run out.*" (Italics are mine.) It is this last sentence that I find most telling and most frustrating. This is how we treat our history: casually, shruggingly, with no eye to the future. For the ostensible want of something as plentiful as time, so many names and stories have been lost, lost not just to the likes of me, a nosy parker who happens to be passing through, but lost to those who have a legitimate, profound connection to a place, even if that connection is anchored in something as banal and as random as the coincident accidents of birth and geography. Age comes and brings with it its particular hungers. We start to hanker for the past, and not just our own, either. As we gain perspective on our own stories — as the distance lengthens between our ever-shifting present age and our long ago fixed beginnings — we need to look at ourselves in the broader context of family and community. Even if this longing is not yet manifest in the individual, he or she should be able to look around and garner from example that it will one day come to roost, along with such geriatric inevitabilities as white hair and creaky knees.

Once, while I was visiting my parents in Winnipeg, I saw that my father was reading the local real estate paper. I asked him why, as I was sure he and my mother had no immediate plans to move or put their house up for sale. He told me that he just likes to keep abreast of the market, and that he was always curious to see if the house of his boyhood might be among the listings. That, he told me, was the very house he saw in his dreams, at least on those nights when a house was among the props his dreams required.

I see nothing sentimental or muddied about such nostalgia. It has less to do with a misty-eyed longing to capture the innocence of the past than with establishing connections, with creating the necessary linkages that give our lives their narrative sense and shape: the beginning, the middle, the developing end. Go into any library or archive anywhere in this country, and there you will see people, generally "of a certain age," cranking their way through microfilms of old newspapers, combing through birth and baptismal registers, absorbed by the work of learning and telling their family's or their community's own story. With this in mind, I have to say that I feel a twinge of sympathy for those erstwhile Englehartians, or their kin, who will turn up one day with their pencils sharpened and their hearts brimming with an eagerness to get a clear fix on their own compasses, only to learn that some of the best bits, the context-enriching curiosities, have been excluded from the record, and all because the allotted time ran out. True enough, they'll learn about Percy, learn at least that once he was, and that he committed petty felonies in order to have a warm place to sleep in the winter. And they'll have the redux version of Nellee as a bicycle-riding, tobacco-chewing codger who favoured frocks over overalls. But as for the *pourquoi* of their lives — well, if that's what they're after, they're out of luck.

Of course, this is not a situation that is unique to Englehart. It's everywhere the same. The fields of the past are richly layered with all the strata of everything that's been ploughed under before it was properly examined, before concerned conservationists had the chance to sift through and say: this is worth saving; this is worth holding up to the light; this merits elucidation through the simple question why? Merlin Black says he'd like to have fifteen minutes with Nellee, a mere quarter-hour to ask some of the same questions I would put to him, the questions nobody thought or wanted to ask Nellee in the moment, either because they were too polite, or too reserved, or because they didn't care, or because it just didn't seem to matter, or because they had more pressing concerns, or because it was none of their damn business. Nellee? What was to ask about Nellee? Nellee was there, had always been there, had always been the way he was; Nellee wore a dress, so what, that was Nellee's way, Nellee's thing, what was to fuss about Nellee, anyway, he was common as dirt, a farm labourer, a neighbourhood kook, a fringe-dweller; Nellee was no big deal.

Such bald acceptance is a legitimate way of accommodating the world. I do it myself with such things as household appliances. I have not devoted a minute of my life, which has already gone on for quite a long time, to understanding what it is that keeps a refrigerator cold. It's enough for me that it happens and that I can rely on it to protect the mayonnaise from bacterial invasion. But when it comes to questions of human comportment and behaviour, my inclinations are less complacent, and more speculative and analytical. Give me a bone like Nellee, and I will gnaw on it for all it's worth, even if it proves to be completely hollow, even if the flavour of its marrow is hallucinatory, a product of nothing more than my own overheated, needy imagination. Such leanings are not necessarily ingredients in a recipe for happy, healthy living. "Tu te complexe!" I remember some French friends saying to me once, in their wonderfully reflexive way, when they were swilling champagne and sucking back oysters and I was wrecking the party by knitting my brow

over some insoluble thing or other. "This week," said a therapist I'd consulted in a fragile moment, never once suspecting
that I'd be given homework assignments, "I'd like you to spend
as much time as you can living outside your own head." What?
And abandon my long habit of reading words backwards and
making up lives for people I see on the bus or in the supermar-
ket line-up? Forget it! I was cured. I never went back to therapy.

There are other traces of Nellee, though none of them is
exactly fresh. An administrator at the North Bay Psychiatric
Hospital, who asked that he not be named, told me that Jack
Reid died on July 30, 1959. His birth year had been recorded
as 1863. The usual patient-confidentiality regulations restrict
access to records or other information. There are a few clippings in a file in the Englehart library, including an article by a
journalist named Ian Ball. A handwritten addendum to the
piece attributes it, incorrectly, to the *The Temiskaming Speaker*,
July 31, 1958. It contains some intriguing notes, including the
startling information that Nellee got his start as a full-time
cross-dresser when he was a boy, and happened to be playing
the bagpipes on the balcony of a hotel in Woodstock, Ontario.
He was wearing a kilt, of course, and his appearance and performance so impressed the owner of a travelling circus, that
Nellee was hired on and billed as "The World's Only Girl
Bagpipe Player." Nellee got to like wearing a kilt, and as time
went on, his taste in costumes matured to "fancy dresses, fashionable suits, charming hats. Even when he enlisted for the Boer
War he refused to surrender his individuality: he joined a high-
land regiment. After the war he became, by turns, farmer, lum-
berman, construction hand, prospector and railroad fireman.
He was an object of derision for his colleagues, but he stuck
by his skirts. When he married the daughter of a circus per-
former (she was later killed in a railroad accident) he was
resplendent in the frilliest costume he could buy....Apart from
dress-making, he has only one other hobby: cats. If it weren't
for the attraction of his appearance, Nellee Jessee Reid would
probably be known as the Cat Man. He always has at least a

dozen around the house and, believe it or not, he trains them to hunt rabbits."

Earl Houghton, who now lives in London, Ontario, grew up in the Englehart area, and he knew Nellee well. Nellee was a regular guest at the Houghton house. For years he came around for both lunch and supper. He would sit in the kitchen and talk and talk, telling stories about his Boer War adventures and his far-flung travels. He was always loquacious. Earl says that his mouth was swollen not because he had a double set of teeth, but because his gums had been so badly poisoned. He imagines that his parents were one of the few constants in Nellee's life. They were his friends, or at least they were accepting of him and generous towards him. Nellee would order dresses from their Eaton's mail-order catalogue. Once, he received some fur cuffs he didn't like. He sent them back with a note saying something like, "Nellee has an old bull he could kill that would make better cuffs than these." Eaton's responded by sending him in exchange the very best they had.

Nellee was lucky to have the Houghtons, as there were many others he'd alienated with his fits of temper. He was often on the outs with people who'd hired him to do odd jobs, and there were times when he showed a vindictive streak. Perhaps he'd strip a wagon of its wheels, or set a living room on fire, an act of vengeance for a slight that might be real or imagined.

As Earl tells it, "He was smart as a whip and could be dangerous. He had a fight with a neighbour who'd given him a job looking after his horses, and not long after that the man was found dead in his house. These were early days, rough and tough, and policing wasn't what it is now. No charges were ever laid, but Dad figured he'd been strangled, and I guess he figured he knew who'd done it, too."

Earl remembers the cats, and agrees that rabbit was the mainstay of their diet. It was Nellee who did the hunting, however. He'd pick off the bunnies with his rifle, open them up, and leave them for the cats to devour. After a season of this, the ground would be thick with rabbit fur. Nellee was also known to take random pot-shots at passers-by, for no apparent reason. Earl himself once came under fire, and had to take cover in a ditch until Nellee's trigger-happy urges were satisfied. He can't say why Nellee should have launched such a volley. He was unpredictable, and he wasn't necessarily harmless, but he was absolutely himself. He was Nellee, and there was no one like him.

"I have never known an eccentric like him in my lifetime," said Mr. Houghton when we spoke by phone, "and we knew he was, of course; knew he was eccentric. But over time he just grew on us, like grass, and we never really got into why he was the way he was."

And that's about all. That's everything that's left of Nellee Jessee Reid, the cross-dressing, itinerant farm worker, the skirt-wearing ditch digger, the cat fancier who might have been a murderer. That's everything I have been able to find, in any case. I rather wanted to prolong my stay in Englehart, in part to see if I could mine some new Nellee nugget, and in part to see who would win the 1997 Bachelor of the Year Contest. The eleven finalists were featured in a full-page spread of the *The Temiskaming Speaker* on January 29. Most of them had been nominated, or so I would guess, by family and friends who had submitted their names along with photos and short biographical sketches. There was Gilles, age 28, "outdoorsy, 'built' and a real 'slush puppy.'" There was Keith, 24, who "likes animals and driving around in his car." Trinh, at 23, "enjoys loud music," and Robert, 52, who had evidently put forward his own name, wrote: "I enjoy being a bachelor. I go to all the bingos." I wished with all my heart that I were an area resident, and therefore eligible to vote for Charles, age 46, a pleasant-looking man in a plaid shirt, posed against pine panelling, and whose write-up, in its entirety, read: "He never had a girlfriend all his life and he is our son." Charles, I felt, needed my support. I wondered if there might not be some point in calling him up, some pretext for phoning, wondered if he might have something revelatory to say about Nellee, or other pertinent information he might care to share. In the end, I thought better of it and decided simply to wish him well telepathically as I headed out of town. I wondered how long the Bachelor of the Year Contest had been a part of the social life of Englehart, Earlton, and New Liskeard; wondered if Nellee himself had ever entered, submitting maybe one of the photos I saw of him in the museum. What would he have had to say for himself? "This button-stealing manure shoveller loves nothing more than the sound of a well-chewed plug landing squarely in a spitoon, and the rustle of his own petticoats as he goes upstairs to bed. Can he bake a cherry pie? You bet, and he sews a straight seam to boot!"

Nellee, Nellee. I am thinking of you as I drive south, *en route* to Sudbury. It's later than would be ideal for such a long journey, a Grenville Kleiser hour of the day, *an evening of great silences and spaces*, wholly tranquil with *piles of golden clouds just peering above the horizon, the blue bowl of the sky, all glorious with the blaze of a million worlds, the empurpled hills standing up, solemn and sharp, out of the green gold air* and *the evening star silvery and solitary on the girdle of the early night*. I am thinking of you, Nellee, as I pass a billboard advertising a lingerie shop in Earlton, thinking of you and wondering if you might not have enjoyed having a teddy or some such garment. It is not a picture on which I especially care to dwell, and I take a small detour a few miles down the highway to look at Tomstown. It was named not for cats, as you might expect, but for a turn-of-the-century squatter who was known as "Uncle Tom." Now that I have seen it, I can report that the story of its naming is all there is to say on the subject of present-day Tomstown. There is no plaque marking the place where Nellee's shack once stood, no sign of any kitty descendants from his once-glorious pride, no sign of the bicycle Nellee rode up and down the sandy roads, his labourer's legs still strong at nearly ninety, pumping hard under his beautiful buttoned dresses. Pumping hard, like his strangely inclined, oddly angled heart. Angel heart, angel heart. Once again, I am travelling, driving and driving, listening with all my being for anything that sounds like news, anything that sounds like a rumour of you.

Some Good Shepherds

For he keeps the Lord's watch in
the night against the adversary.
For he counteracts the powers of darkness
by his electrical skin and glaring eyes.
— Christopher Smart, "My Cat, Jeoffrey"

There's Alex, there's Stinky, there's Buddie and Billy, there's Blindy and Sam, and there's Pain-in-the-Ass. There's Fat Fuck and Tigger and Squeaky and Whisky and Smoothie and Freddy and Pinky and Tom. There's Muffin and Stubby and Smokey and Holly, there's Tortoise and Spooky and Lucky and Stray. There's Pumpkin and Softy and Yankee and Yappy and Split Face, there's Cooner and Sky and the three they call Boots. Boots 1. Boots 2. Boots 3. There's Tinkerbell. There's Catherine, who has no teeth. And there's Angel, who's the favourite.

Angel is pure white. Of course she is. What else would you expect of an Angel? Angel looks Persian. Angel is a princess. Angel has her own potty. Angel eats from a dish that is hers alone. Angel dines in the laundry room, next to the washer and dryer. Their thundering guts heave and turn and jive all the live-long day, from Sabbath to Sabbath, as Donna Wright launders every towel and blanket and slip-cover and throw rug in her house. This is just one of the chores she strings together to make a twelve- to fifteen-hour working day, which is how long it takes to keep ahead of the fur and spit and dander and other excreta which are the inevitable, unavoidable, and excusable deposits of the more than 400 cats currently in residence in their house and in whose choir Angel and Catherine and Tinkerbell and Boots 3, 2, and 1, etc., are just a few of the singers.

"Dogs just don't want to come in," says Jack Wright, who is Donna's husband, and who loves every bit as much as she the pitter-patter of 1,600 feet around the house, which, by the way, is an average-size bungalow on a quiet street not far from Queen's University in Kingston, Ontario. Every day, Jack and Donna prise the tops from 180 tins of cat food and pour out 14 kilos of kibble. These are the amounts required to load up the feeding stations strategically placed in most of the rooms. Other than Angel, who is pampered, the cats eat communally. They keep hydrated by sipping from big bowls of ice water. The ice is important, because cats like their liquids well chilled, and a trough warms quickly with the friction of 400 lapping tongues. Likewise, there are plenty of litter boxes round about, the maintenance of which calls to mind the nursery rhyme about seven maids sweeping for seven years. What with the feeding and the cleaning and the vaccinating and the vetting and all the various sundry expenses and capital costs that are incurred by keeping such an ark afloat, the Wrights figure their annual cat bill can be rounded off to something in the vicinity of $110,000. And that doesn't take into account the cost of the turkeys Donna cooks and carves and portions out to her purring brood on festive days such as Christmas, on which occasion they also receive individually wrapped toys.

I turned up at their house unannounced one afternoon in February. I am not a dropping-in kind of visitor, don't like being dropped-in on myself. However, as I had been unable to raise the Wrights on the phone, and as I had only a few hours in Kingston, and as I was eager to see this house about which I'd heard so much, I thought I would set protocol aside, and take my chances on finding them both at home and in a receiving mood. Donna answered the door with a mop in one hand, a cigarette in the other. I explained what I was about, and she was happy to let me in and show me around their operation. I think she must have been relieved to find out that I wasn't yet another desperate soul with yet another cat needing succour and care. The Wrights are famous for never turning an orphan away, and thousands of feline foundlings have been given sanctuary in their home since first they began their missionary work in 1969.

"Oh, come on in, dear," she said, "come on in. It's a good thing you didn't stop by this morning, I just can't see people in the morning, the place is a terrible mess in the morning. Come on in."

I took a deep gulp of air and stepped across the threshold. I confess that I had steeled myself against this moment. I have a cat myself, just one cat, a sweet black cat whom I adore, and who adores me in turn, and without whom there would be no point in going on. I comb her and pet her and feed her and dole out her favourite treats, which happen to be dog biscuits. She rides on my shoulder and she sleeps between my legs and she nibbles on my wrists and she serenades both me and her private god with tuneful hymns of her own composing. We have a good, solid relationship. We are in love. For all that, I am sorry to confess that there have been times when I have been too busy or preoccupied or lame-brained and have forgotten for a day or three about tending to her litter box. It's shocking, but it's true, and I know about the high, ammoniac wafts that rise from the tray of Jonny Cat when it has been less than scrupulously sifted. I know about the limits of those highly touted green, odour-fighting pellets with which the stuff is laced. And it was the prospect of such a full-frontal olfactory assault, but magnified several hundred times, that aroused my fear and trepidation as I entered their hallway, stepped over and around the half-dozen cats who were slaloming between my ankles, and walked into a place that was, much to my surprise, *as peaceful as a village cricket green on Sunday.*

There was an odour in the air, to be sure, but it was more of cleanser than of the acrid ripening that signals cat pee. It was different, the smellscape, but not objectionable, not off-putting. Keep 400 of anything in a smallish house — 400 cool watermelons, say — and I submit that there will be a redolence that reflects that particular presence. The point is that it wasn't what met the nose that was amazing or memorable. It was the visuals that were overwhelming. The first thing anyone will tell you about Jack and Donna Wright is that they give shelter to hundreds of cats, so naturally, it was hundreds of cats that I was prepared to see. But it is impossible to imagine what "hundreds of cats" look like, contained as a group in a small space, until you actually bear witness to the way they move in slow and solemn procession over every available flat surface of the house, kaleidoscopic, a stunning and shifting geometry of whisker and tail.

There were cats in the hallway, cats on the stairs, cats on the tables, and cats on the chairs. There were rusts, greys, blacks, whites, stripes; there was every patchwork permutation and combination of colouring represented among the cats on the microwave, the stove, the counter, and in the cupboards. On the kitchen table alone, which was layered with a couple of towels, I counted seventeen cats. Who would have imagined a kitchen table could have accommodated seventeen cats, curled up so placidly? They looked like commas, spilled from a typographer's tray.

I spent a very pleasant hour or so with the Wrights. I lost track of how many cats scaled my legs, or nuzzled my chin, or purred in my ear. "Which one is this?" I asked, as I felt the tidy grip of claw, and the brush of tail against my cheek. Some cat had just slipped from the top of the fridge and was straddling my shoulders, stole-like, the length of its warm body against my neck.

"Squeaky. That one's Squeaky."

"Do they all have names?"

"Oh, yes. They have to be registered with the city."

"And I imagine they all have personality traits?"

"Sure they do. Over there — that's Sam. Sam just loves Hostess Ripple Chips. And there, that's Pumpkin. Pumpkin has a thing for pork. They all have their stories. You get to know pretty quickly what they're like."

"Do they ever fight? You would think that with so many cats there'd be spats all the time."

"Almost never. Animal psychologists say that, if you have more than twenty-five animals contained in a space, you've got trouble. But they all get along, mostly. It gets tense when there are kittens. One cat will try to steal another's kittens and then we'll have a fight."

"Do they ever go out?"

"There's a fenced area out the back of the house, like a gazebo. They can go out there safely."

"Do they ever escape?"

"Once, somebody cut through the fence. I don't know who, some kind of animal-liberation activist, I guess. There was a knock on the door. I answered, and it was a nun. She asked, 'Are those your cats?' And all the roofs, all around, were just covered with cats."

"It's a big responsibility, four hundred cats."

"Oh, God. Oh, it sure is."

"Do you ever get away? On vacation?"

"Donna got away once, for a day. That was when she went on "The Phil Donahue Show." She called home every hour or so to check on her babies."

Jack and Donna have often been on television. They've made the news in Japan, in the United States, and in France, as well as in Canada. They have been featured in magazines and newspapers, and in tabloids such as *The National Enquirer*. Such exposure will usually bring in some donations, which is a good thing, since the house-painting business that sustains them has suffered of late, and there have been more than a few times when the demands placed on them by their 400 dependents have brought them close to the financial brink. The problem is, every time the Wrights are advertised to the world as the couple who just can't say no to a cat in need, they can count on taking delivery of the one commodity for which they have no further need. Cats have been packed up and sent north across the border. Bulk orders of cats have arrived from the country, shipped to the city by owners who didn't know where else to turn when they had to leave their farms.

"Could you not just say no?"

"Where else are they going to go? We just can't stand the thought of them being hurt or euthanized."

"But it's taken over your whole life."

"I know, I know," says Donna, whose every day is spent mopping, washing, feeding, cleaning, petting. "Sometimes you think it'll make you crazy. We can't get away. Who's going to look after them? I cry just about every day in the summertime. But who else is going to do it?"

Cats and cats and still more cats. Sitting in the sink, sprawling on the sofa, spilling from the settee and the sills. What can it be like there at night, when everything's settled and still? When everything's settled and everything's still, what is it like at night? How many cats are on the bed of Jack and Donna Wright?

"I'd say forty, wouldn't you Jack?"

"At least. Oh, at least."

Their delicate paws tucked under their chests. The neat, quick beat of their small and happy hearts. The rumble of their breathing. The low and flickering wattage of their dreams.

It has been Jack and Donna Wright's experience — and they should know — that a cat, when it is ready to die, will seek you out. It will come to you. It wants you as a vigil sitter. When Jack Marriott's cat came to him for the last time, it was already dead. Then again, so was Jack.

The cat was called Po. Old Po. White Po. Deaf Po. One-eyed Po. He and Jack are buried in the Starr's Point Cemetery, near Wolfville, Nova Scotia. Only Jack's name is mentioned on the marker, but Po is with him. Although I wasn't there to witness the interment, I have it on good authority that this is so. Jack and Po went down together, nestled side by each in a satin-lined, yellow pine coffin, which was just the right length but unnecessarily deep. There's a photo of the pair of them sequestered there. It's about as still a still life as anyone could imagine:

dead man, dead cat, each insensible to the other's presence, but looking nonetheless pleased with the arrangement, somehow, like two old friends snuggling up for a chaste wee nap. Jack is wrapped up in a favourite blanket, and Po is cuddled on his left chest, guarding his silent heart. Once they were arranged in the casket; once the lid was hammered down, and their earthly remains were lowered into the ground, everyone who braved the winter day to attend the service took a turn heaping dirt on the coffin. A local fellow had designed and built it, a cabinet maker, and it had stood for years in Jack's parlour. Likewise, the stone had been in place for some time, chiselled with both his birth year, 1888, and death year, 1988. That Jack Marriott caused the year of his demise to be literally carved in stone before the fact tells us how confident he was that he would live to be a centenarian. As it turned out, he died on December 28, 1986. Even though he was ready to go — he'd horrified his friends by asking them to help him die by driving a knitting needle through his ribs — it must have been a disappointment to him that his ferry across the Styx turned up two years in advance of its anticipated run. 1888–1988. Such a nice round number! Such gestalt! Luckily for Jack, the same friends who declined to pierce his heart — or to smother him with a pillow, or to set him on the edge of his bed and help him fall face forward onto the floor — saw to it that the stone was not altered to conform to the death certificate. Thanks to his friends, Jack was granted his hundred-year wish, at least insofar as the most visible and weather-resistant of the public records was concerned.

Jack's friends. He more than relied on their kindness. He demanded it. He orchestrated it. His attention-getting ploys were both transparent and effective. For the most part, he got his way. He was, in the words of one man who knew him, who was his neighbour, and who didn't like him, "an irascible old bastard." Irascible is one of many words that might be used to parse the man. Controlling, lascivious, fanciful, deluded, brilliant, charming, manipulative, and aggravating could also serve. David Sheppard, a high-school teacher in Wolfville, alerted me to Jack's story in a letter dated July 14, 1996, which would have been Jack's 108th birthday. I quote it here in part.

"In response to your request for material about Canadian eccentrics, I am sending you this manuscript about Henry John Burton Marriott, an Englishman who came to Canada in 1921 and settled into an unconventional life in the Annapolis Valley of Nova Scotia. I was Jack's best male friend, his secretary and agent, as well as the executor of his estate. His station in life was Artist, but the realities of his life meant he worked as a clerk, a farmer, a customs officer. Nothing meant more to him than his music, his photography, his enjoyment of Nature. He kept detailed diaries for fifty years. There are paradoxes in his life, which was, in some ways, a failure. He believed he achieved true happiness and friendship, but he paid a terrible price in lost friends, a dysfunctional and lost family, and personal disability. He believed his music and photography to be exemplary yet some of his critics are kind to use words like mediocre. He contributed to his community by organizing community theatre, concerts, picnics, spelling bees and the like, yet they ostracized him because he took nude pictures of women and girls. He believed that human friendship was the greatest Truth there was, yet by the end of his life he had decided that cats were vastly superior to humans as friends. Believing in the freedom of the individual, he determined that his death would be based on *his* dictates, not those of the status quo. The cat and the coffin story are the epitome of this individualism."

I went to Port Williams, near Wolfville, and spent a long and very pleasant evening hearing stories about Jack Marriott from David Sheppard and Jennie Sheito. Jennie also knew him well. She was his close neighbour, and was involved with his care in the last years of his life. She and her husband, Allen, literally bought into their relationship with Jack. He sold them his house on the condition that he be allowed to remain there undisturbed and unmolested until his death or failing health dictated his removal. Now, it has been restored it to its full Georgian splendour. It's a provincial heritage site, and they run it as the Planters' Barracks Inn. If ever you visit, you must ask to look at the "before" pictures. They will give you graphic insight not only into what is possible with hammer, nail, and elbow grease, but into the world of Jack Marriott. No life is simple. Jack's was not only longer than most, it was notably more baroque and variegated. His story is daunting in its complexities, but in order to set the cat and the coffin in context, here is a vastly pared-down version, gleaned from my conversation with David and Jennie.

Eighteen eighty-eight. Jack is born into a straight-laced Victorian family that was part of the emerging upper middle class. His father was a financier with a seat on the London stock exchange. Jack was a dreamer. He spent his time painting, sketching, writing, composing music, or cycling around the countryside. He fell under the influence of Maeterlinck. He adored Beethoven. They were the masters he venerated his whole life long. There was nothing in his temperament to suggest that he would make a success of the job his father found him when he left school. For sixteen years he worked as a clerk in the Bank of England, a dead-end job for which he was patently unsuited, and in which he had no hope of advancing. He married a young woman named Leila Talbot, of whom his family disapproved. When Jack was thirty-two and Leila twenty-eight, they had decided that they should take their two daughters and seek their fortune away from England. They settled on Canada and sailed from Liverpool on April 15, 1921, on the S.S. *Sachem*. They came to Port Williams, where they bought the house they would call "Acaciacroft" for about $7,500.

Jack thought he would be able to make a living as an orchardist, selling the Valley's famous apples. When that proved impossible, he took to fur farming. He raised foxes and chinchillas, and still the family barely scraped by. There were other setbacks. Their children embodied the lesson that there's nothing quite so cruel and capricious as genetics. Jack had failed to acquire his father's business sense, but he had inherited, recessively, the family diabetes. He was not affected, but both his daughters were, and severely, too. They were among the first insulin users in Canada. The drug didn't come cheap, and this compounded the family's stress level. It didn't take long for the community to come around to the opinion that Jack was ineffectual, flighty, a poor provider.

When the girls grew up and left home, the marriage dissolved. Leila moved on. Jack stayed put and lived alone in Acaciacroft for over forty years. At the age of fifty, he secured a job as a customs officer. It was not demanding work and he earned a decent wage. There was time to develop other hobbies, photography in particular. He took thousands of yearbook portraits for Acadia University. That was useful, innocuous work. He won his infamy by taking nude portraits of young women. Jack always insisted that his work was completely above board, that there was always a chaperone present, that he never importuned his models. Nonetheless, tongues wagged. It was a small, rural community, after all. He became someone to watch out for, someone to avoid. A dirty old man. The neighbourhood pornographer. At one point, he was banned from a local tea room. Still, for all his notoriety, he managed to find models. He would be smitten with some of them, would photograph them, and write about them obsessively. There was Joyce, who was fifteen when he fell in love with her. Then there was Mary Lou. Others followed. Always, he said, the relationships were Platonic.

Fifteen cats kept Jack company at Acaciacroft in his declining years. Fifteen was the number he required, he said, in order to sustain his diet. He lived for years on a broth made from chicken necks he purchased in bulk from a nearby processing plant. He would take thirty-three necks —

Jack Marriott, Po, and Beethoven.

and it was always thirty-three — and stew them. These he would feed to the cats. He sustained himself on the broth, using it as a stock for a soup that he would keep on the go for weeks on end, adding more water, and another batch of necks as required.

From the road, Acaciacroft looked like a haunted house: a magnificent, crumbling edifice surrounded by shrubs and every noxious weed native to Nova Scotia. Young people were attracted to it, and to Jack. They saw him as an old Bohemian, saw his house as a place to crash. Some came to take advantage, to rob him of his stamps and coins. Others helped out. Jack was already quite blind when David Sheppard met him. He needed "a secretary," someone to read to him, to write the letters he would dictate. Sheppard — Jack always called him by his surname — took on the job. At the beginning, he visited once a week, stopping by to chat, to jot down a letter or two. Jack, however, exerted a powerful fascination, and as time went by, his increasing demands began to take precedence for Sheppard over the needs of his own family.

"In a sense," said Sheppard, "I was suckered. He made it so that I was absolutely essential to him. He could be incredibly insensitive. When my mother died, I didn't go to visit him as scheduled, and he didn't understand at all. It was completely irrelevant to him that she had died. He couldn't see past the fact that it was a day that we were meant to have been together, and I hadn't come. That was one of the days it almost ended, as it had for so many of his friends. But I'm a bit of an odd bird myself, and I said, 'I'm going to stick this out. You're not going to drive me away like you did everyone else.'"

Jack was ninety-four when blindness and ill health finally forced his hand, and he had to move to a care facility. Sheppard, dogged as ever, visited him every day. They settled into a routine that revolved around reading aloud from the diaries that Jack had kept from the time he was a young man. Day after day, they would review his life, his philosophies, his loves, his disappointments. It took them fourteen months to get through the dozens of little notebooks.

For every good reason, death was more and more on Jack's mind. He spent many happy hours with Sheppard, planning his funeral. "We could spend a whole Sunday afternoon talking about his pallbearers, and he would change them at his whim. I pride myself on keeping promises and I agreed that he would have a hand-dug grave, that there would be no backhoe used, that he wouldn't be embalmed, that there would be no formal display of the body, that he would be lowered into the ground by hand. It was one thing to promise that I would take his photograph. But he wanted to be buried naked. I asked, why naked, and he said he wanted everyone to stand around in a circle and place their hands on him. I said, 'Jack, your daughter Joan is in her late seventies. If she comes to the funeral and I have the lid off that casket and you're naked, she's going to be shocked.' He said that was just what he wanted. I said, 'Jack, I can do everything but bury you naked. I'll photograph you, I'll put the flowers on the grave, I'll put the things you want in the casket, like the picture of Joyce and the special grey blanket and the cat, but I just can't see burying you naked.'"

Jack's plan had been to die at home. He saw just how it would be. He would be lifted from his bed before rigor set in, carried downstairs, and placed in the waiting coffin. From there it would be just a short hop across the midsummer fields to the Starr's Point Cemetery, his waiting gravestone, and his view of the Minas Basin. He knew that a fast burial would be required if he wanted to sidestep the indignity of embalming. He was not someone who would gladly suffer hitches. He did not take his illness or the nursing home into account when he began to visualize his funeral; nor did it ever occur to him that he would die in the winter, when the ground would be frozen, making it impossible to dig a grave by hand, or that the graveyard itself might be inaccessible, the whole operation therefore requiring more than the thirty-six hours the health department will allow before a body has to be buried, burned, or shot full of preservatives. It was up to Sheppard to raise these troublesome possibilities.

"Jack, what if you die in the winter?"

"Why, you could carry the casket in on a sled, leave it there, I'd freeze solid, and you could bury me in the spring."

"No one will want to look at the casket all winter, Jack. And anyway, what about the coyotes?"

"Coyotes?"

"Sure, they'd get in there and drag you all over the dyke."

"Then I'll just have to die in the summer."

When Jack was removed to the nursing home, and the ongoing maintenance of his cats proved impossible, a local handyman was hired to take care of them, which he did, one by one by one. Finally, only Old Po was left, the sole inhabitant of the huge house. Jennie came to feed him, but he was going mad with loneliness. It was a dilemma. As Jack wanted the cat as a coffin buddy, and as there was no way to coordinate the two deaths, it was decided that Po would be put down and frozen, then exhumed for the funeral, a kitty cube in waiting. David Sheppard remembers — and who could forget? — how he took the cat in to be needled, and handed the vet a freezer bag. "I told him to tuck the cat up nicely so that nothing would break off. I took him home and placed him in our freezer, with the frozen strawberries, the hamburger, the vegetables. From time to time, Jack would ask me how his deceased pet was doing, and I would say he looked fine, even though he was a mass of matted fur with ice, freezer burn, and a grotesque look of horror on his face. When Jack learned that my family was upset about having Po next to the strawberries, he told me to get a second small freezer, and gave me the money to do so. I bought one second-hand, transferred the cat, then one day noticed a pool around the base. It had broken down, so Po went back in with the strawberries."

As Jack was no longer able to write, but wanted to document his life to the last, he began to make his diary entries on a tape recorder. When he spilled milk on his machine and it short-circuited, and when he was too weak to push the buttons, his visitors were encouraged to record their thoughts and observations so that some kind of diary, however scant, could be maintained to the end.

"Good visit. Talked about memories."

"Seemed out of it."

"He's wearing his teeth and can speak clearer."

"Jack well today. I visited his cemetery plot and reported how his stone looks. He was pleased to hear how nice the Starr's Point Cemetery is."

Towards the end, he was often in pain. It was then that he began to think longingly of knitting needles and pillows. But thankfully, his systems shut down one by one, of their own accord, and he surrendered himself peacefully, and with grace.

The weather was mild for the end of December. The grave was easily opened. Sheppard, as per their agreement, laid out the corpse. True to his word, he did not let Jack go to earth naked. He dressed the shell of his friend, wrapped him in his old blanket, placed him in the coffin, and then remembered Po.

"The one thing none of us had taken into account was how long it would take to thaw a cat. He was a big cat, too. We considered the microwave, but we just couldn't do it. There was nothing I could do but get him from the freezer and put him in the coffin with that dreadful look on his face. I like to think that maybe he thawed into a fond embrace."

"Jack was a misfit in many ways," said Jennie, as our evening wound down. "He seemed to be in the wrong time and place. He would have loved his funeral, though, the way the clouds parted and that light came down from the sky."

Sheppard said, "He thought the most important thing in the world was friendship, and I don't think he had any idea how many people despised him. Certainly we were completely shocked by the number of people who turned up at the funeral. There must have been 150. There were very few of the young people he'd attracted, they'd been gone for years. Mostly, they were people he'd known in the forties and fifties. Almost no one to whom he left things has ever claimed them. He was someone who had a great deal of talent, and none of it ever really went anywhere. In the end, I don't think you can say that he really left a legacy."

"No," said Jennie, "which is sad. He could have accomplished so much. In some ways, his life was like the ultimate failure."

In some ways, perhaps. On the other hand, we talked about Jack Marriott for three solid hours, and could easily have gone on. If his life didn't measure up to his own grandiose plans for it; if the world never saw or understood the full range of his imagined genius, he nevertheless, with all his vanity and all his silliness, left a seemingly inexhaustible supply of anecdotes, stories, and speculation. These have no *material* worth, but perhaps they are enough. And though his family life might have been a failure, and the passions of his middle and old age unrequited, and even misdirected, it's certainly true that he touched David Sheppard's life in a profound and lasting way. It was Sheppard who delivered the eulogy. At Jack's suggestion, he read from the diaries, including this excerpt from 1969:

"I drive back alone in the rain and think how good life is. I have dreamed and dreamed that life could be good and happy and sensible, but was afraid to believe my dream.... Surely the end of my life is coming, for what more is there? For all has come to my life that I have looked for, all the joy and beauty and sense that I have dreamed of; it has come bit by bit and then suddenly [it was] completed. There is no more. I want no more. I see everything now, I think. I feel nearer to the real truth and to the real God than ever before..."

And what is all this pother about?
The piquancy of the pageant of life
Awaiting his summons to the eternal silence

Chapter Twelve

Job's Excellent Vacation

Mark me, and be astonished . . .
— Book of Job 21:5

Job and Jean-Paul Sartre met one day at the gym. They were on adjacent treadmills. Job said, "Hey, J.-P.! Walking, walking, going nowhere. Remind you of anything?" Jean-Paul squinted at him over his copy of *Le Monde*. He pursed his lizard lips and grunted by way of acknowledgment. He had never been one for banter, and ever since the introduction of the Heaven-wide smoking ban, he'd been on the testy side. Job pressed on, undeterred. He was enjoying an endorphine-generated high, and was momentarily insensible to signs of either suffering or indifference. He cranked his speed up a couple of notches and asked, "So, tell me J.-P., how are you finding all this nothingness? Is it everything you imagined it might be?" Jean-Paul folded his paper and calibrated his machine down to zero. He knew a losing battle when he saw one. Not that he was surprised. It was always like this with these biblical celebrities. They just wanted to drive a tent-peg into your heart, pin you down, and have at you hammer and tongs. Yammer, yammer, yammer, they never knew when to quit. Once a proselytizer always a proselytizer. The only one of that crowd he found even passingly tolerable was the Apostle Paul. He was appealing in his austerity, but also looked as though he'd once known how to have a good time. It was a combination of traits Sartre had always admired.

"*Franchement, mon ami,*" said Jean-Paul, dismounting from what he and his weight-room buddy William Blake privately called "the dark satanic mill"; "*franchement,* I'd rather the Champs-Elysées than the Elyssian Fields."

"Miss the old stomping grounds, eh?"

"Ah, oui. La nostalgie de la boue."

"Say what?"

"Longing for the mud. Hard to translate exactly. It's a French kind of thing. *Au revoir.*"

"A la prochaine!" chimed Job, rather pleased that he had such a phrase available to him.

"Sainte vierge, qu' il n'y aura pas une prochaine!"

"Say what?" asked Job. But J.-P. feigned not to hear. He had picked up his towel and was heading for the steam room.

"*Nostalgie de la boue. Nostalgie de la boue,*" Job repeated to himself as he moved to the StairMaster. "I must remember to make a note of that. *Nostalgie de la boue.*" He was forever borrowing books from the library on how to increase his word power. He knew it was important to work new additions to his vocabulary into day-to-day chat as often as possible. It was the only way they would ever take hold. There had even been occasions when he would misrepresent the absolute truth or steer a conversation off on wild tangents just to have the chance to lob a bright new ball into his interlocutor's court. Mendacious. Egregious. Cotyloid. Polymorphous. Disingenuous. It was amazing, the things that would come out of his mouth.

"You're quiet, Job," God remarked that night when they met for their weekly chess game. "Anything wrong?"

"Yes, well, you know. Just a little *nostalgie de la boue.*"

"Those old muddy cravings. Well, that's easy enough to fix. It's been a while since you've had a break from Heaven, with its uniformly egg-white walls and its relentlessly temperate climes. It can be a tad monochromatic here, it's true. How'd you like a working vacation? There's a particular assignment I have in mind."

"Oh?" Job asked, rather hesitantly. The last time he'd been sent on a "particular assignment" he'd wound up dying on St. Helena, the consequence of slow poisoning. Or so he believed.

Worse still was that he'd spent that whole lifetime perfecting his French only to have it all wiped out when he was X-rayed prior to re-entry.

"Ever heard of Manitoba?"

"Can't say it rings a bell."

"You'll love it. It's a friendly place with ample recreational possibilities, and all the mud you'd want to see in a lifetime. And it's a short-term posting as these things go."

"How short?"

"Eighty, maybe. Ninety at the max."

"Are we talking dog years?"

"Not this time."

"What ever happened to three score and ten?"

"Improved health care. Don't fret. It'll fly by. You'll hardly know you've been away."

"What about my plants? My goldfish?"

"I'll see they're looked after. Checkmate."

So it was that Job descended once again to go to and fro on the earth, to walk up and down upon it. And once again, as was his well-established wont, he wandered hand in hand with bad luck. Even the most advanced and practised of souls, when they slip back into the atmosphere, experience a wholesale letting-go, a generalized forgetting of everything they've learned in Paradise. Over the course of their time on earth, the more refined among them will slowly recover a few of the more ringing eternal tenets and verities. It took Job fully half the length of his most recent tenure on the planet to get back to something that even approximated his name. He started out as Wuketsewitz, and eventually wound up with Bog. Paul Bog. If ever there was a life that could be understood as a prescription to counteract the effects of *nostalgie de la boue* it would be his. Back in Heaven, during his debriefing, Job would use the word "ruderal" to describe his Manitoba incarnation. For twenty years, he lived under a manure pile near Petersfield, about 100 kilometres north of Winnipeg, in the neighbourhood of Winnipeg Beach. I went there to hear the story of his life from Mickey

Donohoe, in whose barn Paul spent the last six winters of his life, who knew Paul Bog as well as anyone, and who in many ways has become the guardian of his story.

My conversation with Mickey took place — as was so often the case on this trip — over coffee, in a kitchen. The safe, domestic heart of the house. A good place for storytelling. Mickey was rather more cautious than most of the other narrators I met, and I wasn't sure if his diffidence was a product of shyness, or concern that I would in some way misappropriate his information. I had the clear sense that he had made deliberate choices about what he would and would not divulge. As it was also evident that Paul Bog was a man for whom he felt and feels a genuine fondness and kinship, I can understand well enough why he might have been so protective, even proprietary, about the Bog legend. After all, it was to Mickey that Paul had confided, in bits and pieces, his sad and bizarre story. Mickey, I imagine, feels he carries the responsibility of stewardship. He is the living repository of this eccentric man's memory. He was one of the locals who saw to it that the road to Paul's place was renamed Paul Bog Road.

Paul Wuketsewitz's story, before he came to Canada, and before he became Paul Bog, is sketchy. We have it only in broad strokes. He was born early in the century in Austria. According to Mickey, he lived in Vienna and had a secure (and rather prognosticatory) job working in the city's sewer system. Somehow, for some reason, he was cheated by his family out of his rightful share of his inheritance. Around the time of that considerable discouragement, he fell prey to the ministrations of an immigration propagandist who made him believe that a homesteading life on the Canadian flatlands would be like heaven on earth.

"He came here in the late twenties, thinking he would find the land of milk and honey," said Mickey. "He got here and there was nothing. He went to Saskatchewan and was employed on a farm. He was there for about two years and he asked the farmer to hold onto his wages. Then the Depression came along, the farmer went out of business, and he lost everything, so there was no way Paul was able to get the money out of him. I also heard he had a girl once, but she ran off with a neighbour. I don't know if he was married to her, but he did not like women at all. If a lady happened to walk into the barn he'd get mad.

"He came here early in the thirties. He'd got this piece of land, somehow. He came out here in the wintertime and had to stay with a neighbour and his wife. They had some kind of falling-out. I think it was because the woman was afraid of him, because of the hatred in his eyes. I'm sure they had a conflict and he had to get out. I'm awfully sure of that."

Mickey's sense is that Paul was a loner during those early years. His relationships with his neighbours were civil, for the most part, but distant. With some he had ongoing feuds. There are stories that he would chase unwanted visitors off his property with a pitchfork. He built a small house. He lived as a subsistence farmer, relying on fairly primitive, but reliable, agricultural techniques. He had a team of horses and a wagon, but got around the countryside on an old bicycle, the tires filled with twine, not air. He'd ride eleven miles to the store, even in the wintertime. And all that time he was Wuketsewitz. It was a fire that brought about the circumstances that earned him the nickname "Bog."

"His place burned down in 1960 on New Year's. I'm awfully sure it happened on the first of January. His place burned down and that was when he moved underground. He moved in with his two horses. He'd dug a shelter for them under the manure pile, a shelter for the horses."

(What follows is a transcription of our conversation. My first question is a marvel of journalistic acumen.)

"What's a manure pile look like?"

"Like a pile of manure."

"Like a mound?"

"Yeah. It's a mound."

"Would that have been a usual thing? To dig underneath one and keep horses there?"

"No. But heck, it was excellent. Hot in the winter. Insulation. You're out of the wind."

"How deep? It must have been deep to accommodate horses."

"Yeah. I was in there a lot. Just one of the horses was left there by that time. The steps he had were straight up and down and even now I'm not able to imagine how he got his horse in and out. Up is easy, but to go down!"

"What were the horse's names?"

"The horses didn't have names. One of his horses died in the summertime. Paul asked a local trucker to come over and pick up his horse and haul it into Winnipeg for him. He goes over and it's all chopped up in pieces and it's about two weeks old and it's the summer! The guy with the truck said, Paul I'm not takin' that. So he ate his horse the rest of the summer."

"He ate the horse?"

"He ate the horse."

"Oh. Well, what did it look like down there? Was there any light?"

"No, there was nothing. To open the door was a big thing. To open it from the inside was a big job. You'd give it a pull and the whole thing would fall down the steps and it would take him half an hour to haul it back up. He put sticks and hay around it. For heat, he had a drum and a pipe through the

Paul Bog in front of his manure pile.

top. There wasn't much down there. He had whatever he needed. There was a post in the middle to hold the horse off to the side, and he used to lie on the straw right beside the horse. But the post had to be there so that if the animal moved in the night he wouldn't land up on top of him. And he had cats, too. Oodles of cats. As long as I knew him he always had a bunch."

"How did he feed them?"

"In those days I don't know. But after I got to know him, when he was living in my barn, they ate the same thing he ate."

"What was that?"

"Evaporated milk, eggs, tea, coffee, sugar, rice, beans all in one pot. He'd mix it all up and he'd eat that for one week, in the summertime too. Then when it was empty, he'd make himself up another bunch of everything in one pot. Bag of tea, half a pound of coffee, half a bag of sugar."

"He'd heat it up?"

"At my place he used to heat it up for a day. Then off went the heat and he'd eat out of that big pot with a knife. He'd just scoop in there with this big knife that he had. It must have been okay. He was eighty-six when he died."

"Did you ever taste it?"

"No. I wouldn't taste that. In the summertime? In the heat? Almost a week old? I wouldn't ever try that."

"What did it smell like in his house?"

"Not awfully bad. On the smoky side. The manure from the horse I don't mind at all. Mostly just smoke and the horse."

"How often did the horse get out?"

"In the spring he went out. In the fall he came in."

"Did the horse seem okay?"

"Oh, yeah."

"How long did Paul stay underground?"

"A long time. Twenty years. And then the manure pile burned down. At the time he didn't have his last horse any more, he'd eaten him too. The place burned down in the fall, in the cold, and that was when he moved to my barn. He was there for about six years, but only in the winter."

"His place burned?"

"Yeah. The fire department ended up there, and an ambulance, and they hauled him away and he got mad. I mean, him, he was excellent, but the police were there too, and they just threw him in the ambulance, took him to the hospital. Two hours after that he had an argument in there and he said, 'I'm goin' home!' They dropped him off here at the farm. He just told me, 'I'm gonna come to your barn, now.' He didn't ask me or anything! I said, 'Okay, Paul.' He asked if I had a spade; then he asked me to go with him back to his house. The fire was all out now. Everything was all under water, you know, what with the fire department being there. He started lookin' around and he said to me, 'Here. Dig here. There's something down there.' So I dug there for most of the afternoon. Then I hit something. It was a garbage bag. Then another. They were both full of money. We went back to the barn and I set him up there for the night. And in the morning when I went back he had all his money, individual bills, lying all over the floor, drying, because of course they got so soaked. He had $34,000! It was old, some of that money. It was all excellent, all straight in lines up and down.

"That afternoon, I talked to a few of the neighbours, because I didn't want that much money there in the barn. I told him he had to take it to the bank, and he said he wouldn't. Finally I convinced him and made arrangements with the bank manager to meet me at the door at 10 a.m. exactly. I told him to be sure to be ready because this old guy's unpredictable. So at 10.00 sharp I was at the bank with the old guy and these bags of money. The manager opens up the door and the old guy goes running in behind the counter. And I'm after him because he's not supposed to be there, and the manager is after me because I'm not supposed to be there, and we were snaking around all through the bank with his bags full of money. Finally it was all arranged for us to go down in the basement. There was a teller at the table to take the money, but Paul wasn't going to hand it over all at once. He did it a handful at a time. It was all he owned. He knew exactly how much he had — although he was out by $5. He had $5 more than he thought."

"Did he ever spend any money?"

"On groceries, and he liked a drink."

"Did he ever buy clothes?"

"Not clothes. Not as far as I know."

"He wore the same stuff all the time?"

"Oh, yeah. The socks were unbelievable. Those he had to buy, maybe about two pairs a year. When he needed extra socks, he'd just add. He never took his old ones off. At the end, I took eight pairs of socks off him, and the only ones that were okay was the outside pair. All the rest were completely gone from the ankles down. And another thing I had to do that I don't think anyone ever had to do before was to potty-train an eighty-year-old man. The first time he'd ever had to use a toilet was when he moved into my barn. Before, he'd just go outside. I don't know. I mean, if the horse can do it... I told him at the start that on a dairy farm you can't leave a mess around, not any human mess. And I had to show him, from one end to the other, what he had to do in the toilet. I sat down and showed him how, and when I got up he looked, and understood, and then I showed him how to operate the flush. After that, he was okay."

"What kind of a set-up did you have for him in the barn?"

"It was excellent for him. It's a nice barn, huge, with an office in it, and other rooms that were excellent. It was all heated electrically. The heater was in the wall. One day I went in and noticed there were ashes on the floor. It happened like that for a few days, these ashes on the floor, and it turned out that the way he checked to see if the heater was on was to throw in a hunk of paper. If it burned, it was on."

"This was in the winter. Where was he in the summer?"

"He re-dug into the manure pile, this time into the side. It was about four feet wide, eight feet long, six feet high. No, it wouldn't have been that high because I had to duck down when I went in."

"Very cramped!"

"Yeah. One time at my place I gave him a dog, a little one, and he liked it. In the springtime he took it home. In the fall he stayed there too long, out in the cold, him and the cats and that dog all in the little room. When I went to see him I saw the dog wasn't there. I asked him where it was, and he said it had died. I said, 'Well, Paul, how?' And he didn't want to tell me. Finally, he said, 'A stick on the head! No room here for me, my cats, my dog. I kill dog!'"

"What happened to the cats when he went back and forth?"

"He moved with all his cats. They were wild. He'd haul them all over in a bag. Boy, that was something! But he was able to do it, and without anything on his hands. I helped him once, holding the bag, and those cats would scream, and they'd be trying to eat you from inside the bag, and him, he'd be reaching around behind the stove and he'd burn his hand and they'd be chewing at him, but he'd just keep grabbin' his cats, and then he had a bag full of screaming, fighting cats, eight or nine of them."

"Did he read?"

"At my place I used to catch him sometimes, reading. I'd go out after supper to look at the cows, and there he'd be in the dark with the newspaper opened up. Another thing was his handwriting, the finest I've ever seen. Whenever he had to sign his name it would be a half-hour job, everything had to be just so, all these accent marks above every other letter. But boy, did that man have a signature! It was just perfect. Unbelievable."

"How'd he die?"

"Old age."

"Was it fast?"

"Yeah. He was excellent, and then one day in the fall I noticed that the pot on the stove was still the same height every day, and he was not up and around as much. The next day I asked a nurse to come and look at him, and he was on the poor side then. I called the RCMP to make sure I wouldn't get in any trouble. They came out and took a look and then they phoned the ambulance and took him in. I had to go to the hospital with him, or else there was no way to take him. I told him I'd be back after milking. That night after supper he died, there in the hospital."

At this point, tears well. Mickey says, "Shit, it's hard talking about this old bugger!" He gets a Kleenex, continues the story.

"I told him I'd be back after milking and to wait for me. So I got there and the nurses were at the door, and they said,

'Hurry up, he's wild, there's something wrong!' And I went in there, and put his hand on mine. And he crawled up my arm with his fingers — like this — and grabbed me, kind of pulled me down, and kissed me on the cheek and then he died. December 2, 1987."

"He loved you, Mickey."

"Yeah. It took him a long time to let me know that he wanted me to lean down to him, and then he gave me a goddam kiss on the cheek and then he died."

A long silence. "What happened to his money?"

"Oh, now that's a story. You're not going to believe this. Of course he'd never made a will. They found some relatives back in Europe, and it all went to them, every last dollar. It went to a bunch of strangers who didn't know anything about him."

Finis Paul Bog, whose life is done, whose money is gone, whose house has become someone's fertile garden. Bog is done. A road bears his name. Bog is over. Close the strange, sad circle.

Earth, and What I Found There: A Post-Mortem, Written in Compliance with the Requirements of the Sabbatical Assessment Committee and Respectfully Submitted by Me, Job.

I will write this quickly and succinctly, in the hope that I will be forgiven whatever stylistic lapses might arise as a consequence of haste. Speed is essential, as I must set this down before the forgetting sets in, as I know it must, according to plan. Already, some of the details are hazy, which must be all to the good, if I can judge my time on earth by the condition of my nails. Praise the Lord, for the mercy of His methods! Still, there is enough man-think left in me to find it strange that so much is gone from me, after so extended a stretch in the field. My assignment lasted eighty-six years, that is, by standard terrestrial measurement. As God is quick to point out, however, time is a crude construct when one of your inventions is eternity, and the whole stretch of my absence didn't give Him time enough to belch or blink. Not that God has ever been known to do either.

But enough of this dilly-dallying. The question I must answer is, essentially, what did I do on my vacation? Well, truth be told, I can't say that it was exactly restful. There was little enough of what anyone would call "leisure." No tanning on the golden sands, no volleyball on the beach, no drinks bedecked with little umbrellas. I had a rough time of it, especially at the beginning. There was deceit, betrayal, disappointment, poverty. There was misanthropy, and I don't refer here to my own. That was easy enough for me to put up with. There was hunger, cold, discomfort, loneliness, and pent-up sexual longing. There was English. I never had an easy time with English. There was a kind of wilful blinkeredness. For the longest time, I understand now, I led what you'd have to call an unexamined life. For this I offer no apology. "What's my purpose here?" is largely a question of the comfortable middle class, as you will quickly realize if ever you find yourself in a situation where you have to think of ways to cook up rotting horse flesh. Oh, I know, I know. I should have been able to rise above it. I should have been buoyed by philosophy, like that know-it-all Boethius, and so on and so forth. I confess, I allowed myself to be sidetracked by brute, physical difficulty. The winters were ugly. The cupboards were bare. It wasn't until I had the notion that I might just as well live under the dung heap that things started looking up, or at least began to fall into perspective. There's nothing like a pile of shit to focus the mind, and that was a good lesson to learn, however late in the day it might have dawned.

"It's a nice place you've got here," said God, the one time He passed through.

"It's cosy," I said, "and the overhead is low."

"Yes," said God, "I can see that's the case."

"And it's not so bad living in close proximity to a horse."

"I've always said it's a wise idea to be close to one's eventual lunch."

"And here's the best thing, God. The way I figure it, I can thank this heap of manure for making me who I am. It's given me an identity. I have become the Bog Man. Paul Bog, they call me, and not always with cheer in their hearts. There are those who mock me. There are those who turn their backs. There are even those who have tried to rob me, though never more than once. That's a pitchfork over in the corner, and I can wield it with an aplomb that would make Satan himself think twice about pillaging my sacks full of loot. I am despised and rejected. But those who have known me will never forget me, if only because I am everything they are not, and everything they could so easily become. How far is anyone from the dung heap, God? Not so very far, as near as I can figure it."

"Ah. So you've acquired a *raison d'être*."

"Don't you get all fancy with me, God. Not down here."

"I mean, you've uncovered a purpose, Job."

"Bog."

"Bog, of course."

And indeed that's exactly what I found on earth. A purpose. It might have been odd, and it might have been obscure, but no one could ever call it small. On earth I found purpose, and along the way I found peace, of a kind. It was a here-and-there kind of happenstance, I grant you, but every now and again, I found peace. Peace and purpose, and in rare moments, though often enough to be significant, I saw the certain evidence of goodwill. Once, before I died, there was something I wouldn't hesitate to call love. Unstinting, unthinking love. It was all I required. It is all anyone needs. Love came, and it was time to take my leave. Just a kiss and goodbye. And that's about it. That is all I have to report. I have been gone. Once again, I've returned. My name is Job. At last, I am home.

Through the Hermitage Window

There is a shadow there that sings and calls
But not for you.
    — Charlotte Mew, "The Forest Road"

There should be a word in English to describe the state of mild apprehension that comes over the solitary traveller when he opens the door to his hotel room — with a key, with a card — and steps from the public forum of the hallway into what will be his hermitage for the night. From the moment of his first arrival at the inn, from the very instant he sets foot over that threshold and braves the lobby, he has been plugged in to a source of low-voltage angst. There is so much that can go awry, so many niggling interrogatives: Will there be a vacancy? Will it be affordable? Will the credit card still have room in its heart to accommodate one more swipe through that know-it-all fiscal verifier? Will the desk clerk size you up with her practised eye and know that you are a fraud, that you have no business being here, that travel for you is just a masquerade, an avoidance, that you should really be in school with the rest of the kids? Who do you think you are, playing truant like this? You are on the road only because you are running from something, which you know to be true, even though you can't say exactly what. Will she test you in some way when you ask for the corporate rate, will she think "Corporate, my ass!" and demand a few stock tips, or say that she will have to check with your boss, or your mother, before she can give you a preferred tariff; will she roll her eyes at the hovering bellman who is asking if he can

take your bags, and, if you let him have his way with your suit-
cases, will there be the agonizing ride in the elevator while you
make small talk, and he calls you "sir," making you feel as if
you were in your forties or something, which of course you are?
And after all that, will you have to tip him, and find that you
only have a twenty that you will feel obliged to press on him
in a cavalier, offhand way, as though money oozes by way of
osmosis into your wallet from your right buttock, which is
made of not of flesh but of crisp, surplus bills? If you decline,
will he curl his lip and sneer at you when your back is turned
and you lumber off to your room, which now you stand outside, having just opened the door? Will this be the time you find
a corpse in the bathtub?

Of course, there is nothing. There is always nothing. You
fumble for the light switch and illumine a room you've never
seen but is just as you knew it would be, a room that is in most
ways indistinguishable from the one you were in last night, and
the night before that, and the night before that, in a different
city, in a different town, in a different province. *Déjà, déjà, déjà
vu*: not the gift of prophecy, just the unwavering regard of habit.
Look, look.

Look and see. See if you can find any trace whatsoever of
the last person or persons to occupy this room. Chances are you
won't. Every whiff of them has been expunged. No curly hairs
in the tub, no cigarette butts in the ashtray, no favourite passages
underlined in the Gideon Bible, no helpful notes sharing intelligence on the quirks of the shower or the thermostat, or advis-
ing you to avoid the conditioner, because it will just make your
hair greasy. There is no communal dream book in which the
transient residents of, say, room 310 at the Old Orchard Inn in
Wolfville, can jot down the wellings of their subconscious for
the amusement and delectation of others. It's all so tidy! The
sheets are bleached, the towels hang in regimental lines, everything is arranged to make you believe that no one has gone here
before, that all the bedding and so on is newly purchased from
the Bay. Why should the weary pilgrim tarnish his dreams of

Canterbury by meditating for even a second on the hundreds of passers-through who have used the very mattress on which he stretches out, face down, inhaling the Sanforized freshness of the puckered quilting; used it, and not always for the most savoury of purposes? Why should he exacerbate the loneliness of the road by imagining how eager and maybe adulterous lovers have romped on this very bedspread, not even waiting to pull it back and slide between the sheets before carrying out their sweaty exertions? Before screwing their brains out?

The most overt administrative acknowledgment of the hotel room's illicit potential is the selection of skin flicks which a broad-minded management makes available for about nine bucks a pop. I have occasionally viewed these on my various travels, never out of sociological interest, but more because of some untargeted randiness that required a focus. Of course, these movies are the most innocuous of pornographic excursions, as predictable and as involving as the compulsory-figures portion of a skating competition, or the dressage event of an equestrian meet. They all seem to be shot poolside, or in an adjacent cabana somewhere in California, and everyone looks pretty much the same, and performs pretty much the same acts in pretty much the same order with pretty much the same effect. The soundtracks are also indistinguishable one from the other. Once, I was lying in bed reading, and heard the tell-tale moans and the signifying drone of the synthesized strings and the drum machine bleeding through the wall from the room next to mine. Out of perverse solidarity I put down my book, picked up the remote, and surfed the naughty waves till I found the matching soundscape. An attractive young couple were splayed on top of an office desk, and flailed there happily. She still had her heels on, a remarkable oversight, potentially damaging to the shiny gloss of varnish beneath the blotter. I regretted missing the opening sequence, as I couldn't imagine the circumstances leading up to such a moment. I felt a strange bond, a weird communion of the road with whoever was watching beyond the eastern wall. I half wondered if I might be part of a group process, if the resident of the room on the western side might have heard my television and switched on, and if the same scene was possibly being repeated all down the long hall, that we were all part of a voyeuristic daisy-chain. I thought of how, if I were ever to make a porn movie, I would start it with just such a scene, and imagined for longer than was strictly necessary how I would develop the plot. I might very well have wasted an hour or more in such fruitless contemplation had not some Presbyterian angel whispered admonitions to the contrary in my ear. I turned off the movie, abandoned my next-door soul mate to his miscreant pleasures, and returned to my book, which was the *SAS Survival Guide*.

One measure of my dull ineptitude is that when I was preparing to make my dead-of-winter visits to Canadian eccentrics, I spent more more time fretting about what I would take to read than what I would take to wear. Travel guides, histories, biographies, poetry, diverting novels: I weighed the virtue of many genres and made my selections. On the day before I left Vancouver, I was wrestling with whether or not it would be worthwhile to pack along the *Dictionary of Canadian Biography*, which is a reference tool I have long cherished. I opened Volume One randomly, looking for some sign or advice, and there scanned the story of Anne de Noüe. Anne, who was a fellow, was born under the sign of Leo, near Rheims in 1587. He spent some time in the court of Henry IV, where he was known as "the handsome page." Around the age of twenty-five, he decided the Jesuit life was just the ticket, and signed up. Eventually, his duties took him to New France. He didn't find it an altogether commodious place. He was apparently a skilled angler, which stood him in good stead with his fish-loving colleagues, but was totally inept at learning the Native languages, and was never fully appreciative of their way of life. In 1646, while trekking through snow to administer the sacrament to the garrison at Sorel, he was overtaken by a blizzard and lost his way. He was found, kneeling, bare-headed, frozen solid, six miles upstream from his intended destination. His eyes were turned towards Heaven, as though in chilly supplication. A sad last turning of the handsome page. *Sic transit pulchritude.*

I had sought a sign, and sure enough I received one, a timely reminder that I was travelling to *le vrai Canada* at an intemperate time of year. With Anne's frosty finish in mind, I decided it would be prudent to leave the thirteen thick volumes of the DCB behind, and take instead some combination underwear, which is just about as bulky, and many times more confusing. The thermal suit I purchased — the first I've ever owned — came in a package with no instructions or schematic diagram. It took me the better part of an hour to figure out how such voluminous undies were actually applied, and longer still to acclimatize myself to looking like an overextended icing bag. For the first two weeks of my travelling, the weather in the East was relatively mild, and the unflattering swaddling lay wadded away under the tomes I couldn't bear to leave behind. It wasn't until I went to pay a call on a hermit who lives in the deep backwoods of Nova Scotia that I thought the time had come to forgo frivolous fears of fashion *faux pas* in favour of forestalling frigidity. When I exhumed the lumpen undies from my valise, they disgorged from their deep and many folds the SAS *Survival Guide.* How odd! I vaguely recalled buying it, couldn't remember packing it.

Ostensibly, this palm-sized book is meant to comfort élite airmen whose planes go down in Antarctic wastes or in the jungles of Borneo. It's full of diagrams showing how to signal a passing ship, or dig a trench latrine, or give yourself the Heimlich manoeuvre by hurling yourself against a stump. The point is that the SAS *Guide* was concealed in my thermal suit, and it pleased the heck out of me to for once find a useful tool folded up in my underwear. As I am not impervious to such cosmic *billets doux*, I pocketed the thing, and headed out to meet the hermit, K.

Hector MacKenzie, bless him, had agreed to be my guide. He is one of an informal ad hoc group that looks out for K. Hector is a well-known fiddle player in and around Pictou

County. He has deep roots there. He was born in the same house as his great-grandfather, and on the same day to boot. The old man was also called Hector. In fact, five MacKenzie lads over succeeding generations have carried that name. He lives with his wife, Eleanor, in a pretty house on the highway, not far from New Glasgow. They moved there a few years ago from a place called Salt Springs, leaving the handsome manse house where they spent most of their married life and raised their children. Their property was expropriated for road construction. They harbour no resentment about this forced displacement. They are happy where they've landed. It's a bright and comfy place, with a wood stove in the kitchen, and a glassed-in front room that gets so warm on a sunny winter's day that there's no need to bother cranking up the heat.

Hector had been puttering about in his workshop, sorting through the material accumulation of the years, winnowing oddments for a future garage sale. There were the usual small appliances, in varying states of repair. There were books and board games. There was a black bear, a real one, rearing up on his hind legs, a look of permanent surprise on his face. "Make me an offer!" he said, when I admired it, and I would have, were the road ahead of me not so long and fraught with uncertainty. Some things were not for barter, such as his scale model of the MacKenzie castle, and the sundry taxidermy treasures he and Eleanor have carted home from the far-flung travels they've enjoyed in retirement. On the day I visited, Eleanor was seeing to the renewal of their passports, preparatory to going to Venezuela. From other trips south, they've brought back a coiled cobra, twined around a pole, a turtle's head, mounted on a plaque, and a stuffed armadillo. Protruding from one wall was the hind end of a deer with a red light-bulb stuck in its butt hole. Plug it in and the light flashes. Adjacent to this arresting conversation piece hung a big framed photograph, a treasured memento, not for sale at any price, a blown-up colour shot of a bearded man sitting outside a tiny cabin, playing what is plainly a homespun guitar.

"That's him," said Hector. "That's K. Must have been taken twenty years ago. He looks pretty clean, there. I knew him from the time he was a teenager. He was always a little strange. He had this big dog with him all the time, and they'd just disappear into the woods, wouldn't come back for a couple of days. He was always musical and a good fiddle player. So was his father. Him they called Fiddle Foot."

Eleanor poured tea and set out slices of excellent Christmas fruit cake while Hector traced for me the outline of the hermit's progress. It's a simple story. More than fifty years ago, K. became an unwilling army conscript. He was on a troop train, *en route* to Halifax, from where he would have been shipped to war. The train made brief stops at stations and sidings. It was during one of these halts, somewhere around Salem, that K. decided once and for all that the battlegrounds of Europe and the forced camaraderie of service life were not for him. So, he slipped away. He took his army-issue Enfield rifle and high-tailed it into the woods. This was the landscape of his childhood, as familiar to him as the ridges of his teeth against his tongue. He knew of an abandoned cabin, a shanty on the shores of a little lake where his only company would be the trout. It was miles and miles from anything or anyone. That was where he went. That was where he holed up. And that was where he stayed. And stayed. For a long time, no one knew anything of his whereabouts. He hunted. He fished. The forest provided. He had no need of money or commerce. He had no need of medicine. If he was unwell — which he almost never was — he knew what plants, what barks to use to fix himself up. His only real requirement at the beginning was to lie low. In time, of course, the news got out. People in the community round about came to know of him. They accommodated him — it wasn't as if he was a stranger, someone from away. He was different, true; but he still belonged. And anyway, what harm had he done? If word of his whereabouts filtered back to the army, the authorities never bothered following up. Time passed and the tension eased. The war was long done. Over the years, K. moved from fugitive to fixture. He kept mostly to himself and was left alone, although he wasn't averse to social contact when it was required. He got by. He maintained a trapline and his rifle, could sell furs or venison or moose if he needed some money. Sometimes, he'd carve axe handles.

"How old is he?"

"I don't really know. I'd say he's probably got a year or two on me and I'm seventy-eight."

"That's old to be living alone in the woods."

"It is, though he's always been fit as a fiddle. You'll see that he's pretty bright, considering all the time he's spent alone. Lately, there's been some concern about K. from the social services people. Some folks have even got together and built him this nice little place, not too far from where he's been. It's a good set-up, brand new, closer to the road and to help if he needs it, closer to the store where he gets his groceries. Every so often, he picks up a few staples, flour, rice, tea, and so on. The storekeeper looks out for him, keeps track of everything on a running tab. Problem is, he's just not interested in moving. They're having a devil of a time convincing him he should. You'll see when we get up there. By the way, have you got a four-wheel drive?"

With one penetrating question, Hector had pierced right to the heart of my rented Mystique's every inadequacy. "Well, not to worry. We should be able to manage, long as the road's not too slicky underneath."

Hector suited up, and I took a covert squinny at the SAS *Survival Guide*'s directions for cooking reptiles. "Gut, then cook in their skins. Place in hot embers, turning continually. When skin splits, meat can be removed and boiled." I glanced at the stuffed armadillo, its baleful regard, then helped myself to another slice of fruit cake and off we went.

"Take a right," said Hector, as we passed the place where a bootlegger had his operation back when Hector was a boy. "Left now," he directed as we skirted the field where there's a MacKenzie cemetery, and where every tenant save one belongs to Hector's clan.

"Yep," he said, "All except for one."

There was a lo-o-o-ng pause.

"You're going to make me ask, aren't you, Hector?"

"Hatch." He chuckled. "A foreigner by the name of Hatch."

How Hatch perished I have no idea, but the name called to mind a heart-rending and highly instructive tale I had read in the *Canadian Alpine Journal* of 1908. That was the year Mary E. Crawford, M.D., had written about the advantages of mountain climbing for women. "There is no recreation which, in all its aspects of surrounding and exercise, will bring about a quicker rejuvenation of worn-out nerves, tired brains, and flabby muscles than mountaineering. It is for women one of the new things under the sun and every fresh mountain is a new delight. Ennui has no place in the vocabulary of the woman who climbs, the words which rout it are enthusiasm and exhilaration. Diseases of the imagination cannot be discovered anywhere on a mountain side, where Nature asserts herself so grandly to the consciousness and with such insistence that the 'ego' with its troubles sinks out of sight."

One young woman who took Dr. Crawford's words to heart was Miss Helen Hatch, of Lethbridge. She was part of the Alpine Club's annual summer camp, which opened on Wednesday, July 8, 1908. The camp was pitched at the summit of the Rogers Pass, at 4,350 feet. Miss Hatch was not an utter novice when it came to mountaineering. In fact, just that spring she had made her way up the Crow's Nest Mountain. The climb that was to be her last, which she undertook with a party from the club, went up the northwest face of Mount Avalanche. The outing was supervised by experienced climbers, and what happened to Helen was freakish in the extreme. What happened to Helen happened before the real climbing began. The group was making its way towards the mountain and had to pass across a snow-filled couloir. They were not yet roped together, as there was nothing about their circumstances or environment suggesting that such a precaution might be necessary. Oliver Wheeler, a youth himself, but a veteran climber, went ahead first, to see if the snow was conducive to crossing. Miss Hatch, exhilarated by the altitude, by the surfeit of fresh air, by the novelty of snow in July, ignored his exhortations to remain back. She chirped, "I am coming. Look out now!" Then she took a little hop and slid on the snow. She "lost her footing and, as Oliver reached the bottom, went by him with tremendous velocity. Hearing her call he checked himself, turned swiftly and grabbed for her. Alas! she had gone wide and he only touched her outstretched hand. She passed on down the slope from ledge to ledge, gathering velocity as she fell and, at a depth of 120 feet, dropped over the final ledge, twenty feet perpendicular, to the snow-filled couloir. She had not uttered a sound and must have fainted at the moment she realized what had happened....A charming and plucky young life had been thrown away owing to a moment of impetuosity."

Plucky, impetuous Helen! Her death in the summer ice provides a grim but satisfying bookend to the fiery finish of Keith Pelton, who died ten years earlier in Yarmouth. Her body, *pale and grave as a sculptured nun*, was lifted from the snow where it lay *pillowed upon its alabaster arms like a child o'erwearied with sweet toil*, and was conveyed on a crude litter back to the base camp. No doubt the Alpinists, over whose summer this untoward incident must have cast a dreadful pall, derived some comfort from telling one another that she'd fainted dead away as soon as her slide commenced and that she couldn't have known what hit her; or rather, what she hit, as she died when she smashed into some projecting rock spurs. I prefer to think that her final moments were in no way anaesthetized, and that her blood was awash with dopamine, or whatever other chemical agent the cells churn out in moments of thrill and danger. Death is never graceful, but to have been so fully alive at the moment of life's ending must have felt like being touched by grace, or something like it.

Helen's story took on a cautionary note as Hector and I slid past the graveyard on our snowy route. With each turn the road became less roadlike. We passed the little house that was built with K. in mind, stopped, and got out to check it over. It was, as Hector had described, a charming chalet, with a sleeping loft, and propane heat and fridge, in a pretty wooded copse. The snow around it was unsullied by footfall. There was no sign that K. had been there, sniffing out his new digs. We drove on and on, and when the path finally petered out altogether, we left the car and prepared to strike out through the trackless woods. A pick-up truck hove into view. The driver, a burly, bearded fellow named Sterling, had followed us down the road. He is also part of the network that keeps an eye out for K.'s well-being. Satisfied that we were not up to mischief, he waved us on our way. Into the woods we went, the soon-to-be-octogenarian Hector bounding along ahead of me with rabbity alacrity, leaping over rivulets gone crusty around their margins, under pine boughs drooping with snow. Within minutes, my long johns were damp with sweat. The *SAS Guide*'s hypothermic warnings pulsed against my girdled groin. At one point, I slipped on a rock and my foot went into a brook.

"Did you get your foot wet?"

"Oh, maybe just a little." I had the idea that this was not a good thing, and Hector quickly confirmed my suspicions.

"Oh, lordy. Oh, lordy. We'd better get you to K.'s and get that dried out!"

I was visited by the memory of being eliminated from a spelling bee by the word "gangrene." Would it again prove my undoing, I wondered as we hurried on, passing all kinds of animal footprints which the *SAS Guide* could certainly have helped me identify had I only the time to refer to it. We hurried on, and in short order, we were there.

K.'s pine-log shack — it's really a lean-to — is in a kind of Lake Isle of Innisfree setting: deep woods, deep peace. Smoke from the tin chimney suggested he might be home. Hector pointed out the fresh cross-country ski tracks. It looked like K. had been on a jaunt of his own. One curious architectural feature of his place is the tree that years ago fell squarely onto K.'s roof, which is plastic sheeting covered with corrugated metal.

For reasons that are either philosophic or aesthetic, K. chose not to move the wasted trunk. It lies there, in the dent of its own making, at a forty-five-degree angle. The shack has no door. Entrance and egress take place through the window on which Hector hammered to announce our arrival. "K.! K.! Are you there, boy? It's me, it's Hector, can we see you?" A pause, a shuffling within, the grating of the window, and then there he was, our hermit, squinting into the light.

Once, I saw a baby born. I had never witnessed anything quite so overwhelming as when the hidden head emerged from the vulvic cave, followed by the shoulders, and then the greasy pell-mell tumble of that new life into the world. That is the image that came to me while watching K. exit his house through his window: head, shoulders, the long, accordion unfolding of his body, and then, there he was before us in the snow: tall, thin, and wiry, his flexibility no doubt sustained by his years of slipping in and out through so modest an aperture. He wore a long blue parka, green gumboots, a sweater of indeterminate, subfusc hue, and matching trousers. His beard and hair were long and wild in the best hermit tradition, and the whole of his being seemed bound together by soot. He was, without a doubt, the sootiest man I have ever seen. He didn't seem surprised or discomfitted to see Hector there, nor to see that he'd brought along a stranger. He shook us each by the hand, and did so with uncommon delicacy, crooking his pinky first around Hector's little finger, then mine.

"Afternoon, K.! I brought you a visitor. He's come all the way from Vancouver!"

"Oh, yes."

"How do you do?" I said, betraying my gift for originality.

"Oh, yes."

"Well, K.! Can we come in? Can you show us your place? The young fellow got his foot wet; he'd better dry his shoe by your stove."

"Oh, yes."

We all piled back through the window into the cabin, a

single room scarcely big enough to accommodate the crowd. Even with one it would feel jammed. It was dim in there in the middle of the day. There was a bench, a cot, and what I took to be the selfsame Enfield rifle K. carried when he skipped the train and went AWOL all those years ago. There were snowshoes, a kerosene lantern, a few cooking tools, and a bucket of sloppy-looking stuff Hector pointed out to me as sourdough starter. It was warm, almost oppressively close. There was an improvised stove dug into the dirt floor, and the rich smell of wood smoke, as heady as I've ever known it, almost asphyxiating at first.

This was turning out to be a day resonant with historical association, for the thick air in K.'s parlour, and the way my eyes teared at the beginning of our visit, summoned up the story of Gabriel Druillettes. Born near Limoges in 1610, he was another of the early Jesuit missionaries, a contemporary of the unfortunate Anne de Noüe. Unlike the handsome page, Gabriel adapted quickly to Indian ways. He was a resourceful fellow. If he felt peckish and there was no ready game in sight, he would boil up the thongs of his snowshoes and chow down on leather. One year, he followed the Montagnais on their winter hunting expeditions. The smoky lodges damaged his eyes. Over time he went blind, and had to be led about by a child who was assigned to him for that purpose. An old medicine woman said she could fix him up, and — in what might be the first recorded cataract operation in Canada — proceeded to scrape at his corneas with a rusty knife. Of course, it was terribly painful and ineffectual both. Finally, he assembled the Christian Montagnais around him, and celebrated a mass of the Virgin Mary. Even before he was done, his sight was miraculously restored. K.'s eyes, I was pleased to see, were bright, and his vision seemed unimpaired. Indeed, apart from his deep griminess — or maybe because of his deep griminess — he seemed remarkably sound overall. I would never have imagined him to be eighty, and Hector told me that a public health nurse who went to examine him as part of the campaign to move him to his new digs was amazed by his level of fitness.

I removed my dampened shoe and set it beside the stove, relieved to find my sock quite dry. We all three sat in companionable silence for a few minutes, just enjoying the sight of one another. K. tamped some tobacco into a long pipe, lit up, drew slowly, showed no curiosity about why we'd intruded on his solitude. Hector spoke first.

"We've just been up looking at your new place. Have you been there lately? They've got it fixed up real nice for you."

"Uh-huh. Mmmmm. Yes."

"Why, I think it would be grand to live there. So much space, right there in the woods. It's close to the store, K. They've got a big woodpile, all cut and stacked and ready. I'd move in there myself if I could. I'd move in tomorrow. Don't you think you should maybe take your stuff over there?"

"Hmmmmm. Well. No. No, I don't think so. No. I'm not much for moving, you know. Not in the winter. Afraid I could catch something. Afraid I could catch a chill. Bad at my age. A chill. No."

"But there's a good heating system up there, K. They've got it all set up with propane."

"Hmmmmmm. Yes. Understand it explodes from time to time."

Hector shrugged, rolled his eyes, grinned. It was just as he thought it would be. The hermit was not for moving. There was another stretch of quiet. I noticed many damp and mouldering books around, and picked up an old volume from the *Reader's Digest* condensed-novel series. It was positioned beneath the window-sill and covered in boot marks.

"You like to read?" I asked.

"Yes. Oh, yes. I've read all these books. I read the Bible most every Sunday. Know how many times the word 'howl' has been used in the Bible? Four. Yes, I read the Bible, and I remember amperisms."

"Amperisms?"

"You know. Little — what would you call them? Little sayings. Robert Louis Stevenson, he said that a purpose in life is the greatest treasure a man can own. Yes. I often wonder what he meant by that."

"Well, I'm not sure…"

"And G. K. Chesterton, he said that the best thing about miracles was that they sometimes happen. Hmmmmmmmm. I often wonder what he meant by that."

"Chesterton said that?"

"Chesterton, yes. And Mark Twain, a woman once said to him that she had both a headache and a toothache and could anything be worse, and he said, yes, rheumatism and St. Vitus's dance. Yes. I like that. Did you ever hear tell of Pan?"

"Pan? Yes. Yes, I guess so. I remember a story about how he chased a nymph and she prayed to be saved from him and was turned into a reed. Pan cut her to make his flute."

"Is that so? Huh! I often wonder if I might not see him here," and he looked out into the woods. "Yes. Pan."

We sat and listened again to the attenuated quiet. It was very pleasant, and I just didn't feel like wrecking the moment with prying questions. What would I want to ask, anyway? I could see how he lived. I could see that he was content. I could see his wry humour in the way he deflected suggestions that he'd be better off elsewhere. No doubt there are thousands of stories he could tell about the life he has chosen to live, abstracted from any regular intercourse with human society, but he was not the sort of man who was going to open up to a stranger, to someone from away with no more than an afternoon to spend. It was enough to be there, and to enjoy the moment. Then Hector spoke. "K.'s quite a fiddle player, aren't you, K.? Remember how I came here once with my grandson and you played and we all danced? Why don't you play something for us?"

"It's broken."

"Well, how about the guitar, then? Could you play us something on the guitar?"

And much to my surprise, he agreed. He took down the guitar he'd made for himself, God knows with what tools, and

played this wonderful, bluesy, loopy tune. It was his own composition, and there was nothing about it that was linear or the-
matic or familiar. It was absolutely original and beautiful. As
was he. It was music that belonged wholly to that place. As did
he. I taped it and played it back for him. He listened carefully,
nodded approvingly. He filled his pipe, looked out his window.
I imagined him there, hours after we would be gone, strumming
his songs in the smoky dark. I imagined him looking from his
window in the morning, studying the fresh prints in the snow.
Strange ones. Nothing a member of the Special Air Service
would be able to identify, not even by thumbing through that
helpful guide. Not bear nor wild cat, not raccoon nor prairie
dog. No, no. These would be the crazy calling-cards of the great
god Pan, all melting, all tangled. For you should know that his
cloven feet are hot as coals, and when he passed by in the thick
of the night, he just couldn't keep himself from dancing.

○○○○○○○○○○
● ● ● ● ● ● ● ● ● ●
● *Chapter* ●
● *Fourteen* ●
● ● ● ● ● ● ● ● ● ●
○○○○○○○○○○

A Woman Clothed with the Sun

And to the woman were given two wings of a great eagle,
that she might fly into the wilderness...
— Revelation 12:14

There are not many words to which I can point and say with
assurance that such was the time and place, such were the circumstances that reigned when this new notch was carved in my
vocabulary. "Derrière" is one such instance, as I have already
said. "Nostalgia" is another. When I turned adolescent, and
every certainty was rattled or shaken loose, I began to read
poetry with the kind of feverish devotion I'd once brought to
the Hardy Boys and Enid Blyton. I can't say why. It just happened. Perhaps it was in part genetic, as my father was also partial to the stuff, and in part environmental, as we had a few
starter anthologies around the house, as well as editions of such
stalwart rhymesters as Kipling and Service and Longfellow and
Omar Khayyám. The home collection that quickly became my
favourite was a squat, fat book called *A Little Treasury of
Modern Poetry*, edited by Oscar Williams. It was published in
1946, and it remains to this day a solid, representative culling
of English and American poetry of the first half of the century.
Certain poems I committed to memory. "The Elephant Is Slow
to Mate," by D.H. Lawrence, "Recuerdo," by Edna St. Vincent
Millay, and Helen Hoyt's "Rain at Night," with its desperate
and fateful final cry, "O love, I had forgot that we must die," a

line which could have been improved only by the addition of an exclamation point.

One summer afternoon, flipping idly through the tubby *Little Treasury*, looking for something lush and improbable to learn by heart, I found a leaf pressed between two pages. It was an autumn leaf, plucked from the cotoneaster that grew by the side of the house. It was tiny and many-hued, orange and red with streaks of yellow. I picked it up, and remembered very clearly that it was I who had placed it there, half a lifetime (i.e., six years) before. I'd intended it as part of a display, a school project of the kind every child who lives in a part of the world where the foliage turns colour must have undertaken at one time or another. Why this leaf had not made the final cut I couldn't guess. Perhaps simply because it had been overlooked, or because there wasn't enough room on the dry-cleaner's cardboard onto which the fallen beauties were attached, or because there was a prettier inclusion from the same bush, or because I was uncertain about how to spell "cotoneaster." I held that leaf in my tender, hairless palm and remembered those far-off, simpler times, when life was unencumbered by the difficulties that were beginning to beset me. A delicious wave of something new washed over me, a dumb longing to reclaim what could never be retrieved. I looked down at the page (227) against which the leaf had languished all those years and read the first lines of the poem printed there — "My soul stands at the window of my room, / And I ten thousand miles away" — then took in its title: "Nostalgia." By Karl Shapiro. Nostalgia. What a soft, pretty word! I went to the dictionary, and was amazed at the dumb, happy accident that caused me to place such a souvenir in such a spot; that had caused me to find it, in that specific then-and-there, to teach me something for which I was past ready. It was a perfect moment. I understood, even then, that I had been given a gift. Could there be a more convincing way of learning the word "nostalgia"? I can't think of one, if there is.

Wallace Stevens and Marianne Moore joined Shapiro in the *Little Treasury*, as did Yeats, Auden, Delmore Schwartz, and

Robinson Jeffers. There was a Jeffers poem I loved and worked hard to learn. In "Cassandra," he aligns the neglected and misapprehended poet with the sad prophetess, who was doomed never to be believed.

> ...Poor bitch, be wise.
> No: you'll still mumble in a corner a crust of truth, to men
> And gods disgusting. — You and I, Cassandra.

This was heady stuff. Unfortunately, there was never an occasion to show off publicly my memorizing of this or other poems. I would speak them to myself in my room, cast them out to my own pimply, pale reflection, captive in the dresser mirror. How I loved to say the words, "Poor bitch be wise," giving the hard, explosive consonants a Gielgudian oomph, savouring especially the outlaw syllable "bitch," a word that in those days would guarantee severe censure and possibly suspension if you were to speak it too loudly on the school playground. "You and I, Cassandra," I would intone after a dramatic pause, forcing my voice into its lowest register, and feel in that instant connected, umbilically, to that great assembly of artists who, over time, have been scorned and dishonoured in their own countries. I was thrilled to be among them! How lucky I was, I thought to myself, then; how lucky to be such close kin to Robinson Jeffers, how lucky to be a player in the Cassandra league. How lucky, lucky, lucky to be me!

"Of course, psychics make mistakes all the time!" says the seer Laura Kay Prophet, who is wiser than Cassandra, as she is not freighted with the expectation that she will always be believed, nor with the conviction that she will always be right. "All the time!" she reaffirms, making a gentle grab for the fledgling robin who has come to roost on her blonde hair. "I know, because believe me, I've made them all!"

She spills this confession while we are talking in her tiny room in a modest, downtown hotel. It's a hard-times kind of place where the enterprising desk clerks have been known to take advantage of a long-term guest's week-long absence by renting out his room on an hour-by-hour basis to hookers and their tricks. The hallways are wide, but scuzzy and ill-lit. The carpets are a colour not found in nature, and have not been swept or vacuumed in a very long time. But step from the common area into Laura Kay's place, and all the Dickensian gloom metamorphoses into Beatrix Potter cheerfulness. Her cubby is cluttered, but tidy and feminine-looking. It measures, I would guess, nine-by-thirteen feet. There's a long vine, I think a philodendron, trailing along one wall. She has a single bed, a pint-size fridge, a sink, a wardrobe, a chair, a coat tree. The several square feet

Laura Kay Prophet at home.

of floor space which are uncolonized by such necessary oddments as these are piled high, in an orderly way, with miscel-
laneous possessions. So are the one or two flat and elevated
surfaces. There's not really so very much stuff, but the minute
space available to it gives the impression of volume.

Laura Kay has tried to beautify her room over the four years
of her tenure by painting the walls and hanging pictures and
cultivating plants and so on. She has finally given up on such
decorating initiatives because every time she gets things just
the way she likes them, a bathtub will overflow upstairs, and
there'll be a flood that will come through the ceiling and ruin
everything, and she'll have to fight with the management to get
it all put right, so really, what's the point? She doesn't like to
press too hard, because she can't risk eviction. Finding another
place would be difficult, since Laura Kay comes with landlord-
aggravating encumbrances and attachments, of which the robin,
with its speckled breast and its cunning trill, is a transient
example. The robin was given to her a week or so ago by a couple of winos who found it after it fell from its nest. They brought
it to her to nurture. Besides the hookers, there are lots of winos
on this stretch of Granville Street, and many of them have tender hearts. A few know about Laura's way with birds. They
have brought her starlings before, too. The robin won't be here
much longer, as it is only a few days shy of being able to fend
for itself. It has made tremendous progress with its flying technique. It flutters about from corner to corner quite happily, with
little recuperative station stops such as the one it has just made
on Laura Kay's noggin. Laura takes the bird on her finger. It
looks her in the eye, leans back its little head, and gargles.

"She's hungry again. Do you want to feed her?"

"Sure."

This is just like a petting zoo! Laura takes a bag of wieners
from her fridge, removes one, slices off a sliver. She shows me
how to break it into pinhead-size pieces and foist the dainty
morsels directly down the robin's throat, which is not as easy to
do as she makes it seem. Then she cuts the remaining meat into

bigger cubes and offers them to Bob. Bob, who is a duck, all dressed in white like a first-communicant, and with a bright yellow bill, gets up out of her wading pool, shakes her little tail, and marches over for her treat, not even breaking stride to noisily expel a stream of liquid brown shit. I am having an education. For one thing, I am surprised at the size of the bird. It's dimensions verge on the goose-ish. That ducks are hot-dog eaters is also a revelation to me. What's more, I have never before seen one excrete at such close quarters. I'm amazed as all heck at the rapid liquidity of the operation, and even though my first thought is that this is surely the kind of incident that might invite managerial wrath, I decide it is my role as a guest to radiate nonchalance, as though this is something that is part of my everyday life as a convinced city dweller. As it turns out, the mess is in no way a problem. It's part and parcel of living with a duck, which I guess I should have figured. It goes with the territory. This, of course, is why the floor of the room is covered with plastic sheeting. Laura rips off a length of paper towel from a roll she keeps handy for just such mishaps, and wipes it up. Presto, it's gone, you'd never know it had been there. As I said, her place is scrupulously neat, and the duck, as it turns out, is as vigilant about such sanitary concerns as is her mistress.

"All my kids are well trained, that's for sure," Laura boasts as she disposes of the towel. "They like cleanliness around them. When we're going along the sidewalk and Bobby makes a poo, she stands right beside it and quacks till I come back to clean it up. Excuse me," she says, and interrupts the flow of the conversation to offer a smidgen of chocolate to her gerbil. Apparently, it is in need of such small consolations as this, for it has been depressed since it was displaced from a more palatial cage by the arrival of two chinchillas. A baby robin, an adult duck and its wading pool, two chinchillas in a stately pleasure dome, a pining gerbil in reduced circumstances, Laura Kay, and me: what a jolly confabulation on a weekday afternoon! Oh — there are also some goldfish, paddling in a largish aquarium.

Laura Kay Prophet and her duck — sometimes, ducks —

have been a fixture in downtown Vancouver for years now. I first met her in 1992. At that time, she was mostly seen on fashionable Robson Street. She would set up shop on the sidewalk in a sheltered spot where she would not obstruct pedestrian traffic, and hang a little placard to advertise her services as a clairvoyante. The duck, an eye-catching prop as well as a faithful companion, would watch from the buggy in which Laura used to push him to and from work. I happened to be living nearby, and would often pass her on my perambulations round about the neighbourhood. I grew accustomed to seeing her there, and came to regard her as one of the more colourful pieces of the urban jigsaw, like the one-tune harmonica player, and the tanned man who sat day after day at the same table outside the same coffee shop, conventionally dressed but for women's shoes and pantyhose, and the twins who looked like the Pillsbury Doughboy and who still wore quilted parkas when most people had switched to shorts. I would see the occasional passer-by stop to seek advice from the sidewalk psychic: tourists with video cameras wanting something out of the ordinary to show the folks back home, or packs of frisky young girls from the suburbs having a giggle with their friends before getting the bus back to Surrey, and so on.

I had recently misplaced my boyfriend and was holding open auditions to secure a replacement. One night, heading home from a song-and-dance session with a promising candidate, I saw Laura Kay sitting in a jeweller's doorway, with her duck at her side, and with time on her hands. I had spoken to her before, just to say hello, or to talk with her about my dog, of whom she was fond, and once I had taken one of her brochures. They were tiny and blue, and contained a capsulized version of her story, beginning with the sentence, "Laura Kay Prophet, a spinster, was born in Sudbury in 1941." That night, when I thought that love might be in the air, was the first time I'd stopped to inquire what the future might hold.

"What's his name?" she asked, when I had explained something of the investigation I hoped she would undertake.

I told her. She took out a pencil and a pad of paper, and began to sketch a goofy cartoon with quick short lines. She talked while she drew.

"Oh! He's *nice*-looking. Strong chin?"

"Yes."

"Dark hair?"

"Yes."

"Very nice! Very, very — Oh. Oh, well. Too bad. Not him. No. Nothing's going to happen."

And she was right, just as she was right the next time, and the next time, and the next. I began to make a habit of seeking her counsel whenever romantic attachment loomed, and always it was the same routine with the same result. The pencil, the pad, the quick cartoon, a wistful smile and a business-like shake of the head. Nope! Not this time. She never apologized for delivering up such sad news, and there was no reason why she should have done so. If it wasn't what I wanted to hear, well, that was nothing to do with her. She was just the messenger, innocent of judgment and malice. She said what she saw or heard — from what source came this news I was never sure — and it was up to the client to believe or disregard as he or she saw fit.

You and I, Cassandra.

Time passed. I formed an attachment with someone about whom I never sought psychic advice. We moved from the neighbourhood. For a couple of years, I saw nothing of Laura Kay. Sometimes I wondered idly where she might be living — when I first met her she and her menagerie were boarding at the Y — and if she was even still in town. During our conversations she had told me that she saw very clearly how she was not long for the city, that she would soon buy a winning lottery ticket, would become an overnight mogul, a millionaire ten times over, and would move to the country. There, she would have a big house, and use it to provide shelter for the families who would be devastated by the earthquake she also knew was in the offing. In this prediction, at least, she was in complete accord with the conventional wisdom offered up by geophysicists, *vis-à-vis* the tectonic future of the West Coast. Laura's specific vision had a Hollywood intensity about it. She saw how Nelson Street (a major east–west thoroughfare) would become a corridor of flames because of exploding gas lines. She saw sheets of plate glass detaching themselves from post-modern skyscrapers all throughout the downtown area, and falling like jagged guillotine blades, delivering fatal nicks to the unfortunates walking beneath. Her eyes, as she told me this, had a fixed and staring quality, as though she might be watching a disaster movie. I remember thinking that it was not so very unlikely a scenario, and was actually jarred into putting together an earthquake survival kit, which, if memory serves, consisted of several bottles of Perrier and many tins of smoked oysters. I was better prepared for unexpected company than for the trembling of the ground, but that's always been my little way. Several people suggested I should track her down when I began my eccentrics hunt. I wrote "Find Laura Kay" on my mental "to do" list. Over the next several months, it would surface for review, then sink again.

Late in the fall of 1996, troubled by a word-processing–induced numbness in my left arm, I began some massage therapy treatments. I was walking along Robson Street after the first of these sessions, heading east towards the office in the vaguely altered state of mind that can settle on one after being forcefully and corporally manipulated by a complete stranger. I was floating over the pavement, calm as a clam, meditating on the koan "The medium is the massage," when, at the corner of Granville Street, I crossed paths with a woman carrying a shopping bag across which was emblazoned the single word "Bliss." This was almost as happy an encounter as my long-ago meeting with "nostalgia." The cosmos hummed all the louder when she passed me by, and who should prove to be travelling in her slipstream but Laura Kay Prophet, looking as blonde and as fresh and as sweet as ever she did. Laura Kay, with her amazingly youthful skin, and her sweet, sweet smile, as *bright as the*

coming forth of the morning, in the cloud of an early shower.
The medium and the massage. You could have knocked me over
with a feather.

Feathers were once an important part of her psychic regalia.
That was back in the days of Harvey, who was her duck before
Webster and Holly, who were her ducks before Bob. "God
always gives me ducks," she tells me, while preparing a tomato
and lettuce salad for Bob, "and He always gives me miracle
ducks. Even though I love them, I sometimes say, 'God, why
me? Why ducks?' They cost me a fortune, and not just in
money, either. I pay the price of my privacy. It's like having a little baby. You can never be away from them, and you can't just
trust any sitter to look after them. Believe me, there are things
I'd rather be doing than spending my whole day wiping up duck
shit, but I'm never gone for more than two hours, and when we
go out together we have to walk. You can't take a duck on the
bus. I could in Calgary, but not here. Not in Vancouver."

It was while living in Calgary, in 1980, back in the days
when she had an apartment in a nice high-rise, that Laura Kay
hooked up with Harvey. He was the first of the several fowls
who have complicated and enriched her life on earth. She pref-
aces her story with the caveat that it might sound crazy, but this
is exactly how it happened. Laura learned through a dream that
she would have a duck who would be both magic and lucky.
One day she visited a hatchery. Baby ducks were being pulled
from the incubator. The operations supervisor would not let her
take just one chick. He told her she must leave with two. She
selected a runt who was cute, but who was destined not to live
for more than a few weeks. The hatchery man insisted she take
a big bruiser of a duckling he picked out for her, and this was
Harvey. It was not long before Harvey began to show just how
wondrous a creature he was. For one thing, he seemed to live in
a state of perpetual moult. He was forever shedding his feathers, of which he had a great many more than the average duck.
He could easily cast off a hundred on any given day. As well,
these feathers turned out to be more than commonly lucky. The

first of Harvey's miracles was that people's wishes came true when they made them on his feathers.

"If I told you some of the things, you wouldn't believe me."

"Try me."

"Okay, but you have to remember that these are miracles, and miracles don't make sense. You have to remember that nothing is impossible, just improbable."

And she tells about how wishes made on Harvey's feathers brought together young lovers. She tells about an old lady who'd been sick all winter and who was finally well enough to go out and who started going to bingo again, and who always lost until she got a feather, at which point she began to win every time. She won so much and she won so often that she came back for more feathers. She would take them to the games and share her luck, would rub Harvey's plumage on the shoulders of the people playing around her, and they started winning, too. And once — this was after she and Harvey moved to Vancouver — she got to talking to some boys who were skating on the Robson Square rink. One told her that he had a wish, but that it was impossible. "Only improbable," she assured him, and he went home with a Harvey token. A few months later, he found her again, and told her what had happened. His mother had died, and the impossible wish he had made on the feather had been to see her again, just once more. He was having a terrible time at school. One day he came home, downtrodden and discouraged and full of hurt, and there was his mother. She was standing before him, "as real as if she could have been real, as if he could touch her and everything, and she said, 'Everything is going to be all right, dear, I'm always with you, even though you can't see me, and you know I love you.' And then she just sort of evaporated."

Harvey also had the miracle of healing. Once, for instance, Laura and Harvey were in a welfare office in Vancouver, and they met a little girl who was wearing winter gloves, even though it was the middle of summer. Laura always knew when to expect a healing episode, because a deep, booming voice would alert her before she left the house that one was scheduled for that day. She had had such a warning and sensed that this child was to be the recipient of the miracle. Laura approached her.

"Would you like to pet the duck? He's magic, you know."

Her father wasn't keen. He explained that for the last several months the child had been plagued by blisters on the backs of both her hands. The little girl removed one glove, and there were indeed lesions that were horrible to behold. The doctors had been powerless to help.

"But I still told her to pet him, to feel his nice feathers. Harvey was just full of healing energy. His feet and his bill were unbelievably hot with it, like they were on fire, and when people were around he'd just squat and let them touch him, sometimes several at a time. It was like he was meditating. He did a lot of meditating, even at home, and this whistling sound would come out of him, kind of like: O-o-o-o-o. O-o-o-o-o. Anyway, he sat there, very still, and she petted him, and she laughed, and the next day I got a phone call from her mother. I'd given the father a card with my number. She told me that when the little girl got up that next morning her hands were healed. Her mother said, 'Jesus healed you. Praise the Lord.' And her daughter said, 'No, it wasn't Jesus. It was Harvey the Duck.' And you know, it never occurred to me to get their last name or telephone number to ask them if we could publicize this and do the media thing, so that I could maybe make some money. I mean, these ducks eat me out of house and home. They are terribly wasteful. Really, there are times when I wind up eating their leftovers!

"Harvey's third miracle was that he came to talk. I'd always known he was going to, but I couldn't understand how. It didn't make sense to me. The first few times I thought I was hearing things, but he did learn to say his name. He would say 'Harv, Harv.' And if I left the room, he'd go 'Mom! Mom!' And if you gave him a treat, he'd say 'W-o-o-o-w.' Of course, he didn't do it every time; when the media were around he'd never say it."

Harvey died in her arms on his sixth birthday, in April

1986. His spirit returned to her almost immediately in the form of a baby pigeon someone brought her to look after, although she didn't know at the time the baby bird was a revenant. It was only afterwards, when she thought of how it had gone straight away for Harvey's favourite toys, and how it shared Harvey's habit of watching her out of one eye, that she understood he had returned to her as a sign, a reassurance that their connection was far from severed. In the very near future, Harvey will be with her again, first as Harvey II, and then as Harvey III. Harvey III will be the big miracle, his healing power intensified many times over.

For the nonce, though, there is Bob, who has the miracle of tears. When Bob began to ovulate, she had a very hard time of it. Her eyes would stream for half an hour before and half an hour after laying an egg. The vet has witnessed this anomaly, and even tried to take a photograph of it, but for some reason wasn't able to. And before Bob, there was the tandem team of Webster and Holly. They came along in 1988, and were given to her by a couple of kids who couldn't properly see to their needs. Both ducks were gravely ill when they came to Laura, but she nurtured them till they were whole, and well enough to fulfil their rakish destinies.

"I had a dream they were coming, and I knew the male would be called Webster. Now, the spirits had told me that he was going to be an artist, and I thought, 'Oh great, he's going to make some great little abstracts and I'll get some money off of them.' One day I said to him, 'You're supposed to be an artist, so paint a picture.' And all I did was to put down the background. I spread it on a big paper with my hand, and he walked through the paint, and when he finished there was an amazing painting, with himself at the top, as a duck, but he was a duck that had artist clothes on: the baggy trousers, and the belt hanging. That was like his penis. He was oversexed. I felt sorry for Holly. He drew Holly facing him as a pretty girl, because she was beautiful. That was all she had going for her. She was not sweet-tempered, she was always bitching about something. Then there was a picture of me, kind of looming at the side, and you could see their special cup, the one with the Christmas goose on it, and he did the vines we had in the kitchen then. I was amazed at the detail. I mean, there was muscle tone! I can't even paint that well, and I'm quite a good artist. It took him about three minutes. He always did a poor piddle on the paper first, so I'd have to wipe it up. It would make a smear, which would become part of the painting, and also his signature!"

Laura Kay shows me a photograph of one of Webster's paintings, and with her guidance I can see how it looks sort of like a clown. She is skilled at interpreting this kind of symbology, since the cartoons she draws as a vehicle for expressing her clairvoyance look like so much hen scratch until she tells you what the various lines and curlicues signify. This she will do in a voice that is, by her own description, like a little girl's. There is much about Laura that is childlike, but she is not an innocent. She has lived for years in this flophouse hotel on a dangerous street, has seen plenty of unsavoury comings and goings, and has developed the set of survival skills you require when you live on and from the streets. There was a time when she supported herself as an exotic dancer, doing a Salome routine with seven veils. She's nobody's fool, she knows where to find the bottom line, and she can look after herself. At the same time, she has managed to hang on to an essential optimism that is both charming and, in some ways, alarming. She has made her little room into an enchanted forest where miracles are commonplace, a place of hanging vines, singing robins, magic ducks, flouncy curtains, and granted wishes. It is a mean place with which she has done her best and that she knows is just a stop along the way to something altogether more glorious. "I've got no damn past that's interesting," she says, "and my present is hell, so the future is all I've got to look forward to. I say, hey! there are better days ahead."

In fact, her past, as she relates it, is far from dull. It has about it the fairy-tale quality of her here and now, and like many such tales it contains more than a whiff of adversity. Once upon a time there was a pretty little girl called Betty. Her father was in the navy. The family travelled. They moved every year until she was five or so. Then, they settled in Edmonton, where her memories really begin. Some are happy. Many are not. Her mother liked to flirt, and when she flirted it was with intent. When her father found out she was sleeping around, he'd be furious. Her mother learned to save herself by diverting his anger. She would push little Betty at the raging man. He liked to beat her with his belt. Years and years later, she would say that it was as if there was something almost sexual about those whippings. He would take the strap to her while she lay naked on his bed. She couldn't understand why her parents treated her like this. She did her best to be good. She worked hard at being good. She loved them, but, over time, her heart grew full of rage.

One night, when she lay in her own bed, covered in welts, she had the first of two white-light experiences. An angel, maybe it was even God, came into her room and enveloped her in a warm, loving hug. The light spoke to her in a voice that was deep, fatherly, and genuine. Betty understood instinctively then that the man who beat her was not her real father. No, it was this kind visitor who was her true parent. He had come to show her how her life was going to be. He showed her everything, and it was like watching a movie. She saw that she would have to stay nearby her parents for the first thirty years of her life, even though they would abuse her and call her "it." She saw how they would treat her like a slave, like Cinderella, saw how her mother would try to keep her down, would not allow her to grow up. She saw that she would eventually get away from them and forge her own life. She understood that she was there to serve them as scapegoat, that their cruelty came from their own deep unhappiness, their own frustrated longings. The angel offered her this insight, and all the rage melted from her heart. In the morning, every welt had vanished. It was as if they had never been there.

Betty was a pretty child, with ringlets in her hair. She had lots of energy. She took dance classes and gave recitals. In the sixth grade, she choreographed a ballet for her class that won a prize in a festival. She was fond of singing, and could make her voice heard at the back of the room, without need of amplification. She excelled in athletics, especially the fifty-yard dash. She won track trophies for the school. She was a fine badminton player, unbeatable, even by the boys. She had such stamina and drive that she slept only for a few hours each night. When she grew up and left school, she got a job in an office. She moved from her parents' house into her own apartment, although they did their best to keep their hooks in her. Finally, in order to escape, she had an affair with a man she didn't love, and moved away to Calgary. It didn't last, but it served its purpose. At the age of thirty, she was rid of the family that had never been hers. It happened just as the white light had shown her it would. To make the severance complete, she decided to change her name. She'd had a dream. In this dream there was a big hall full of people, and she was coming up out of the audience to address the crowd. A deep, manly voice announced, "Ladies and gentlemen, the prophet Laura Kay!" He was lifting the veil on what was to be. Her real life could now begin.

After Laura Kay Prophet has told me about her early days, she looks at me and says something that makes me wonder if she might be in league with Elly May, who back in Toronto had confided in me the cosmetic usefulness of spirit gum. "Those lines around your eyes. You know, they're exactly the same as the lines I have. Those are the markings of someone for whom nothing happens in the right time. You see the same thing with a lot of movie stars and big shots. We're the kind of people who come not to have Christmas like everybody else, but to celebrate it in a different way. We're the ones who don't work the usual day jobs. I love stories about people who become something after being nothing, about people whose big chance came along at the worst possible moment, but they made it. Those people have our markings. There are other people with hardly any lines at all, or they might have itty-bitty short lines only.

They're the ones who go to school in the right years, they get courting in the right year, they have the baby in the right year, they get their business developed in the right year, and they drop dead in the right year. Everything happens like it's supposed to! But with us, it doesn't."

Laura Kay thinks a lot about timing, and no wonder. Coming up with an accurate schedule of events is a psychic's greatest challenge. It's one thing to be able to see a sequence of happenings before it unfolds, but pinpointing when that sequence begins and ends and how much time elapses between acts is something else altogether. I am sympathetic to this difficulty, for as Laura and I are talking, I find I have some difficulty keeping track of the chronology of her life and career. Our conversation ricochets so frequently off the signposts of the past, the present, and the future that I'm never sure in what direction I should be looking to see the action. However, I think I have it right when I say that around the time she was preparing to leave Edmonton and discard her family, Laura began to have some health problems. She found her energy was quickly depleted. She lost her motor skills. Sometimes, she couldn't bring a fork to her mouth. There would be days on end when she couldn't get out of bed, when she was so weak she could scarcely raise her arm. She began to have difficulty breathing and swallowing. Sometimes, her vision would blur to the point that she was effectively blind. Her hearing was no longer acute. She would soil herself when she coughed or sneezed. Then she would be well again, although for shorter and shorter periods of time. Doctors, she says, dismissed her complaints, or couldn't come up with a diagnosis. Eventually, she stopped seeking their advice. What good was it doing?

One day, in 1979, when her condition was as bleak as it had ever been, she was visited again by the white light. Again, she was shown the movie of her life. This time, she saw that it was to include these magic ducks, and that many, many miracles would be worked through her agency. She would be the focus of intense media scrutiny. And in order that she be able to sustain all this activity, she would be made well. It would not happen hocus-pocus, holus-bolus all at once, but gradually, in stages and degrees. She was told that she would soon meet a man in a wheelchair, and that if she found out what afflicted him, she would have the name of her illness.

The healing began as soon as the white light left her. It wasn't long before she was up and around. One day, in a nearby park, she met a man in wheelchair. On inquiry, he told her that he had multiple sclerosis. His symptoms were identical to her own. She had never heard of MS before, but was satisfied from his description that his pathology matched her own and that this was indeed the illness from which she had suffered. She was not concerned when he said there was no known cure, for she had the assurance of the angel to the contrary. That was more than fifteen years ago, and the healing is not yet complete. On the day of our meeting, she looks very well, lively, enthusiastic, full of beans. She still has bad days when she must stay in bed, but says her energy reserves are much more quickly replenished. Her breathing is noticeably laboured; it comes sometimes in gasps, and she must use a ventilator to handle the congestion in her lungs and bronchia. One day, though, the affliction will be lifted from her absolutely, and her remission will become permanent. This she deeply believes. This she has been shown. And she has to get her full strength back soon, because she has so much to accomplish before the end of the millennium.

In the present, she is occupied with a foundation she has established, Duck Soup. Through it, she would like to raise money and awareness to ease the plight of the homeless. But if the movie of her life, shown her all those years ago, holds true to the plot as she remembers it, she will soon have much, much more on her plate. She sees that her big lottery win will happen in the near future, and it will be followed by her move to the country. She looks forward to that, to moving into a place where she will have room for all her animals, where she doesn't have to scrub out the fridge and the stove, and clean up the mess from the last people before she can be comfortable. After the country move comes the earthquake. Then she will have to spearhead her humanitarian relief efforts. That will use up most of her money. There will be changes in the feathered personnel, too. Bob, she sees, will pass on. Then Harvey II will materialize. He won't last long, but will die (in a gas leak, she says) to make way for the big miracle of Harvey III. This duck's arrival will usher in a golden age of spiritual growth and renewal, when she will have to deal with the demands put on her by the wide public acclaim that will come her way when she is a celebrated guru, bringing her message of peace and reconciliation to audiences around the world. She sees that she will get caught up in some bad business deals, and at some point will be married to a man she calls "Prince Charming." This is not just a fond endearment, for he is actually of royal blood. He too, she has been shown, will treat her badly. It's a mixed bag, that's for sure, but there is no way out of any of this for Laura Kay. This is the work she is destined to do. She has seen the life she is meant to lead.

"How would you feel," she asks, "if you knew that you were born just to fulfil a prophecy in the Bible for a bunch of weird people who have to see it to believe it?" The prophecy she believes she was born to make flesh is that of Revelation (12:1–2, 5): "And there appeared a great wonder in heaven; a woman clothed with the sun, and the moon under her feet, and upon her head a crown of twelve stars: And she being with child cried, travailing in birth, and pained to be delivered.... And she brought forth a man child, who was to rule all nations with a rod of iron: and her child was caught up unto God, and to his throne."

"You don't even know," she says, "the miracles that are going to happen to me. I've already had one. It happened when I was six, and that was walking on air. I've never been able to do it since, although I've been able to levitate off the scale to get myself down by five or six pounds. I know that I am here to walk on air again, and I do it during the time I am preg-a-nant with twins, and Harvey III, yellow as he can be, is walking on air behind me. Harvey III is not a reincarnation of Harvey I and II, but an actual resurrection. He is found by that fountain that's between Christ Church Cathedral and the government building with the number 666, and the man who finds him starts breathing fire as soon as he picks him up. I've seen the headline, 'Fire-breathing Man Finds Duck.' When we walk on air, we are in Toronto, and it's a cold, miserable day. It's standing room only, and you see all the cameras flashing as we walk. I've got this pretty yellow dress, and long ringlets."

"Laura, how old are you now?"

"Fifty-six and a half."

"But pregnancy isn't something that usually happens after you're say, fifty. I mean, unless you really work at it."

"Oh, I know. And I know it sounds crazy. But it's going to happen. I'll be strong and healthy, too. I'll have twins, but the girl will die. The boy will grow up to be a leader among men. He'll marry, and I won't like his wife. I'll die, alone in my bed, at the age of eighty-two. Oh, there'll be lots else, too. So many miracles! You know, my life is full of miracles."

I think about the impossibility–improbability ratio, and look out her window. It gives onto the alley. The view is of brick and of pigeons. It might be bleak, but this room — with its greenery and its wildlife, with its little robin who throbs with new life — has something of the oasis about it. It is peaceful here. Sometimes, the more raucous sounds of Granville Street filter in. A car horn. A harsh curse. Now, an ambulance speeds by, siren howling. It speeds past the drunks and the addicts and the hookers and the runaways, speeds past the doctors and the notaries and the stenos, speeds past everyone doing what we all of us do, in our time, in our way, while we're here, which is nothing more than trying to get by. It speeds past the cheap repertory cinemas where Laura likes to go when she can get a break from Bob, with her emotional and gustatory demands. None of the offerings at any of these theatres is as inventive or as promising as the movie of her future, the pageant of her days yet to come. Nonetheless, she goes and watches the movie of someone else's life for two hours. That's as long as she can risk being away from her duck, but so much can happen in that time. A robin could fall from its nest. A prince might arrive in the lobby, with her name on his lips. Her lottery number might be drawn. She could step back into the street and find the world totally rearranged. She might step into the rainy afternoon only to find she has been given eagle wings to take her to the wilderness. She might step into the chill of the night and find she is a woman clothed with the sun.

La Belle et La Bête

She looked like the picture of a young rapt saint,
lost in heavenly musing.
— Grenville Kleiser, *Fifteen Thousand Useful Phrases*

When I am feeling limber of neck or when the chiropractor tells me I must, I give my head a yogic twist. I look over one shoulder or the other, and study the steady retreat of the present moment. On such Lot's-wife occasions as these, with the panorama of the past in plain view, I like to reflect on my days on earth. Sometimes, I remember a game I enjoyed as a child, a diversion I made up when I was passing through a cumulative-thinking phase. It was a silly solipsistic pastime called "How Much? How Many?" To play, you simply ask yourself as many total-tally questions as you can before you collapse laughing. For example, in my life to date, how much money have I made, how much have I spent, how many people have I met, how many miles have I walked, how many words have I read, spoken, written? You press on in this vein, and the laughter typically comes when you reach the bodily fluid questions. It's always a great time-waster, and I enjoy it until I get around to wondering how many brain cells I've lost, and if they could be amassed and laid end to end would they equal the distance to Moscow, to the moon, or to Mercury. At this point, "How much? How many?" ceases to be amusing, and I hurry to reswivel my head.

The horror! All those brain cells, dead and done, and God only knows what they've taken away with them. So many years

in school, and what have I retained of the specific theorems, for-
mulae, and equations I worked so hard to master? What about
the dates? The Diet of Worms. The Defenestration of Prague.
Where have they gone? Once they were inscribed on the register, but try as I might, I can no longer call them up. Even the
nine times-table eludes me, most days. I squeeze and squeeze the
constipated medulla, and all that oozes from between its folds
is the first stanza of "Excelsior" and four lines of dialogue from
a seventh-grade French text I think was called *Parler et lire*.

    «*Paul et Louise, comment vont-ils?*»
    «*Paul va fort bien, mais Louise est malade.*»
    «*Que c'est dommage!*»
    «*Oh, ce n'est pas grave.*»

This dumb blandishment, so seemingly forgettable, was a
feature of my very first French lesson. As such, it's taken on a
symbolic weight that is disproportionate to its straightforward
meaning and narrow import. Over the years, it's become a key
I use to unlock the door to what little French remains from the
days when I could actually get by. I repeat those few lines over
and over, a mantra, a spell, concentrating on their rhythm, their
music. I use them to prime the pump, and to invoke the spirits
of Paul *et* Louise. Whenever I am in Montreal, I ask them to
stand up for me and assist me as I try to negotiate my way
through the world in a language that is not my own.

Why I persist with this, I'll never know. *The whole truth,
naked, cold, and fatal as a patriot's blade* is that, as a linguistic lubricant, such an exercise is completely ineffective. Paul *et*
Louise are of limited utility. They are interested only in talking
about their respective states of health. What good are they to
me when I have to engage the desk clerk in a mangled back-and-
forth about whether or not my room is equipped to handle the
requirements of a modem? "Que c'est dommage!" I say when
she tells me that, no, their phone lines can't accommodate such
a pesky innovation and that, furthermore, the last pernicious ass-
hole who tried to send or receive an e-mail in his room brought
the whole system down and caused considerable inconvenience

to the hotel management, the other guests, and the phone company, too. "Oh! C'est grave!" I say, sympathetically, and she nods agreement before saying in English, "So don't try it, okay?"

Hélas! It's always this way for me in Montreal, a city that is pretty much my whole experience of Quebec. My conversational partners will put up with my blundering for a minute or two, and then slip into an easy, vernacular English. It invariably happens, and I invariably take it as a stiff rebuke. Would it be too much to play along? I have always been a convinced federalist and booster of official bilingualism. I want to do my bit to sustain the cultural underpinnings of the nation, want to show myself willing to make an extraordinary effort to keep the union from coming unseamed. But every time I am rebuffed, terrible red-neck whinings of the kind usually heard on private radio phone-in shows in Calgary insinuate themselves into my thoughts. "Well, phooey on you, Quebec," I come perilously close to saying. "If no one on your side of the linguistic divide is willing to play along, then what's the point in even trying? Go ahead and cash in your sovereignty chips for all I care!" But then I rally. Ever the optimist, I press on, and continue to measure out my Montreal days in encounters of four lines or less.

"Pourriez-vous me dire où se trouve l'Université de McGill?"

"Oh, sure, just a few blocks further on."

"Merci."

"No prob."

Or:

"Excusez-moi, monsieur, le métro, est-il loin d'ici?"

"Nope. There's the entrance over there."

"Ah, oui. Je vois bien. Merci, monsieur. Vous êtes très gentil. Prière agréer l'expression de mes sentiments les plus respectueux."

"Glad to be of help! Where ya from? Berlin or something?"

Given this history, and my exquisite sensitivity to the mere perception of a slight, you can readily imagine my delight when I called up Sylvie Longpré to request a viewing of her many Barbie dolls, and learned that she speaks almost no English. "Fort bien!" I said, and I meant it, too.

"Pourriez-vous m'expliquer comment je faire pour aller à Repentigny?" I asked the young woman at the car rental. Repentigny is the suburb where Sylvie lives.

"Repentigny? Oh, God. No one goes there. Why would anyone want to go to Repentigny?"

"J'y vais pour voir Barbie."

"Barbie? In this snow? It's your funeral, I guess. Go east on Sherbrooke. It'll take you right there. Eventually."

She was such a supercilious know-it-all that I almost hated to credit how her adumbrations were not without foundation, meteorologically speaking. However, by the time I was willing to say uncle, I was stuck smack dab in the middle of an industrial wasteland, in a blinding blizzard, in an absurdly long line of traffic that was *creeping like a snail, unwillingly to school*. To make things worse, Paul *et* Louise — who were in the back seat — were joined by the ghost of Grenville Kleiser. He was spunky and full of beans and eager to demonstrate that there are many more useful phrases available to conscientious users of the language than the famous 15,000 on which his reputation rests. *The car is like one segment of a parasitic worm clogging the intestine of the highway*, he sang, turning down the radio in order that I might hear him the better. *The traffic-bound drivers are squirming like young rabbits, eager for release from the magician's top hat. All the world is wearing a veil as white and as sticky as that of a young noviciate emptying a honeycomb.*

I was an hour and a half late getting to Sylvie's house. "Je suis désolé d'être tellement en retard," I began, but she kindly deflected all my sorry bleatings by making *ce n'est pas grave* noises. She apologized herself for the inconvenience of the weather, assuming total responsibility for it, the way we all will when we meet someone from away in less than clement circumstances. Sylvie is a lively woman, vibrant and gracious, radiant with good health. She broadcasts the kind of energy that belongs to someone whose reserves are regularly replenished by such vigorous activities as snowmobiling, which she adores. In the summer, she goes boating, and drives her four-by-four on lost and rutted roads. We met on a Friday evening, and she was as perky and outgoing as any human being has a right to be, especially after a long work week of teaching business principles. Her long blonde hair was swept back and held in place with barrettes. Her attractive face had a tan-in-a-tube bronziness about it, and she was very prettily dressed. She wore a navel-exposing white angora halter-top — it was a puffy, girlish aureole, like a dandelion seed-pod — and leopard-skin tights cinched at her tiny waist. She had on open-toed sandals, and she looked exactly like Barbie. Exactly.

In 1995, David Weeks published a book called *Eccentrics: A Study of Sanity and Strangeness*. Dr. Weeks, an American neuropsychologist working in Edinburgh, observed that psychiatric literature has by and large overlooked eccentricity as a discrete and discernible condition. Three out of four of the best-known standard texts, he noted, made no mention of eccentricity whatsoever, and it had never been described clinically. He set out to remedy the situation, and brought the weight of scientific method to bear on his investigation. My mythopoeic reliance on luck, rumour, and coincidence pales next to his standardized methods of data gathering and analysis. I tried to avoid "in general" reductions, tried to avoid drawing conclusions, while he identifies particular descriptors or signposts of eccentric behaviour. These included devotion to nonconforming behaviour, and a supercharged sense of creativity, curiosity, and idealism. He found that eccentrics often had more than one obsession, were intelligent and confident in their opinions, had peculiar eating habits or living arrangments, were more often single than partnered, and were frequently bad spellers. I suppose I saw signs of many of these symptoms on my travels, save for the spelling, for which ability I didn't have the nerve or foresight to test. I was also struck by the presence of animal companions — cats, in particular — and by the use of clutter as decorating technique; I visited many amply strewn rooms. However, while it piques my interest to see such characteristics spelled out in a list, I remain stubbornly resistant to the idea of delineating an eccentric "norm." It pleased me to see that, if such a thing could be said to exist, Sylvie Longpré deviates from it in several key respects.

Repentigny is a suburb unremarakble in everything save its expansiveness. Sylvie and her co-vivant live on a quiet street in a very spiffy and neatly organized split-level house. It is tasteful in its appointments, subdued even, and you would never be able to guess from a cursory look around the living room or dining room or kitchen anything of the depths of Sylvie's obsession, which has to do with Barbie. There are no framed pictures of Barbie on the walls, no Barbies propped up on chairs, none of the many publications of interest to Barbie aficionados — collector's magazines, sales catalogues, lavish commemorative albums, and so on — fanned on the coffee table. You might note that her boyfriend, Pierre, who is trim, handsome, and neatly coiffed, looks more than a little like Ken. But you won't get the whole picture until he has disappeared downstairs to play with his sound equipment, and Sylvie has led you into the guest bedroom that is Barbie Central. The atmosphere there is hushed and reverential, as it should be. This is her sanctuary. This is where she becomes her truest self: a priestess venerating a goddess who is infinite in her incarnations, and in whose being the perfection of all possibilities is manifest. Barbie complete. Barbie regenerative. Barbie forever.

Now, there are plenty of Barbie enthusiasts in the world. I've met several of them, women and men both. They have Web sites and newsletters. They hold international conferences. They talk knowledgably and often about the arcane minutiae that is the basis of their shared experience: such things as dates of issue and regional variants in product and the small defects of packaging that can greatly enhance the value of a doll. Packaging overall is important. Take Barbie from her box, and the second she hits the air, her value goes down by twenty per cent. They all know the Barbie gospel, know that she was first marketed by Mattel in 1959 (one year before the birth of Sylvie), and right from the beginning she was a hit. Right from the beginning, she was desired. Of course she was! Everything about her appealed to collectors with a populist sensibility. As collectibles go, she is pretty darn democratic. There is enough "Barbie-ana" that is accessible and cheap to allow anyone to make a start, and there is enough that is rare and far-flung and impossibly expensive that you always have something to hope for, a reason to persist in your quest, a Grail to hold in your sights. You can be as expansive or as focused as you wish, for Barbie is bigger than Barbie alone. Barbie is also Ken and Skipper and Midge and Francie and Ellie and Teresa and Julia and Steven and all the other friends and hangers-on of diverse colours and abilities that she has admitted to her magic circle over the years. Barbie is All Of Us, and herein lies the reason behind her tremendous and enduring, her almost mystical magnetism. She is perfect, immaculate, and eternal. She is sister and mother, sun and moon. She is yin and yang, animus and anima. She is every ethnicity, she is all things womanly, the universal feminine principle. She is the source of our nourishment, though not one single drop of milk has ever been wrung from her impossibly conical, rigid

Sylvie Longpré in Barbie Land.

breasts. She is the ideal date, though never has a tongue — not Ken's, not even her own — slipped between her lips. Why would she need a tongue? Her communication is instant and telepathic. Intact and impenetrable, she is the fecund virgin who never stops giving birth. She is the tangle of incongruities that makes perfect sense. She is logic and confusion. She is Love. In a word, she is Barbie.

As we entered the temple, Sylvie apologized for certain lamentable absences. Some of her dolls, the rarest of the rare, were on loan to an important toy show at Olympic Stadium. She sat on the floor and motioned for me to do likewise. This was not as straightforward as it sounds. It required very careful positioning. There was not a surfeit of unstaked turf. There were collectible Barbies beaming from their boxes, and there were the free-range Barbies who were out and about, striding fearlessly through the world. Here was Barbie in one of her several dream houses, casually dressed as though for a picnic, coming down a spiral staircase to greet her friends, all of them looking up at her adoringly. There was Barbie emerging from a stable into her corral, a cowgirl for all seasons, and with roping and branding on her mind. If she were to be diverted from her purpose (which could never happen, her concentration is that pure), and if she were to look to her right or to her left, she would see herself laughing in a snowmobile, or speeding along in a flashy car. She would see herself swaddled in surgical greens, ready to perform a delicate surgery, or dressed for a wedding, her own, of course. Flight attendant, lawyer, teacher, lifeguard, missionary: there was nothing she couldn't do or be, since, for Barbie, thought and action are one. She only has to wish for it, and it is so. Ballerina Barbie, Hawaiian Barbie, Superstar Barbie, Beach Fun Barbie, Equestrienne Barbie, Disco Barbie, Club California Barbie, Gold Medal Skier Barbie, they were all there. It was grand! In the middle of January, in the middle of Repentigny, I'd fallen down the rabbit hole and ended up in Barbie Land, in the country of one citizen. I felt overcome with the same vertigo that seizes me when I look in one of those image-duplicating fun-house mirrors. I put down my right hand to steady myself and felt the digging of ten perfect toes against my palm. To whom could they belong? Why, to Barbie, of course. And what was she wearing? A pretty angora halter-top sweater, leopard-skin tights, and sandals. Her hair was held back with barrettes. *Déjà vu.* Where had I seen such an outfit before?

Outside, the storm raged. Inside, Sylvie talked, and the torrent of her words had a "leaves that before the wild hurricane fly" quality to them. She had so much to say about Barbie, so much to show me. Look at this one, see how her legs bend, that's what makes her special. And with this one it's the bangs that are important, and with this one it's her bubble cut. There were Barbies from every land, Australian Barbie, Korean Barbie, even Inuit Barbie. Every so often I would ask a question in my misshapen French, and Sylvie would graciously answer, though sometimes a mist of puzzlement would cloud her blue eyes, as though I had posed a non sequitur. Which probably I had, a consequence of not having taken in everything that had gone before. Sylvie's speech was rapid and colloquial. Still, I think I got the gist of it.

It was her mother, Audette, who launched Sylvie on her Barbie path when she was a little girl. That's a familiar story. Millions could tell it. Unlike most of her contemporaries, Sylvie never passed out of the phase, never lost her fondness for the doll. Her fascination began to compound as she grew older and she started acquiring more and more Barbies (and Skipper and Midge and all the gang) along with their licensed accessories. Nor was this so very bizarre. If one has the constitution of a collector, then that acquisitive urge will find an out. Teaspoons, vintage aircraft, salt and pepper shakers, Barbies: there's nothing that distinguishes one from the other in any moral or procedural sense. Whatever the object of your affection, you develop a keen eye, and a specialized, spongy intelligence, a breadth of knowledge, and a cool savvy.

Sylvie is steeped in Barbie lore. She knows every pertinent detail about Barbie's early days as a fashion queen, knows that her "Gay Parisienne" outfit was a pin-dot taffeta bubble dress in deep blue, along with a veiled hat in blue tulle, a rabbit-fur stole, long white tricot gloves, open-toed pumps, pearls and matching earrings, and a gold velvet clutch. Ask and she will be able to tell you about Ken's bath-time "Terry Tog" assemblage that came out in 1961: the blue terry robe with the "K" monogram, the white briefs, the tie belt, the blue sponge, the bar of pink soap, the razor, the comb, the slippers. She will know about how the "His" on his towel washed out if you weren't careful. You could not stump her with a question pertaining to the components of the "Leather Limelight" ensemble, or Francie's "Fur-Out" costume. Sylvie knows it all.

I liked Sylvie very much. I was charmed by her, completely caught up in the leghold trap of her enthusiasm. I was struck by her intelligence and good humour, but mostly by her depth of feeling. She spoke so lovingly, so breathlessly about Barbie, and about all the confections within her collection. Her eyes at times would roll back in her head as she described the profound, the really sensual pleasure that was hers when she found an elusive doll or wardrobe item to supplement her huge holdings. Listening to Sylvie talk was like witnessing the donning of a mantle of holiness, like watching a transcendent moment in *The Song of Bernadette*. But what really sets her apart from the garden-variety Barbie enthusiast is that the doll has become her role model. Unlike Pinocchio, the puppet/doll who wanted to become a real live boy, Sylvie, a flesh-and-blood woman, wants to become a real Barbie. More than a doll, she is an object of emulation. The angora sweater/leopard-skin tights combo was just one of many Barbie-inspired ensembles Sylvie owns, and costume is not the whole extent of it.

Every waking day, when she goes out into the world, Sylvie does her best to lead a Barbie kind of life. She gets up in the morning and fixes her hair. She owns several wigs, made in Italy, that she can style to match the Barbie do of the moment. She goes to her closet and decides what to wear. Many of her clothes have been made by her mother and are exact duplicates, in their every particular, of Barbie's outfits. She has done her best to match the jewellery too, as well as the shoes, the handbags. She also has some of the more exotic collations, that are not strictly suitable as classroom attire, like the all-white, all-fur trappings of Snow Queen Barbie. Before Sylvie leaves for work, she must walk her two dogs, Charlie and Stinger. They are Afghan hounds, which she acquired after Barbie turned up on the shelves with Afghan hounds. She kisses Pierre–cum–Ken goodbye and gets into her car. It is a Corvette. You needn't wonder why she drives a Corvette.

"But don't people think you're crazy?" I asked.

"Sure, they do! They have every right to think I'm crazy, just as I have every right to do what makes me happy. It's just the way I am. I see someone I admire and I want to become that person. I study every detail — her walk, her make-up, her style of dress — and then I copy it. I've just always loved Barbie. I feel comfortable in her skin. I make friends this way. It makes people smile. Children love it. Sometimes, I even go to visit them in the hospital. You should hear the little girls when they see Barbie come in the door. You should hear how they laugh!" She laughed herself and *let the soft waves of her deep hair fall like flowers from Paradise.*

Another "symptom" of eccentricity, or at least one that I observed, is a "greater than average need to exert control over an environment." Think of Charles Henry Danielle, determined to manipulate every detail of his laying-out and his funeral. Think of Fred Sauer, with the happy clutter of his inventions and his need to know whether or not Big Dukie's in Bed. Think of Glenn Gould, how he guarded his own privacy, shut people out, and called his friends at his own convenience, at two, three, four in the morning. Think of Sylvie Longpré, with her great sense of fun and style, and her commanding eye for detail, investing her considerable energy and imagination in the decorating of her temple, and in the crafting of a world where perfection is, in fact, attainable; a Barbie world where no hair is ever out of place, no nail is ever chipped, no dream is ever dashed. Barbie is a garden where fantasies grow. Barbie is a moulded palimpsest on which Sylvie can write the story of her own life. Why not have what Barbie has: independence; loyal friends; fast cars; great hair; a good man with limited ambition, a sculpted chest, and rock-hard thighs; and her own body that will never, ever change? All this, and universal adoration, too. Life as Icon is not without its appeal.

Sylvie told me as I was leaving, and as I was apologizing yet again for my broken French, that she wishes she had more English. She feels trapped, sometimes, for where can she go outside of Quebec and feel confident that she will be understood? The U.S. is problematic, no one speaks her language there. She was planning to attend a big Barbie congress in Detroit, and she wondered how that would go, how easy a time she would have of it. Heavens, even Toronto would be dodgy from the point of view of language. Not that her life is ever dull when she just stays put. Far from it! She can get in her Corvette any old time and head out of town, get in some off-road motoring, some snowmobiling, some boating. And there will always be subliminal escapes via Barbie. Barbie is an astronaut. Barbie is a time traveller. Barbie thinks nothing of changing the colour of her skin. Barbie adapts herself to any linguistic circumstance. Barbie does everything except get older. What if she did? What would she look like at forty? Fifty? What would be the complexion of Pensioner Barbie? Through Sylvie Longpré, goddess made woman, come to live on earth among us as Barbie's exact contemporary, we might yet find out. I told her *merci*, I wished her *bonne nuit. She seemed happy as a wave that dances on the sea.*

Outside, deep snow. Inside, the lights clicked off in the dream house. I watched them wink out, one by one by one. I wondered, as I stood in the dark and scraped the ice from the windshield with a credit card, what it was about Sylvie — other than language — that made her seem so very Quebec. Could she exist anywhere else? Was she, just maybe, a product of the "distinct society" about which we've heard so very, very much?

Oh-oh! Distinct society! It had been my hope that nowhere in these pages would I use those words in tandem, and now I've gone and done it. May I say how sorry I am? I thought I'd make it through without such a spillage. Anyone who spends more than five minutes in Canada and who pays even the scantiest attention to the ongoing and incredibly tedious bun toss that passes for secessionist–federalist dialogue in this country will appreciate how the rhetorical moo of "distinct society" can coax the gag reflex into dancing a hornpipe. Like most of the catch-phrases that are conceived by policy wonks, gestated in think-tanks, and then forced upon the public for suckling, "distinct society" has come to mean too much and too little. It is intended, of course, to have some bearing on the thwarted aspirations and disputations of Quebec. But by now, so many politicians and patriots and academics and commentators have passed that way and sown their seed in its soil, and so much has grown from it that is hybrid and out of control, that it has become impossible to penetrate the brambles. "Distinct society." What does it mean? Language, religion, the Napoleonic Code, the ready availability of the cholesterolic mess called "poutine," the creative use of greystone, shelves of liquor in the grocery stores, the absence of newspaper boxes on the streets of Montreal, and the fact that you can't turn right on a red but can still smoke in a restaurant: any of these might be trotted out to demonstrate that this place is essentially different from the rest of the country. Just try it, though, and see what a hoo-ha ensues! See what a lot of scrabbling and hoarding and bean-counting and recrimination-tossing gets loosed. It's been going on for centuries. It will never, ever change. Every goddam year we're subjected to yet another take on "Hey, ho, away we go, donkey riding, donkey riding." It makes one pine for Greenland.

I am one of those Canadians who has never lived in the province of Quebec but for whom an open-handed and unstinting acceptance of the notion of "distinct society" has never been a question, issue, problem. Lamentably, I am also a simpleton whose opinion counts for nothing, and properly so. I can't explain my feelings in this regard in a way that will make any difference to anyone. I go to Quebec and my response to the place is both psychic and visceral. Distinct? Sure it is! But I could never support the ringings in my ear or the rumblings in my gut that tell me this is so in a debate or other public forum, could never validate them in the way one must by pointing to the demonstrable or the quantifiable. What do I feel? *Je ne sais quoi.* It's the surge beneath my feet, the direction of the wind, the colour of the river, the slant of sleet and snow. And more than anything else, it's the clothes on people's backs.

Yes, when all is said and done, it's fashion more than anything that makes my barometer of distinctiveness point to "really, really, really different." I walk along St-Denis or St-Laurent, look in the stores and the restaurants, study what people are wearing, and time and time again it is driven home to me that, even if I could speak flawless, Quebec-accented French, I would never belong here. Not only am I too Anglo in speech and outlook, I am too dumpy by half, too much of a shlump, and there is nothing God nor make-over specialist could do to change that. I hasten to add that this is not a class distinction, not some white-collar Sunday-afternoon-at-the-gallery, Saturday-night-on-the-Main phenomenon. I notice it everywhere: on the Metro, in the library, even here, in a dough-nut shop on Beaubien, in Montreal's gritty east side. The place is inhabited by senior citizens, women for the most part. Each and every one of them sports something deliberately distinctive, like a pretty aquamarine scarf, or a shocking-pink tam, or a slightly outlandish set of spectacles: cat's eyes, rhinestones. They are fun-loving gals and you can tell from their easy banter with the waitresses that they are regulars here. They are gossiping avidly about the tabloid news. While I wait to make the rendezvous that has brought me to this unlikely place — unlikely for me, anyway; I don't even like doughnuts — I eavesdrop on their to and fro, and learn more than I ever thought I might about the pop diva Céline Dion and her alleged difficulties achieving gravidity.

"She needs to put on weight!" says one.

"She needs to spend more time at home!" says another.

"Her husband is not so young any more!" says a third, and they all fall about, cackling.

Distinct society? Can anyone imagine a clutch of women of similar age and circumstances sitting in a Salisbury House in Winnipeg or a Tim Horton's in Ottawa and carrying on in the same clucking and maternal and uproarious way about Alanis Morissette? Or Anne Murray, God save us. It would never happen. They could never care enough. Québécois(es) are legendary for their loyalty to their home-grown talent. They ply their indigenous celebrities with all the fawning courtesies and teasing disrespect that elsewhere in the world would be accorded only to royalty and truly international film stars. So caught up am I in the tragedy of Céline and her putative infertility that I don't even feel the earth tremble when the man I am here to meet comes through the door, surveys the scene, and makes his way in my direction. He knows where to go. It doesn't take him a second to spot the stranger, the one who obviously doesn't belong, the one who smells like an Englishman. With a Fee, and a Fie, and a Fo, and Fum, he comes, he comes, he comes, he comes, a Golem of a man who, seen from a satellite, might be mistaken for a European principality. Mountainous Andorra, maybe. He comes lumbering in my direction, rending the air before him, pushing his mass through the narrow spaces between the tables like an ice-breaker smashing its way through the floes.

Enter the Great Antonio, senior citizen, neighbourhood landmark, and living legend. Enter the Great Antonio, with his ankle-length, Rasta-thick braid tucked inside his blue parka, and the Ionic columns of his legs contained by an enormity of denim. Enter the Great Antonio, The World's Strongest Man, all 510 pounds of him, the very man who once fought eighteen wrestlers in a single ring in Fort Worth, Texas. And won. Enter the Great Antonio with his green garbage bag full of newspaper clippings tucked under his arm, the Great Antonio, six feet, four inches, who claims to be descended from extraterrestrials, who is as tough and as unplaned and as lumpen as a meteor latterly fallen to earth. With his white haystack of a beard and his gorgeous turnip of a nose (*covered with vegetation in wild luxuriance*) he might be a root cellar made animate. He is a force of nature, he is the reason we have the word "monolithic," he is hoarily alpine, he is his very own distinct society, and he has come here for one reason only. He has come here to talk. To me. He has come here to talk to me in English.

"Hello," I say brightly, "you must be the Great Antonio."

"YES! I am G-r-r-r-r-e-e-e-a-a-a-t ANTONIO!"

All of his verbal artillery is high decibel and rapid fire, but certain words seem to shoot from him with the weight and velocity of cannon balls. I hold my smile and extend my hand. He ignores it. He yanks back the table as far as it will go without toppling over the doughnut eaters who are adjacent to us. He wedges himself in next to the wall, squeezes into a space that is scarcely wide enough to accommodate both him and his shadow, and hovers for an instant over the long banquette that is about to receive the gift of his bulk. He lets gravity take over, shudders into a hunkering posture, quivers as he lands and his mass spreads out like a jelly salad, untimely sprung from its mould onto a too-warm plate. He begins to fuss with his bag, muttering as he removes its rolled and wadded contents. I try to pick up the conversation, and am taken aback at the sound of my voice as it falls from my mouth. I am nauseatingly chipper, and I start to blather with the forced cheerfulness of a dental assistant reassuring a patient before a root canal.

"It's so good to meet you, everyone has told me so much about you. Can I get you a cup of coffee? A doughnut, maybe?"

"NO! Not now COFFEE! Coffee LATER! Now, you SIT! You SIT, I SHOW!"

"Heh, heh, heh. Why, sure!"

In short order, his biography lies before me. The table is stacked, is overbrimming with prunings from the world press. There are sheaves and sheaves of clippings, originals, photocopies, all well examined, some smudgy with thumb prints, some tattooed with coffee stains. They impressively document the glorious life and expansive career of Antonio Barichievich, known to all and sundry as the Great Antonio. He was born in Yugoslavia in 1925, came to Canada in 1946, and began to work right away at his chosen vocation, which is that of Strong Man. Those were the days when it was not an overcrowded field — unlike today, when steroids are as readily available as Popsicles — and word of his deeds of derring-do spread quickly. He was soon well known in Montreal and beyond for his feats

The Great Antonio with Liza Minnelli.

of strength, nerve, and endurance. A dyed-in-the-wool exhibitionist, he liked nothing better than to show off in public. He wasn't — isn't — the kind of guy who could be satisfied hidden away in some gym, bench-pressing 500 pounds with only a few muscle-bound buddies to look on and applaud his brawny displays. No, he wanted to be out on the street, as visible as possible, attracting an appreciative crowd by doing something big and outlandish and unlikely, such as pulling something really, really heavy. Such as a loaded bus.

Buses, in fact, were his specialty, his habit. Sometimes, several buses were corralled so that he could prove his prowess.

On at least one occasion there were as many as four linked together. There are photos — he has them — of the Great Antonio yoked to a colossal bracelet on which buses are the only charms, straining as he pulls them down the road, his face a study of joyous agony and maniacal intent. This was how Samson looked when he prepared to pull down the pillars and wreak havoc on the Philistines, you can count on it. The G.A. performed this stunt so often, to such acclaim, and with such aplomb, that there was a time when one could hardly say "The

The Great Antonio (left) captures the attention of Sophia Loren.

Great Antonio" without pronouncing "bus" in the same breath. The two concepts became regionally synonymous. You can test this by mentioning his name to anyone who has lived in Montreal since the war, and who takes public transportation. They will know exactly who he is, and they will almost certainly say, "Oh, yeah. I was late for a movie once because of him. It was the strangest thing. I was taking the bus, and all of a sudden the driver just came to a dead stop, right in the middle of St-Catherine. There was kind of commotion up front, and it turned out to be the Great Antonio. He'd step into the road and stop these buses and attach a chain and haul it along for a block or two. Then, he'd pass the hat. I think he also sold postcards of himself. That was a long time ago. Isn't he dead?"

Many Montrealers to whom I mentioned his name wondered if Antonio had passed from the world. Absolutely not! He is very much among us, and, what's more, he remains preternaturally vigorous. At seventy-two, he is no longer interested in dragging buses up and down St-Catherine with a chain, but you could never call him inactive. Spreading his own legend is pretty much a full-time job. In fact, simply maintaining the archive is a chore to tax a strong man. So much paper! His is a well-documented life, amazingly so, really. No one gets that kind of slavering attention from news hounds unless he is deliberate about casting out attractive lures. Anyone who cared to court the attention of the media would be well advised to take a page from Great Antonio's book. As recipes for fame go, his is easy to follow. Stop a bus, attach a chain, haul the thing down the street, and every journalist in town will beat a path to your door. Pull four buses and they'll make a return visit. Pull four elephants — somewhere along the line he claims to have done that, too — and you can pretty much join the press club.

"EVEN AS A BOY, GREAT ANTONIO WAS A TITAN"
"STUNNED AUDIENCE WATCHES ANTONIO EAT 25 CHICKENS"
"GREAT ANTONIO — HIS MUSCLE IS 10 HORSEPOWER"
"THE GREAT ANTONIO TAKES A BUS"

The headlines just keep on spilling, one after the other, all of them clamouring to be heard after their confinement in the green garbage bag. All the clippings tell more or less the same story. International travel. Meetings with celebrities. Movie roles in films that required convincing autochtones, such as *Quest for Fire* and *The Abominable Snowman*. As Antonio shows off his impressive collection of cullings, one by one by one, he annotates the stories in his associative, rambling, stream-of-consciousness style. He gets very loud. A Strong Man show 'n' yell unfolds right there, in the middle of Montreal in the middle of the afternoon in the middle of Dunkin' Donuts. He is uninhibited by middle-class, born-of-therapy conventions like "respect for personal space and boundaries." He exudes a sense of proprietorship in this place, which is one of his regular haunts. He lives nearby, and this is where he comes "to take a meeting." All the other regulars are habituated to his tail-fanning displays and pay him no mind. They continue to gossip about Céline, and are unmoved by his voluble exuberance. Apparently, they've seen and heard it all before. As his monologue — and it is a monologue; he won't brook questions while he's talking about himself — gathers momentum, his language becomes harder to penetrate, not so much because of his accent but because his sentences swallow one another, eliding together as he thunders out the litany of his accomplishments. One thing that emerges from his prolix spewing is that he is especially proud of his foreign press, and his close encounters with movie stars.

"Here, here, ANTONIO in JAPAN, I go Japan FOUR times, pull buses for 14 MILLION people, 14 MILLION, you understand, POPE he get 50,000, MADONNA she get 60,000, Antonio he get 14 MILLION, MADONNA she come to Montreal, she want to MEET me, but I OUT of town, too BAD, some day maybe I GO to Los Angeles meet MADONNA, here is Antonio with MICHAEL JACKSON, he come here, much, MUCH security, MANY, many BODYGUARD, I only ONE he let in to SEE him, there is picture, he SMART man, very intelligent, people TALK about him, I DON'T give a SHIT what he does, I don't give a FUCK he very smart guy, there is Antonio with JOHNNY CARSON, with SOPHIA LOREN, with GREEK lady, what her name, NANA MOUSKOURI, yes, I, the GREAT ANTONIO, strongest man in WORLD, I pull buses with my HAIR, I never tell anyone how I get such STRONG hair, this a SECRET, old woman taught me, she TOLD me I come from EXTRATERRESTRIALS, maybe some day NASA come test my HAIR, test my BLOOD see why I got such strong blood, my BLOOD too strong for PEOPLE on this PLANET, one day the GREAT ANTONIO perform in Little Rock, PERFORM for CLINTON, I try to get him to COME to Montreal, he come SOON to see ME, see, here, SEE, I get this LETTER from his WIFE."

He pushes this piece of rare correspondence at me. I read it while he rears up and goes, at last, to get some coffee.

June 15, 1993

Dear Mr. Barichievich:

Thank you for inviting President Clinton to visit Montreal, Quebec. The President asked me to convey his appreciation for your kind invitation and to apologize for being unable to make a commitment to your request at this time.

During the Clinton–Gore campaign, the President had the opportunity to visit many towns and cities across our nation. Now, as he implements a national agenda to move our country forward, he does not have the opportunity to travel to as many places as he would like. However, the President is committed to staying in touch with the concerns of the American people. He hopes this will include a visit to Montreal.

Please be assured that I will keep your letter on file for further consideration. Your continued interest and support are both encouraged and appreciated.

Sincerely,
Marcia L. Hale, Assistant to the President
Director of Scheduling and Advance

Oh, dear. Oh, dear. Oh, dear. Marcia Hale, who obviously graduated in Tactful Studies from some Ivy League school, did herself proud with this reply to what must have been a bizarre invitation; though probably no more bizarre than many that fly over the White House transom. What "concerns of the American people" might be addressed by an audience with the Great Antonio? Would the President come to Dunkin' Donuts and use his considerable powers of persuasion to convince The World's Strongest Man to part with his hermetic and closely guarded formula for making his hair so strong he can use it to pull a bus? Well, why not? He does have an impressive mop, and surely such a secret might have a role to play in the development of post–cold war, national-defence strategies.

While Antonio is tanking up at the coffee counter, I begin to rehearse my "it's been swell but I gotta hit the road now" spiel. I've listened for more than an hour to what is plainly a well practised rant and feel that I know what it is to be a punching bag. I am completely enervated. I am flaccid and drained. I hear the words "sad and empty as a bereft belfry from which the bats have recently flown," and look around for Grenville, but he is nowhere to be found. A bad sign. When Kleiserisms surface in the absence of the master, you know you need a nap in the worst possible way. It's time to say goodbye, for there is nothing to be gained from lingering.

Such questions as I've tried to ask the Great Antonio during those rare spaces that opened up when he breached and gasped for air he has ignored or deflected with a wave of his paw. I think I get the picture, now. Strong man past his prime, grappling to come to terms with his present reality, anchored in the past, reliving his glory days, obsessed with his own record. In fact, he is not dissimilar from many men who are retired and struggle to find a way to reconcile their memorable then with their lacklustre now. I was reminded of a study I saw described somewhere, which had to do with a particularly male need for approval. Some scientists figured out how to lavish on rats the kinds of compliments only rats appreciate. They did this with a group of male rats and they did this with a group of female rats. The treatment went on long enough for rats of both sexes to get used to it, to like it, to think of it as the norm, to believe that life was just one big flattering banquet. Then, without warning or reason, the source of approval — whatever it was — was cauterized. The well-spring dried up. The rats no longer received external signs of approbation. And what happened? Well, the girls shrugged and got on with their lives. They looked within and found they had resources enough to adapt to the change. Not the boys, though. The boys languished. The boys got depressed. The boys thought that life wasn't worth living. I wouldn't be surprised to learn that some of them tried to enlist in experiments where they would be fed known carcinogens, if only to get it over with. If only to end the pain.

What can we extrapolate from this? How vast is the chasm between rat and man? Is the Great Antonio, "descending from extraterrestrial universal champion of the world," merely demonstrating a biological imperative when he saws so endlessly on his one-string fiddle? Does he just want reassurance that he is remembered, that he is still loved? There's nothing wrong with that. There's nothing wrong with that at all. And perhaps it's not so surprising that he chooses to dwell in the marble halls of his halcyon days. He trails a magnificent past, that's for sure, and God knows he worked hard for whatever rewards he has received, as any of the bus-pulling photos can attest. He worked hard with what he had, with strength, nerve, and more than a little gall. What did Liza Minnelli, Sophia Loren, Clint Eastwood, or Luciano Pavarotti think when this self-confessed scion of space creatures — who lists on his CV such accomplishments as "lifts 2 horses from the ground and kills many animals with his bare hands," and who claims in the same sentence to be a "dancing playboy" — muscled into their post-concert or film-festival parties and cosied up close for a photo opportunity? Doubtless they were surprised or amused, maybe even slightly alarmed, in the minute. An hour later, they'd have forgotten all about it. Another fan. Another photo. Ho-hum. None of them know, nor would they care, that the Great Antonio now carries around their smiling faces in his green garbage bag, and passes them out with indiscriminate abandon to total strangers in the Dunkin' Donuts on Beaubien.

When the Great Antonio returns to his seat, I begin to excuse myself, to make the usual "it was a pleasure" noises. I put Sophia and Liza and Clint and Johnny Carson into my bag. I stand to go and again extend my hand. This time he takes it, and I notice what very fine fingers he has. Huge, yes, but beautifully shaped and proportioned. They're smooth, too. Pianist fingers. Painter fingers. We shake, gravely, but when I try to reclaim my hand from his firm, firm grip, he doesn't let go. Instead, he gives a gentle tug. Gentle for him, that is. Gentle for a man who used to pull four buses and could still grind my bones to make his bread if he chose to. Which is the subtext of the gesture, I'm sure. *I am the GREAT Antonio and YOU are but a FEATHER! See?* He tugs, gently, and I am caught off guard, all balance is gone. Powerless to stop myself, I fall forward, or start to. I teeter. I totter. I am on my way to landing, squarely in the coffee spills and the doughnut crumbs, which would be an ignominious end to our meeting. There's a moment of giddy disequilibrium before I meet the resistance of his steadying hand, and he shoves me back in the contrary direction, just as gently as he had tugged me down, and lo and behold I am again on my feet. It is over in a second. No camera could have caught it, and for that I'm sorry. I would like to be able to send him a picture. I would like him to remember that once we met.

Still and Moving Images

My friends...expended much eloquence —
eloquence wasted in vain! —
in endeavouring to dissuade me
from a winter journey to Canada.
> — Anna Brownell Jameson, *Winter Studies and Summer Rambles in Canada*

Two days before I was scheduled to hit the road, when the stores were still teeming with post-Christmas bargain hunters, I was overtaken by the urgent need to acquire supplies for my journey. The simple act of packing had drawn my attention to some of the gaps in my readiness, and idle fantasizing about whatever perils might await me as I sailed over the edge of the world accounted for some of the perceived, and more far-fetched, oversights. While I stopped short of including on my "must get" list a barrel of salt cod and a score of limes, I saw with feverish clarity that I would certainly have to invest in more than just combination underwear if I hoped to incur a minimum of psychic and physical damage over my two-months voyage. The prospect and the dread of leaving behind all that was familiar somehow stripped me of the remembrance that this is a world where remote jungle tribes have Coke machines and Metallica T-shirts, and that therefore I would surely be able to find a tube of toothpaste or a stationer in, say, St. John's. Such are the fitful delusions that settle upon the anticipatory traveller, *as gently as the flower gives forth its perfume,* and it was under their influence that I sallied forth on my charger,

Acquisitive. There was much that I required. I was intent on finding notebooks of several sizes and configurations, as well as pens in many colours, figuring that I would devise some codified and efficient way of record-keeping that would make such an investment worthwhile. I had to seek out such toiletries as bath balms and moisturizers and exfoliants, so that I could keep ahead of the dead and flaking skin cells that are so much a part of our northern winter, particularly in the drier climes. I needed new gloves, and a good winter hat, one of those seen-at-the-Kremlin models with the ursine earflaps. I had to have boots, for heaven's sake, boots that would cushion my feet (with their resident plantar warts) from the treacherous ice and snow I knew I would find everywhere in abundance, and yet be stylish enough so as not to attract hateful stares if worn out for dinner on St-Denis. And then there was the suitcase! None of the five or six valises available to me at home had anything like the requisite number of pockets, compartments, straps, wheels, and there was no doubt in my mind that I would need a bag that was fully loaded with every option.

I cut a wide swath through a mall in downtown Vancouver, sucking up supplies with all the indiscriminate and merry abandon of a black hole with its first credit card. I was on the verge of heading home — already courting a hernia with the poundage of my purchases — when I passed a camera counter, and lingered just long enough for the persuasive salesman to send out his suctioning tentacles. Five minutes later, I was the proud owner of a Pentax Espio Jr. with AF Zoom, an autofocus window, a self-timer lamp, and an infinity landscape button. This camera is about the size of my kneecap and is fully twice as smart and self-actualized as I'll ever be. It adapts itself instantly to any light, any place, any situation, with no fuss, no fear, no flash. It is unfailingly honest, and demonstrates no inclination to stretch or completely realign the facts to suit its own purposes. It is what I hope to be when I grow up.

Why I allowed myself to be persuaded that this was a gadget without which I couldn't live another day, I can't say. Of course, there was every good reason to take along a camera on an excursion such as the one before me, and many advisers had told me that I must. On the other hand, my incompetence as a photographer is so pronounced and has so often been proven that it could almost be called a disability. Cameras have always been a mystery to me, and the capacity to peer through a lens, compose a photo, press a button, and come up with anything that looks even remotely like the intended subject simply does not live in me. Anyone unfamiliar with our world, and who might try to understand it by leafing through my albums, would surmise that the planet is populated by beings whose heads end at the eyebrows, and who are ghostly in their smudginess.

"I guarantee you," said the clerk to whom I had explained all this, as he rang up the Espio Jr., "that all you'll need to do with this little baby is point and shoot, and you'll have professional-quality pictures every time." So convincingly did he deliver this assertion, and with such an authentic air of *bonhomie*, and so completely had my brain given itself over to the particular dementia engendered by dallying too long at the Christmas-week sales, that I actually believed him. I remembered that salesman and his windy promises just a few days later, as I prepared for my point-and-shoot début. This was in Toronto's Mount Pleasant Cemetery, where, you will recall, I had gone to stand before the grave of Glenn Gould. The dead don't squirm, which is one of the qualities that recommend them to novice shutterbugs.

I sized up the headstone through the view-finder, and wondered how long it had taken the earliest photographers to start chasing after images that were either sexual or death-related: seaside bathing beauties showing a bit of cleavage; Auntie in her coffin with her hands folded over her breasts. And I thought of how sex and death are the active agents in every photograph: you smile for the camera, you seduce it, are seduced by it, then you freeze the moment, defeat time, live forever as you are. This cosmic and wide-ranging line of inquiry brought on a Zen-ish state, that white-hot purity of thought that presages transcendence. I began to feel I had attained a mystic oneness with Glenn, and that, when my film was developed, I would see not just the grave itself, but the translucent form of its most famous tenant, looking on with detached humour. Just as I was poised to click the shutter, and take what I hoped would be the first picture of many, the Espio leapt from my hands with Tosca-like élan and decisiveness, and plummeted to the snow. I'm very much afraid that I might have said "Fuck!" or something quite like it, right there on sacred ground and with all the dear departed lying round about, helpless to stop their ears. I picked up the Pentax, brushed it off, tried to blow the powder out of its crevices, and hoped against hope that no permanent damage had been done to its red eye–reduction flash button or zooming lever. The lens was completely misted over, but nonetheless I prepared to shoot a second time. Once again, the camera slipped — flew is more like it — from my hands. Now, I am fumble-fingered, but not so maladroit as all that. This was a ton-of-bricks message from the beyond, if ever I've received one. These were the spirits flipping me a bird. Back off, Mr. Paparazzi Man, they said in their loudest spirit voices. Back off and leave us in peace! And I did just that.

It was too late for the Espio, though, and in some ways it was too late for me. Mild, but irreversible, damage had been done. Certain claims had been laid. The fog never did relinquish its hold on the autofocus window. I never did assimilate the miracle that is the infinity landscape button. Nor was I ever able to shake the feeling, from that moment on, that I was travelling in the company of ghosts. There were times over the next couple of months, especially when I was driving, that I felt they were sitting beside me, distracting me from my autofocus, pointing me towards an infinity landscape.

I am exactly the sort of driver after whom the recruitment officers for Death and Son come running, their attaché cases bulging with offers of immediate and permanent employment, all the while touting the advantages of their generous benefits packages. I am exactly the sort of driver who, if he were inclined to use one of those automotive air fresheners, would look for the scent called "Whiffs of Mortality." I am exactly the sort of driver who shouldn't drive at all and who, for the most part, doesn't. It's not that I drive too fast, or drive too slow, or take unnecessary risks, or lean from the window to whistle at construction workers. No, I am a cautious driver, a courteous driver, a defensive driver. Above all, I am an aware driver: too aware for my own good.

Every time I get behind the wheel of a car I'm invaded by the oppressive certainty that I am a weak, mortal creature who is at the helm of an instrument of potential mass destruction. The question "what if?" is never far from the surface of my awareness. What if vital cables snap, what if a wheel becomes disengaged, what if a swarm of killer bees flies through the window? Such terrible apocalyptic visions as these occupy a corner of my eye, *like a dew-drop, ill-fitted to sustain unkindly shocks.* Even more likely than a mechanical foul-up is the momentary lapse of attention or a failure of the fallible flesh that will lead to a slaughter of the innocents. Children in school buses, babies in strollers, old people in wheelchairs, young lovers planning their weddings while enjoying a cappuccino in a sidewalk café: any of these are potential victims of the stroke or seizure or unstoppable sneezing fit or detached retina that might take me while I am in charge of a ton or two of sculpted metal, filled with litre upon litre of volatile liquid. What good would such prophylactic agents as a red light, a crossing guard, a two-inch curb do in such a circumstance? These things happen. They happen every day. Why take a chance? Walk, don't drive along Tranquillity Street, and happiness will be yours.

I had stupidly hoped that I would be able to make my dead-of-winter crossing of the country without recourse to the automobile. I imagined following a light-hearted, Kerouacian trajectory. I saw myself in the plush embrace of a Greyhound seat, chug-chug-chugging along two-lane country roads, admiring the picturesque farms and the pokey little villages, their red barns and tall steeples glimpsed across white, unsullied fields.

My predominant emotion would be wistfulness: kind of lonely, yet kind of not; kind of detached, yet kind of engaged. I would incline my head against the window, expel hot breath on the plexiglass, and write haiku in the mist. Delicious! Now and again, I would take one of my several notebooks and jot down something exquisite in a legible hand, something aphoristic and Kleiserian:

> Like a locomotive engine with unsound lungs
> Like a long arrow through the dark the train is darting
> Like a troop of boys let loose from school,
> the adventurers went by.

But I was wrong. Oh, how I was wrong. *Bienvenue au Canada*, land of impossible bus connections and no trains whatsoever. Once I was into the thick of it, a rental car proved the only sensible option. All the ghosts who trailed me clapped their insubstantial hands. They tumbled into the backseat. I turned the key. I drove. Someone — not I — took a few pictures. Shall we see the phantom slides? Lights please. Thank you. Begin.

CLICK

Oh. This is a good one, yes. I remember this very well. January 6, 1997. Sydney, Nova Scotia. If I look a little bleary-eyed, it's because I've just got off the ferry from Newfoundland. An all-nighter. Look at that weather! Execrable. Slush by the cupful from a dung-coloured sky. That's Mert, my cab driver. He's taking me to the car-rental place. Mert's radio is blaring. It has to be loud because he's deaf, or getting that way. The announcer reads a chilly litany of school closures, event cancellations.

"I guess the driving's going to be pretty bad on the highway."

"Eh?"

"I said — I GUESS THE DRIVING'S GOING TO BE PRETTY BAD!"

"Ah, no. Piece of cake! Take 'er easy and you'll be fine!"

Mert squints through the woolly blanket of sleet, notices a stop sign, tries to brake, and sails right on through.

"Whoops! Guess I've forgotten how to drive in this stuff. I've just moved back from California."

"What were you doing in California?"

"Eh?"

"IN CALIFORNIA! WHAT WERE YOU DOING?"

"Tuning pianos. What's your name?"

"Bill."

"Eh?"

I look out at the harbour and think about Bill Jamieson, a local man whom I never met, but of whom I've read, and who has very recently gone to his reward. He took part in a New Year's Day "polar bear swim," and the sad aftermath was reported in the St. John's *Evening Telegram*.

"Bill Jamieson, 65, was one of 29 people who dunked themselves in the harbor at nearby South Bar in –7 degree temperatures watched by more than 1000 people.

"Jamieson stepped out of the water, went to his truck, got dressed and drove to the local firehall before he collapsed behind the wheel. Attempts to revive him failed and he was pronounced dead in hospital and his body released.

"Eddie MacDougall was with his friend when they went into the water near South Bar wharf where the waters were relatively calm....

"'I have no doubt in my mind it is the way he wanted to go,' said MacDougall."

"So, Phil, what brings you to Cape Breton?"

"I'm writing — I'M WRITING A BOOK ABOUT ECCENTRICS!"

"Ha! Like who?"

"Like a man — A MAN WHO COLLECTS SHRUNKEN HEADS!"

"No kidding? Who's that?"

"BILL JAMIESON!"

"Bill Jamieson. Bill Jamieson. Where've I heard that name before?"

Here we are in Bill Jamieson's apartment. This Bill Jamieson, unlike the other, still maintains his flesh-and-blood status. He's in his early forties, and he lives in downtown Toronto, and we're going to look at his shrunken heads, of which he has a dozen or so. First, take a gander around these rooms. Gorgeous, no? Such deep colours, these golds, these reds. Such eclecticism, so much stuff! A Tamara de Lempicka print, a big carved mahogany palm tree (from some night club in Cuba, apparently), and many beautiful Art Deco pieces, including a sideboard for which I'd give up a kidney, lamps, statues, mirrors, a collection of microphones that make for very unusual accent pieces. All that gilt and chrome, all those sleek lines that are so much a product of a highly rarefied and European sensibility achieve a surprising homogeneity with his various jungle artifacts: the leopard skins, the zebra rug, the elephant foot, the tribal masks, the ostrich. Bridging the gap between the Deco pieces and the shrunken heads (we're getting there, be patient!) is the funerary collection. There's a coffin (again!) in the hallway; there's a grotesque dagger with a human hip joint for a handle; and in the bedroom, affixed to the wall, is the back end of a Victorian hearse, ingeniously adapted to serve as a salt-water aquarium. That's a pretty angel fish that dangles dead centre, all languorous and calm, not a care in the world, hanging as though suspended by a silken thread, hanging as easily as might a shrivelled head from the belt of an Amazonian tribesman.

"Different cultures hunted heads for different reasons," Bill will gladly tell you, "but for the most part, they were trophies. You can see why. They're light and easy to carry and everybody has one."

Had one, anyway. There's no denying their portability: by the hair; by the ears; or bowling ball–style, with your fingers inserted into nostrils and mouth. Truth be told, you'd have a hard time getting an index finger or thumb into these mouths, as they have been stitched shut, crudely, after the fashion of the day. Let's move in for a closer look. There, you can see them, the heads that is, daydreaming under their bell jars. They are about the size of and about as wizened as last fall's potatoes. You can lift up the glass if you'd like. Be prepared for a light and musty odour, an earthy, cellarish, old-potato smell. This is so different from the smell of Bill's Egyptian mummy head, which is thousands of years old, and is still lightly scented with the spices used in its embalming. Be informed that all these *objets de mort* are the real thing, not some fun-house knock-offs. You have to be careful, when you're in the market for shrunken heads especially, not to be taken in by the fakes, of which there are plenty out there. Do you want to know a sure way of distinguishing a real shrunken head from a bogus one? The nose hair. You just can't fake the nose hair.

Bill Jamieson became interested in head-hunting culture when he went to the Amazon on a kind of Carlos Castaneda pursuit of a powerful herbal hallucinogen called *ayahuasca*. It is ingested as part of the spiritual observances of the Jivaro tribe, in Ecuador. *Ayahuasca* opens the door from this world to the next, and the next, and the next. It is apparently dynamite stuff. Bill immersed himself in Jivaro lore, learning about the tribe's unstinting ferocity, and its reputation for nicking the heads of enemies at the slightest provocation. Such larceny was outlawed in the twenties, but is said to have been carried out until much more recently. Bill, who was touched by this, began to collect his heads after he returned to Toronto. He placed a discreet ad in the paper. It said something like "Authentic Shrunken Heads Wanted." The phone began to ring. His head-hunting career was under way.

Each of the heads is different. Wrinkled and stitched and stunned as they are, you can get a sense of individuality of appearance. Something lingers of happier days in the humid rain forest. Most of these relics have brown skin in common, and all of them look surprised. Taken aback. This is especially true of the one blotchy and pale-skinned model. He is a man who looks to have had Celtic antecedents. His moustache is red, and there is something about the whole set of his countenance that suggests he just can't believe this is happening to him. Him! Of all people! Why did they never warn him about such an eventuality when he was at Eton? Mommy will be so upset! Daddy will be — WHACK!

CLICK

What a lucky boy I am! Bill Jamieson gave me this T-shirt as I was leaving his place. That's me, modelling it. Pardon? Yes, I know a day or two at the gym wouldn't be time misspent, thank you very much for pointing it out. The front of the shirt is decorated with a shrunken head. On the back is the recipe:

Beheading
The warrior cut off his enemy's head with a lance as close to the shoulders as possible.

Removal of the Skull
He cut a vertical slit at the back of the head and peeled the skin from the skull. The eyes, lips, and back of the neck were then sewn shut.

Shrinking
He soaked and simmered the boneless head in a pot of hot chichipi plant juice for about 2 hours, reducing it to about one third of its natural size.

Drying and Hardening
He placed hot rocks in the head cavity while he smoothed the face with a small stone to preserve its natural proportions. He filled the cavity with hot sand when the head and neck became too small for stones to complete the drying process.

Blackening
He suspended the head in the smoke of a fire all night.

Polishing

He washed the hair and rubbed the skin with a cloth to make it shine.

Apparently, the whole operation took about twenty hours from beginning to end. Should you care to try it sometime, you might be interested in these complementary instructions for cooking brain, which appear in the aforementioned *SAS Survival Guide*: "Skin head and boil, simmering for ninety minutes. Strip all flesh from the skull including the eyes, tongue and ears. Blood: collect in a container and leave covered until a clear liquid comes to the top. When separation seems complete drain it off. Dry the residue by the fire to form a firm cake. Use to enrich soups and stews."

And now you know.

CLICK

What? Another picture of me? This was also taken on Cape Breton Island. I'm on my way to Cheticamp, and have stopped to stretch my legs by the side of the road. The car is a white Mystique, which is fitting for one of my colour and sensibility. I'm looking skyward because I'm counting crows. One crow for sorrow, two for joy, three for a wedding, four for a boy, five for silver, six for gold, seven crows a secret, never to be told. Which is fine and dandy as far as it goes. But what about eight? What does that get you? Eight crows a cream puff? Eight crows a lay-off notice? Eight crows a flat tire, a bad cold, a runny omelette, a wooden nickel? Eight crows a shin splint? If there's anything of prognosticatory value to be wrung from counting crows, eight is the number I need, since there is an octave of the birds (just the black keys) perched in their formal attire along the utility wire that runs parallel to the highway, near the field where Joe Delaney's scarecrows are hibernating.

In the summer, they would never be so bold, those crows, not when the field is full of scary totems, more than a hundred scarecrows, some in rags, some in tags, some dressed as Marilyn Monroe. Joe Delaney, who was well known in the Cheticamp area as a *bon vivant*, a community organizer, and as the janitor at the high school, put up a few scarecrows in 1984, just as a way of diverting birds from a vegetable patch. They attracted the attention of passers-by, who would stop to talk, which appealed to Joe's gregarious nature. The next year, he planted a whole garden of scarecrows, with stuffed-stocking faces and decked out in a wild array of Sally Ann chic, each bearing a card stating the character's name and occupation. Word of his enterprise spread. Tourists began to flock. There were more than 18,000 visitors in 1986.

Then came the massacre. "Le massacre de 1986." Vandals came in the night. They unseamed the scarecrows from stem to stern, from nave to chops. They left the field strewn with parts. Incomprehensible! "They really did it dirty," remembers Joe's daughter, Ethel. "The only one who was left standing was a scarecrow called Rory. For a while, our father was very discouraged. But he began to get messages of support from all over the world. So, he decided to rebuild. He was inspired by Rory. Rory lead the charge."

Joe Delaney died on February 7, 1996. Ethel and her brothers decided to keep up the scarecrow field, as a tribute to their father, and to stick with their father's free-admission policy. But it's a lot of work. They make nothing from it, and there is considerable outlay. How long can it go on, one wonders, without the singular devotion of the man whose odd inspiration it was?

CLICK

A brief detour here for a cautionary tale. We are in the Humber Heights district of Cornerbrook, Newfoundland, standing inside what is left of the Sticks and Stones House. This small bungalow was Clyde Farnell's castle and fantasy world. It was his recreation. It was his oblique pathway to reconciliation.

Mr. Farnell was born in 1919 and died around the time of

the scarecrow massacre. For many years, his life was circum-
scribed by the ordinary. He was a married man with five children.
He was a worker, with jobs on the railway and as a carpenter.
In his spare time he sketched and painted, as many will. He was
a foot-soldier in the army of the day-to-day, marching, marching, and all the while, something was simmering. The lid blew
off the pot in the mid-sixties after the death of his wife, Leta.
When he was on his own, everything began to change. Perhaps
it stopped mattering to him what people might think. Perhaps
he woke up one morning and understood that names would
never hurt him. As if to prove it, he began gathering sticks and
stones. Using these as design elements, he undertook a wholesale transformation of his home environment.

The stones were pebbles, culled from the beach. The sticks,
which were the most conspicuous element of his new household
aesthetic, were once the spines of Popsicles. Over the years, he
used hundreds of thousands of Popsicle sticks to line the walls
of his house. He would pay neighbourhood children some nom-
inal amount to gather them up and bring them to him. Then, he
cut them, shaped them, and arranged them in various patterns.
The basic effect was that of a mosaic. When they were burnished
a tawny gold, it was a sight to behold. He began to add on layers, arranging sticks on sticks in floral patterns, geometric
shapes, and star clusters. These he painted a variety of shades.
The pebbles were incorporated into his stick configurations,
and used throughout the house to provide a granular texture.

I like to think of him placing the very first stick, think of
him standing back to study the result, and understanding that
yes, yes, it would work. The die was cast. There was nothing for
him to do but press on. When the foundation of sticks was laid,
Mr. Farnell proceeded to cover almost every square inch of that
corrugated foundation with something of his own creation:
paintings, collages, found objects. There were nautical scenes
and forest scenes, there were many, many renderings of flowers.
Often they were relief pieces, three-dimensional, incorporating
all manner of found objects, from matchsticks to hub-caps,

from busted spectacles to shell casings. Some of the pieces, the paintings in particular, were magnificent pieces of folk art, whimsical and altogether original. When they were all hung in one smallish dwelling — and there were thousands vying for space on the wall — it must have been dizzying to survey, and for some years, the Sticks and Stones House was a popular tourist attraction in Cornerbrook.

Sadly, the family was unable to maintain it for many years after Mr. Farnell's death. They just couldn't keep up with the maintenance and the staffing requirements, and so closed the house and broke up the collection. Now, there is hardly anything left. The bathroom is still more or less intact, and it is a thing of such weird beauty that it breaks your heart to think of what has been lost.

It breaks your heart to think of Mr. Farnell, working out what I suppose to have been his deeper purpose. He was blinded in one eye by a flying Popsicle stick when he was a child. In the subsequent years, he had ample time to reflect on what he had lost, to sift through the layers of anger, regret, resignation. I like to think that what he did in his home was to find a constructive way to bend his oppressor and assailant to his will. He built a palace of Byzantine splendour from dangerous dross. It was more reconciliation than revenge. The innocuous wand that plucked out his eye is not destroyed but transformed, and made to please the eye that remains. That the tangible record of Clyde Farnell's obsession, his one-of-a-kind inventiveness, the key to his secret oddness, has been removed from us is a terrible thing. It is not his family's fault, of course. They are living people with practical needs and concerns. But someone should have done something. Someone should have had both eyes open. Someone should have seen.

CLICK

Back to Cape Breton and Joe Delaney's field. A scarecrow's work is seasonal. When summer's done and the tourists disperse, their job is over. A period of hiatus ensues. This is a picture of the metal trailer where they come to sleep, huddled together in this rude shed. Huddled together all winter along, against the wind, a tangle of fabric and stocking and stick. Huddled together, while, outside, the harsh crows bark and palaver. Nine of them now. Nine crows a murder.

If ever there came a time, during their long hibernation, when these loony effigies would want to spring to life, it would be at Lent. In this part of the world, the solemn weeks leading up to Easter are broken by an observance called *mi-câreme*, that is, "midway through Lent." At *mi-câreme*, all the fasting and introspection of that austere season is set aside for a carnival night. People dress up, as at Hallowe'en. They go from house to house. They drink, they dance, they carry on. The object is to keep your identity hidden. The object is to kick up your heels. The object is to thumb your nose at the sacred, to confound propriety. It's purely pagan. It's purely fun, and Joe Delaney's scarecrows have a part to play.

Visitors from away, who come to see them in their summertime field, will be charmed by that unlikely congregation. The crazy hats, the fright wigs, the hobo clothes will make people chuckle and reach for their cameras. But Joe also intended his genial dummies as *mi-câreme* symbols. They have more on their stocking-stuffed minds than frightening crows. In fact, they are dressed up for the express purpose of going door to door as *mi-câreme* celebrants. They are reminders that we require the profane to remember the sacred; that in the midst of all that is holy, you must be ready to invite the devil into your house for a dance. Make him dizzy with a fast spin around the floor, and then send him packing. Joe's scarecrows have a transcendent purpose. They are symbolic, a present reminder of tradition and custom. And we all know how fragile a thing tradition can be in the absence of such touchstones.

Now they doze. Chances are they'll sleep right through *mi-câreme*. And in the spring, when the ground has thawed, Joe's kids will resurrect them, and plant them firmly in the earth.

They have to be well anchored, or they will fall victim to one of the area's dependable vandals, the wind.

In Canada we aren't much given to christening our winds. We content ourselves with generic terms like "squall" or "storm" and leave to others such lovely words as "mistral" or "hubbub"; "libeccio" or "Ox's Eye." Here, in this part of Cape Breton, the wind has a such a personality, they've claimed it with a name. It is *le suete*, so called because it blows from the south east: *le sud-est*. *Suete* is pronounced as "sweat." A hard-scrabble word for a hard-scrabble place. This is a wind that foments its revolutions in the dips and whorls of the worn-down hills. It uses them like the tubing in a brass instrument to pitch its frigid ululations. In the wintertime, it can stampede over the rise at speeds of over 250 kilometres an hour. Houses have to be built against its tantrums, with double shingling, with no windows giving onto the southeast. Even so, from time to time, one will blow right off its foundation and be tumbled down a hill. There's a terrible beauty in such a blow, to be sure, and I am thrilled to think I am experiencing it firsthand as I prepare to make my way south. A great howling wind is careening through Cheticamp, tearing over the fields and around the House of Sleeping Scarecrows.

"Is this *le suete*?" I ask the gas-station attendant, who laughs and laughs. How could I mistake this tickling breeze for that cold slug in the chops? How could I look at a midget and see such a giant? No, no, no, this is not a wind, not a wind at all! I ought to have been around last week! That was when there was a wind!

The story of my life to date: a week too early, or a week too late. In spite of his derision, I can't believe this is the puniest wind he's ever known. Look how it blows the snow! It rattles the car as I pull away from the pump. A trash can is being tossed along the street. The wind has even driven away the crows. Nine have become none. No. Wait. Not quite. There's one, hurling herself against the gale. One crow sorrow. Surely not! Don't let this be the case! In the name of Joe and Rory and the *mi-câreme*, in the name of the hibernating scarecrows, in the name of all that is good and all that is pagan, don't let it end with sorrow! I scan the sky and find another, far across the field, it is true, flying out to sea, but visible nonetheless. It is flying out to sea, where it will bring some mariner bad luck if it passes over his bow. He will look up and see just one crow, and head back to port. But for now, there are two crows and they are mine. Two crows joy. I give my attention to the highway. For the time being, I am through with the sky. It has told me as much as I need to hear or know.

CLICK

The white Mystique can't go on forever, and that is a lesson most of us in the middle class in this country could stand to learn, as the century winds down. I left my Mystique in Halifax. In Ottawa, I picked up a black Cavalier. "Would you like a black Cavalier, Mr. Richardson?" they asked me at the rental place, and believe you me, I had to bite my tongue.

Just the day before, I'd been in Montreal. It was a Sunday, a very cold and windy afternoon, and I'd slipped my way along the rutted, icy roads of the Cimetière Notre-Dame-des-Neiges in Montreal. There was no one in particular I cared to find. I'd simply had one of those hankerings only a graveyard visit will satisfy. Stung by the wind and defeated by the dreadful condition of the pathways, I took shelter in the foyer of the administrative offices, and availed myself of their CD-ROM information services. Post-modern death is a marvel of convenience. The curious passer-by can take a digitized tour of the new mausoleum (accompanied by Handelian music that is aptly funereal), or check into the cost of burial, or locate any extant grave by punching in the name of the tenant. Self-indulgent as always, I looked to see if there were any Bill or William Richardsons on the register. Delighted to find there was none, and thinking I might one day be the first, I printed out the price list. "Cremation done in the presence of the family — $165.00." A bargain! Why, so scant a sum would hardly buy you dinner out. Eternity at Notre-Dame-des-Neiges! An attractive and affordable option. One could do worse, and that's for sure.

Here's the thing. Spend too much time consorting with Death's many concubines, and he thinks you want to be numbered among them. After all, there's always room for one more in his harem. Now, advance the clock, two weeks hence. The picture is of another Sunday drive. Coming down from Sudbury, I stop in Parry Sound for lunch, the one open restaurant, all pub food. I order up the "suicide wings," get back in the black Cavalier, head in the direction of Gravenhurst. I listen to a tape, Shawn Colvin's *A Few Small Repairs*. The roads are slippery, a consequence of the thaw-and-freeze syndrome, as well as freezing rain. I drive slowly, pass through the village of Beatrice, and start to think of Dante. Halfway down the road of life. Lost in a dark wood. Abandon hope all ye who enter here. All that shit. Shawn Colvin is singing "Suicide Alley." I give a little belch, enjoy a gaseous memory of lunch, and the phrase "spread your suicide wings" rises up from the brain's tight folds. I chuckle at the melodrama of it all, to say nothing of the idea of going to Gravenhurst in a rental car. Grave in Hertz. It's all too perfect! Who arranges these things? I press on the brakes while approaching a curve, steer too wide, and the rear end of the Cavalier catches in some slush on the shoulder. A law of motion asserts itself and the car chucks itself into the opposite lane, mercifully nothing oncoming, then back, mercifully nothing behind, then half spins around, then whirls in the opposite direction, seems to pick up speed in spite of my braking. I am asking myself, what is the rule, what is the rule, is it steer into or away from the spin? But neither seems to work, the Cavalier is only going faster, there is nothing but motion and a noise which is the sound of treaded rubber on ice, sand, salt, asphalt, and someone's voice calling out "Jesus!" and the car is hurtling off the road, a crazy trajectory, a second's suspension as it takes to the air and then smashes itself starboard into an enveloping drift, and there is nothing but white against the windshield, nothing but the gunning of the engine as it tries to regain its primacy, the ferocious roar of the two front wheels, spinning, spinning, throwing up the snow. Shawn is still singing, wry and unconcerned. I find the key. Even when the engine is extinguished, the roar lingers in the air a second or two. An echo. Shock, manifesting itself sonically. A howl from some dark quarter. And then — peace. Peace. In less than a minute, I will be standing on the road, waving down a minivan, noting how I missed smashing into the guard rail by mere inches. In an hour I will be at my hotel, and able to appreciate more fully than ever before the beauties of the phrase "came out of it without a scratch." Even the black Cavalier will be unscarred. But in the moment, there is only this deep quiet, only this vista that is nothing but white. A few months from now, I will attribute the fact that I can write down this story to pure, dumb luck, to random rescue. But in the moment, it is like looking at a landscape of mercy, like gazing into the still and blameless heart of something I could never bring myself to believe in, and never hope to again. Our Lady of the snows. Notre-Dame-des-Neiges.

CLICK

Which were the winter roads they drove? Where did they think to go? How can you follow the black Cavalier who leaves no tracks in the snow? Never a track and never a trace to show he was there or here, and none can travel as far as fast as the coal-black Cavalier. No one. Nowhere. No how. Not you. Not me. Not the Great Antonio, with his extraterrestrial connections. Not even Alexis Lapointe could outpace him, and it was his celerity that won him celebrity. Alexis was as much horse as he was man. Or, so they said. Running was so much his game that he was known far and wide as "Alexis Le Trotteur." He was the *surcheval*, the superhorse of La Malbaie. He was said to have had the legs of a horse, with knees and hips that were jointed like a horse's. He had the heart of a horse, the lungs of a horse, the tongue of a horse. He smelled like a horse, and he cantered like a horse. When he was preparing to run, he would throw back his head and he would whinny like a horse. He had a whip with which he would administer a purposeful self-flagellation. When he had heated his chevaline juices to a near boil, when he had worked himself into a good old froth, he would break into a gallop and run like the wind, covering huge distances in a single stride, never flagging, scarcely touching the ground, like Poppy, the Flying Horse of the North, who was his mane-bearing alter ego. He ran against men who were on foot and on bicycle, and he won. He ran against horses, the fastest and best, and he won. Why, he even outpaced Roger Savard's famous grey horse in a race over the ice. The snow was no impediment to him. Once, he ran fourteen miles over winter roads, whinnying all the way, covering the distance in just thirty-five minutes, and all for the sake of fetching a forgotten fiddle so a fête could begin. In true Paul Bunyan fashion, he was able to win contests against trains, speeding alongside, and dashing in front of them, laughing and careless, with hardly a bead of sweat weighing down his withers. That kind of hubris exacts its wages. It was a locomotive that took him out, when he was sixty-five. Some say he was clipped while making one of his intrepid, daredevil cross-overs, and tripped mid-canter on a railway tie. The more credible story is that he was loping across a railway bridge, in man-mode, and didn't hear the approach of the engine until it was too late. Both versions converge on the outcome. His legs were severed and he died a few hours later, his horse-coloured blood drained into the snow, his ghost limbs churning, churning, and the black Cavalier breathing hard down his neck.

Alexis Le Trotteur died in January 1924. Four years later, and more than a thousand miles to the west, Letitia J. Reed joined her twenty-seven classmates and their teacher in a photographer's studio. Ready ladies? Smile!

CLICK

Thank you. This will be our last slide. May I draw your attention to the figure who sits smack dab in the middle, the matron with the rounded edges. That would be the teacher. She's in her mid-forties, or so I'd guess. Her name is Mrs. Johnston. Some of the girls who surround her — the worker bees clustered about the queen — are called Viola, Olga, Phyllis, Pauline, Olive, Tessie, Okie, Lillie, and Hatley. They have left Estevan, Indian Head, North Battleford, Swift Current, and other little Saskatchewan towns and farms; have said goodbye to their families and friends and struck out on their own, putting their girlhoods behind them. They have come to Regina, come to the capital to be formed. They have come for vocational training.

The Graduating Class of the Marvel School of Cosmetology, 1928.

How old are they? Young, for the most part. Sixteen. Seventeen. They are young, but not frivolous. No, they are foresightful and cautious. They are not counting on anything: not counting on inheriting the farm, not counting on the death of a rich aunt that comes in good time, not counting on finding some man who will tend to their needs. They have come here to prepare themselves as best they can for whatever curves life — and their lives stretch on and on before them — might throw.

They are young, but they already haul behind them the ponderous weight of ambition and disappointment. Of course they
do. You can't live even so short a time as they without having
your heart broken at least once, without knowing the forward
impetus that comes from mourning or regret. You can't live that
long without catching a glimmer of what you might be, if you
just have the nerve to seize the chance when it comes along. The
turf that lies between heartbreak and hope is fertile. That is the
ground they have come to Regina to till. Now, after months of
hard work, they have arrived. They are the ladies of the graduating class of the Marvel School of Cosmetology, freshly minted
experts in hairdressing and beauty culture, fully equipped and
qualified to go into the world and practise haircutting, sham-
pooing, marcelling, and permanent waving. "December 13, 1928.
Photog. appt. 11.00. Wear whites!" That might have been the
note Letitia wrote to herself in her daybook. December 13,
1928, is the date on a diploma that swears, in a fine calligraphic
hand, that she has satisfied the requirements of Marvel's "Beauty
Course Complete."

Oh, the Marvel girls! Look at them, wise and vestal virgins,
priestesses of Venus, all dressed in their blameless acolyte robes,
with their hair marcelled to a fare-thee-well, and little kiss-curls
punctuating their foreheads just above their pencilled brows.
They are the fulfilment of prophecies set down long ago in
Kleiser's Holy Book.

Her cheeks are like the blushing cloud
Her eyes, glimmering star-like in her pale face
Her lashes like fans upon her cheek
Her little lips are tremulous as brook-water is
Her skin was as the bark of birches
Her two white hands, like swans on a frozen lake

All the days of the months just gone have been leading up to
this moment. They know one another so well, know the con-
tours of every classmate's face: the plane of cheekbone, the arc of

brow, the droop of chin, the faint line of moustache, the shadow of a nose. They have been one another's guinea pigs. They have willingly surrendered themselves, to one another, to a Platonic ideal, to the suffering that is the midwife of beauty. They came as disciples. Now they are apostles, with a mission. With a gospel to spread. They are the Marvel girls, and they will never forget it. It is 1928, and they are primed and eager to stride out into the dangerous world, the jazz world, the talking-picture world, the flapper world, the nothing-is-impossible world. Their autograph books are full of fond and hopeful inscriptions.

> A half a yard of Georgia crêpe
> A facial and a curl
> Chiffon stockings, eyes that lure,
> Behold! The Marvel girl!

What would they have thought had they looked over their shoulders and seen what was tearing along to catch them up: the dust bowl, the drought, the Depression?

> Choose not your friends from outward show
> For the feathers float and the pearls lie low.

What would the Marvel girls have thought, as they arranged themselves in their ranks in that studio; as they perched on the tiered benches, on that December day, in that overheated room, the air electric with static charge and thick with the grime that had settled over the years on the plush draperies, the trailing, trellised plants that were the photographer's dependable backdrop; what would they have thought as they engaged the camera, as they inhaled the several subtle scents of one another's talcum, or rose-water spray; what would they have thought had they known that one day their portrait would finish up in an antique store on Main Street in Vancouver; that it would come into the hands of a complete stranger who would fall in love with them, who would spend much, much more time than he properly ought, looking into their soft and frozen faces; who would invent their lives?

(See the sweet-faced girl with the long raven hair flipped at the shoulders? She almost failed to get her qualification because she missed two weeks of classes after her father hanged himself in the barn. She had to work hard to catch up when she came back. Nail care she found especially difficult. She just couldn't wrap her mind around nail care.

The girl kneeling on the bear-skin rug? She would tell her landlady she was going out for a malted and all the time she was sneaking into speakeasies. Only last night she caught the eye of a visiting bootlegger with important Mob connections, and she'll be living in Chicago before the year is out.

The two plump girls seated behind the speakeasy moll have formed a special attachment and they think they might go off to Paris together. If not Paris, somewhere, anywhere that's not here. When you have a pot of rouge and you can give a permanent wave, the waves will part before you.

The tall girl, standing on the left, the one with the crimped-up locks, will become a nun, will forswear all vanity, will take her vows in a firm, steadfast voice, but will secretly paint her toenails different colours — red, pink, coral, magenta, turquoise — will do so all her life, and no one will find out until 1981, when she dies at the age of seventy-six, and the removal of her shoes will start the breath of scandal wafting through the convent.

And the heavy-set girl who stands in the third row, at the extreme right of the photograph, the practical-looking young woman who seems to keep herself to herself? She's the one whose name no one could remember. She's the one at whom the photographer took one look and fell in love.)

Cows like apples
Pigs like squash
I like you, Hatley,
I do, by gosh.

Viola, Olga, Phyllis, Pauline, Olive, Tessie, Okie, Lillie, and Hatley. I know their names because Letitia noted them on the back of the photograph. She must have done so in her old age, not long before her death, not long before her goods would be parcelled up and sold at an estate sale, which was how she and her sisters came into my care and keeping. She must have done so in her old age when her memory was failing her and many names had been sundered from faces, as only half the girls are identified. Of course, Letitia did not inscribe her own name. Modesty forbade. Besides, what would have been the point in pointing herself out? She knew perfectly well who she was.

> Any girl would be gay
> In a classy coupé
> In a taxi they all can be jolly.
> But the regular girl
> Is the one who can smile
> While you're taking her home in a trolley.

Which is Letitia? Where is she sitting? Standing? Did she seek out the comfort of the centre? Or did she draw her strength from the edge? It's the girls on the margins I wonder about most, the girls who lean away from the firm but gentle hand, the kindly governance of Mrs. Johnston; who seek to enliven her tried-and-true prescription for beauty with their own saucy combinations. I wonder especially about the siren seated on the far left, at the very end of the second row. Her sceptical glance, her haughty demeanour, her been-around-the-block look that says "Don't give me that watch-the-birdie crap, mister, I've seen your kind before, I've got your number, and your birdie just ain't worth watching!"

I love her two kiss-curls, like tiny, crumpled horns. Check out the Clara Bow mouth, the gypsy hoops that are her earrings, and that gold chain around her neck. From whom was it a gift? What does she remember when she puts it on? She is angled away from the group. She cannot wait for this to be over.

She cannot wait for this suffocation to end, for her life to begin. Her heart is rattling the bars of its cage. It is too big to be contained by convention, by expectation. Her suitcase is packed. She has set it down just out of camera range. As soon as she hears the shutter snap, she will be out the door. Before the others have stopped blinking from the flash, she will have disappeared.

> In the garden of your friendship
> Keep a warm and sunny spot
> Where my fondest wish may blossom
> It is this — forget-me-not.

Years later, Letitia would look back at the Marvel girls. She would remember how she chased Clara Bow (that is what she will call her, in the absence of a name) out of the studio when she saw how she had left her autograph book lying on the floor. She ran after her, into the snowy December street, called Clara! Clara! But Clara only stopped to light a cigarette. She tossed the match over her shoulder and never looked back. Letitia watched as she receded into the future, watched the relentless retreat of her muskrat coat, her seamed stockings, her battered valise, her pert little bob; watched until she turned the corner, and that was the end of her. She left no forwarding address. She never turned up for the reunions. Letitia would sometimes dream of her, of Clara, and in her dreams she was walking, always walking. Clara walking, brisk and purposeful, but with no destination in mind. Walking through the world as if she owned it. Walking as if she were born to it. Walking as if she didn't care that the girls all talked about her when they realized she was gone. Who did she think she was? Little Miss All the Nerve! Little Miss High and Mighty! Little Miss Vanish Into Thin Air! Why, she didn't even trouble to sign my book, and after all that time I spent on her cuticles!

> Think of us now
> Think of us ever

Think of the gang
We are Marvel, forever.

"Ready ladies? Smile!"

CLICK

And then, it was done. Then, it was over. Then, she was gone.

The Forest Primeval

This is the forest primeval; but where are the hearts...
— Longfellow, "Evangeline"

Clara was not alone. In 1928, Lillian Alling — pronounced "ailing" — was likewise walking. One foot in front of the other, for 5,000 miles. Walking, walking, never balking, merrily on she rolled.

"Lillian Alling, steadfast, unfailing, where does your garden grow?" That was what the lonely telegraph linesmen demanded of her as she hiked past their cabins, through the dense British Columbia forest, as fixed on the north as any compass.

"Siberia" was her answer.

"Where are you off to, miss?" asked the police when they stopped her from travelling in the deep-snow country of the Bulkley Valley, alone in the dead of winter.

"Siberia! Let me go. Let me go. I am going to Siberia."

At the New York Public Library, they had been no less incredulous when she told them her plan.

"You want to walk where?"

The librarian was certain she had misheard, or had not been able to make out the request through the young woman's Eastern European accent. Was she Russian? Polish?

"Siberia," answered Lillian, a little too loudly. "Siberia," she whispered, and she carried every available map to the long, varnished table in the hushed reference room. She spread them out. She took out her pencil and notebook. She began to plot her route.

She left New York in the spring of 1927. What was she leaving behind? The throbbing metropolis. Her job as a maid. The usual disappointments. She never said why she turned her back on the bustle and the promise of the city, never said why she had come there in the first place. Adventure, let's suppose. Rumour. Because it was there.

"Siberia" was the answer she gave to anyone who asked as she walked west. Through Chicago, St. Paul, up to Winnipeg, and west across the prairies. Thirty miles a day she walked, in her simple brown skirt and shirt, her sensible boots. If she sang "Val-da-ree, Val-da-rah" as she walked with her knapsack on her back, no one thought to write it down. "Siberia" was Lillian Alling's constant refrain as she walked, through the foothills, over the mountains, all the way to Vancouver. Then she veered north, bearing straight for the Bering Strait. She followed the Cariboo Wagon Road, walked through Ashcroft, Hundred Mile House, 150 Mile House, Quesnel, Prince George, New Hazelton, and Hazelton. She was a thousand miles south of Dawson when she joined up with the telegraph line. Imagine the surprise of the linesmen who heard "Siberia" when she turned up at their cabin doors, thin, ragged, and on fire with determination. Of course she was mad. Why else would she do such a thing? She had to be stopped, she had to be reported, at least. The police were summoned. Questions were asked.

"What do you eat?"

"Berries. Bark."

"Why do you carry that iron bar?"

"Protection."

"Against animals?"

"Against men."

"Where are you going, miss?"

"Siberia."

They took her in. For her own good, they said, they sent her back to Vancouver. She spent a couple of months in jail, serving a sentence for vagrancy. On her release, she got a kitchen job in a restaurant. Spring came, and she put on her walking boots. By mid-July 1928, she was back in Smithers. This time, she would not be deterred.

Lillian Alling followed the line, and the telegraph messages scuttled above her. Telegraph Creek, Sheslay, Nahlin, Nakina, Pike River, Atlin, Carcross, Whitehorse, Fort Selkirk. When she reached Dawson, early in October, she was wearing a different style of men's shoe on each foot. She wintered there. She got a job, slinging hash. She bought a boat and fixed it up. She waited for the thaw. Sometimes, during the twenty-two-hour nights, the northern lights would sing, and Lillian would join in the chorus. Siberia. Siberia.

In the spring of 1929, she launched her skiff and set off up the Yukon River. She was 1,600 miles from the Bering Sea. And that is where her story peters out. There were rumours that she was seen pushing a two-wheeled cart, somewhere near Teller, Alaska. There were rumours that she was apprehended by authorities on the other side. Nothing is known for sure, though. Some say she was homesick, inhabited by a desperate longing for her family, country, language. Some say she was driven half-mad by a love that went wrong. She offered no explanation other than Siberia. When all is said and done, the only certainty is that one day she set out walking.

For a while she had a dog, Bruno. One of the linesmen gave him to her as a guardian and gift. He was a pack dog, and she loved him, but he drank from a poisoned stream and died. It broke her heart. She had him skinned and tanned, and when last she was seen, she was carrying Bruno — who was beyond cure but nonetheless cured — with her, schlepping his pelt on her back. Lillian Alling, what was she trailing, what did she have to show? Her tattered skirt streaked with sweat and dirt and the corpse of a dog in tow. She dragged him behind her, just as St. Simeon Salus had done with his no-name dog, wandering and babbling along the streets of Emesa, 1,600 years before. God's dear fools. Salus and his children. All his sons, and all his daughters, all their funny little ways. Look what I found, Ma! He followed me home. Can I keep him?

July 1, 1997. Just a few hours ago, and for the last time, the Union Jack was lowered in Hong Kong. Never one to shrink from jumping on a bandwagon, I, too, have reverted to china. As recently as last year, it would have been paper plates, disposable forks, and a plastic tumbler of cheap champagne. Not today, though. Not any more. I have acquired standards to which I cleave. I have an image to uphold. Middle-aged. Stodgy. Conservative. Establishment. I have worked hard for this, and I have no intention of throwing it away. Do without china? Unthinkable. Why, if someone should saunter through this meadow and see me eating my Canada Day/St. Simeon Salus picnic from something ersatz like, say, Chinette, I don't know what I'd do. Word would get out. I know it would. There'd be no point in going on.

What a varied array of delicacies I've assembled on my grandmother's Blue Mikado. What a colourful assortment of comestibles! Hummus. Dolmades. Roasted peppers: red, yellow, and orange. A fragrant bread laced with olives and sun-dried tomatoes. Smoked trout. Roasted chicken (free-range) with a tasty little pepper and garlic condiment on the side. A runny Brie (French). A good Fumé Blanc (Californian). Some lemon sorbet, insulated against the warmth of the day with an ice-pack. However did privilege get such a bad name when it's this much fun? My grin is so wide you can see my gums. Which I note is "smug" spelled backwards. Which may or may not be significant. I read less into such coincidences than was once the case.

I am not absolutely alone. My shaggy old dog is with me. She lies beside me, doing her celebrated impersonation of a bath mat. She is not so very long for this world, and I have promised her that she will be spared the post-mortem indignities foisted on their animals by Lillian and Simeon. She gave no outward sign of gladness at this news, though I am confident that in her heart she rejoiced. There are some cows who graze nearby, safely contained in their pasture by an electrified fence. They call to mind Emily Carr, who wrote in *The Book of Small* of how she would sing to the denizens of the cow-yard.

"When Small began to sing the old cow's nose-line shot from straight down to straight out, her chin rose into the air, her jaws rolled. The harder Small sang, the harder the cow chewed and the faster she twiddled her ears around as if stirring the song into the food to be rechewed in the cud along with her breakfast."

How grand it would have been to have had Emily here today. It would be grander still had Glenn Gould been able to come along for the ride. They were both dog fanciers, and Glenn was also known to serenade cows. He turned his back on sold-out concert halls, would not perform for an adoring and paying public, but would happily croon to a select audience on the hoof. There's a photograph of him doing just that in Peter F. Ostwald's book, *Glenn Gould: The Ecstasy and Tragedy of Genius*. It's a fuzzy-edged shot snapped by the soprano Roxolana Roslak. Glenn is perched on a rock, in a field. He wears his overcoat and familiar peaked cap while he vocalizes for some appreciative bovine fans. This was on Manitoulin Island, a place that exerted an Edenic tug on Gould. He fantasized that one day he would buy a farm there and establish a retirement home for beasts who were past their prime.

In fact, my cows — I hold them now in proprietary regard — have been getting the Gould treatment this afternoon. I have brought along a tape-deck and the soundtrack to *Thirty-two Short Films About Glenn Gould*. It contains his performances of music by Strauss, Beethoven, Sibelius, Hindemith, Prokofiev, Schoenberg, as well as several selections by J. S. Bach. Now and again you can hear his guttural, trademark "dum-dum-dum-ming" rumbling through. I am obliged to say that the cattle have not been visibly stirred by his lowing. Nor do they seem responsive to the quintessentially sixties sound of "Downtown." Its inclusion on an otherwise classical album is a tribute to Glenn's fondness for Petula Clark.

Downtown. Manitoulin Island. For Gould, they both held Utopian possibilities. Me, I'm a downtown kind of boy. Mine is not a voice fit for crying in the wilderness. Even to so pastoral a place as this — this meadow on the forest edge, only half an hour from the city — I bring along the trappings of urbanity. I find my peace in concrete and crowds, in fumes and noise. Not for me the forest primeval. Though I admire it in the abstract, and appreciate the important role it plays in the maintenance of the biosphere, and value it as a symbol, there is little that makes me as nervous as a thick tangle of trees. It has ever been thus. As a little child, I would listen to the story of Hansel and Gretel and squirm when they left the safety of their home, when they turned their backs on comfort and civilization and entered that dark and pathless wood. *Don't do it! So much that's bad can happen in there! You don't know what you're up against! Bears, bogs, badgers, witches! You'll get lost! Fools! Fools!* This was what I'd want to shout, to warn them, even though I knew perfectly well it would all work out fine, just fine, in the end. Similarly, the many legends of Robin Hood, and his merry men in Sherwood, made me feel more agitated than elated, and all because of the setting. I could see that it was an expedient environment for a bunch of well-intentioned outlaws, but I couldn't help but wish that they had found some other, more citified place for their redistribution-of-resources initiative. I would have been so much more comfortable, so much more willing to absorb their socialist message, had they robbed from the rich and given to the poor in Chelsea, say. Or Soho. Even downtown Nottingham would have done.

Despite this deep-rooted aversion, I experienced a twinge of sadness when I read in *The New York Times*, on April 8, 1994, an article with the headline "SHADES OF ROBIN! FOREST MAY BE SOLD." The story had to do with the hue and cry that erupted over the then Conservative government's plan to privatize the management of England's woodlands and heaths, including Sherwood Forest. Not that there was much left to manage in Sherwood. Most of the oak, birch, and yew that gave shelter to Robin and company was gone. Where there was any vegetation at all, it tended to be clusters of Mediterranean pine that had been imported after the Great War. By and large, the land had been given over to settlement and industry. It made me glum to think of all the gullible and disappointed pilgrims who must surely visit Nottinghamshire every year, only to have their mind's-eye vision of this brooding, mythic shadowland dashed beyond repair. It made me glum because it reminded me of David Curnick, who will always be linked in my mind with Robin Hood, and who died on January 31, 1994. He was — is — the only murder victim I've ever known.

I cannot say I knew him well. We were peripheral to each other's lives. We met through friends of friends, would intersect at parties and on the street. For a couple of years we lived a few blocks apart and we'd bump into each other fairly regularly. These meetings always took place by chance, never by design, but they happened often enough that our acquaintanceship became more than nodding. David was on the short side, about five feet, six inches, and puckish, the kind of person about whom you'd be tempted to use the phrase "elfin twinkle." He was bright and friendly. He had a keen sense of humour. He was articulate. By the time I met him he was in his mid-forties and had had a varied career. He'd been active as a film maker, had written and/or produced several low-budget features. I'd never seen these, and was under the impression that they had either been held up for years in post-production limbo, or had had only a very limited release. As well, he done some work with the National Film Board. It wasn't lucrative, and he kept body and soul together with a half-time job teaching English at Gladstone Secondary School on Vancouver's east side. He had been there for years, and was well known throughout the school for his unconventional approach to classroom management and for the musical extravaganzas he staged every year. These were elaborate, choreographed mime shows, which featured students lip-synching along with popular tunes.

David had much to recommend him, but he always made me edgy. Wary, sort of. When we had our occasional collisions, he would throw me off balance with the way he could steer the chat away from the bland pleasantries that are usual in such encounters into a voluble disquisition about what was new and vital in his ongoing research into the life and times of Robin Hood. There was an inevitability about the conversational drift that I found both engaging and dispiriting. With David, it was Robin Hood this, Robin Hood that, Robin Hood round the Maypole. He just loved, loved, loved Robin Hood. Ever since his childhood days in England, ever since he first saw the 1950s television series starring Richard Greene, Robin had been his governing passion. It grew with him. It followed him to Canada. He became an avid collector of films and videos and books and articles and visual representations of the Sherwood legends. It spilled over into his every undertaking. While it was lovely to see someone in whom a childhood enthusiasm had not withered, and while this youthful sprightliness inhabiting a middle-aged man presented a charming incongruity, I sniffed a depressing air of hopelessness about his obsession. He was always laying plans, big plans, which had Robin Hood paving David Curnick's path to the glory and recognition he had been denied, and somehow those plans never came to fruition. Of smoke there was plenty, but there was never a sign of flame in the forest.

Whenever I saw him, he would bring me up to date on the Robin Hood documentary he wanted to make but which was caught in a state of perpetual delay. He would give me the latest news about a book he planned to write. He had been talking about the damn thing for years. It was a project on a grand scale, the "definitive" examination of screen treatments of the Robin legend. It was a good idea, and as a film maker and self-made Sherwood Forest authority, he was ideally positioned to bring it off. To his credit, he did more than merely talk about it. He sent query letters to many publishers and received several encouraging expressions of interest. He travelled to England and interviewed some of the actors, directors, and producers who had been involved with film and television presentations of the Sherwood legends. He met and maintained a friendly correspondence with Alan Wheatley, Nickolas Grace, Sidney Cole,

Paul Eddington, and Patricia Driscoll, among others. In 1985, he visited Bristol and landed a walk-on role as a peasant in one of the episodes of *Robin of Sherwood*.

David Curnick aloft as a merry man.

He prepared, and prepared and prepared, but never got around to doing. He was like someone who winds and winds a jack-in-the-box that refuses to pop. David was not oblivious to the tragi-comic aspects of his quixotic tilting. There's a current of irony in the annual report he sent to his various correspondents and confederates, and in which he summarized his progress to date on the book that never was.

"August, 1990. How time flies. Eight years since I contacted most of you and told you of my plans. You'd think I was writing some kind of Decline and Fall."

"August 1991. It seemed that ten whole weeks of summer would provide me with so much time to work on 'the book.' Alas, I was wrong."

"May 1992. Well, I have to reluctantly admit that this is the 10th anniversary of my pronouncement that a book on Robin

Hood in film and on television was happening. I carry on, each year inexorably moving towards…what?"

Looking back from this temporal vantage point — the feast day of St. Simeon Salus, 1997 — I see how there was something dear about all this fudging and delaying and hoping. Something sweet. But at the time, I'm afraid I dismissed David as a bit of a flake, as one of those would-be writers who was more talk than typing; who bag on endlessly about how they long to string words together but never get down to the hard slog of it.

Of course, when I heard David had been murdered, I was jolted by stupid guilt. *I once thought badly of him, and now he is dead.* As if there were some causal connection. As if fondness would have made a difference. I had not seen him for some time. He had moved from the neighbourhood, and it had been a year at least since I had spoken to or of him. At such a remove I responded to the news of his violent passing with more shock than grief. I didn't know him well enough to mourn. But of course I was curious. Murder victims are never people one knows. How could this have happened to David? He was not innocuous, exactly, but he hardly seemed a candidate for harm. How on earth? However on earth?

When I began my winter's wandering, when I undertook to write about Canadian eccentrics, I determined that Rumour would be the pillar of fire I would follow to narrative's promised land. My methodology, such as it was, was passive and reactive. I would make it known, as best I could, that I was looking for stories. I would wait for word to come. Then, I would follow up on proffered leads. In this regard, David Curnick is an aberrant inclusion in the gallery. No one mentioned his name to me. No one spoke of his qualities or nominated him for inclusion. He surfaced in my own meditations early on, and I determined that he would find a place here. In some ways, for me, he came to personify the pleasures and perils of a life abstracted from the centre. Two poles exerted their influence on his compass: the scorned and the beloved.

We admire people who give rein to their passions and obsessions, who fly in the face of convention, who have easy access to an id unmediated by a prissy, stultifying ego. We need them. You could say they have a societal utility. They shake up the old order. They remind us that our familiar priorities, whether personal or political, are arbitrary; the product of unthinking convention, and nothing more. We cherish these outsized characters because they amplify qualities we each of us possess in some small measure. And we love them because they give us stories. When all is said and done, it is stories that keep us buoyant.

On the other hand, we are suspicious of such psychic spaciousness. It makes us uneasy. It can be messy and inconvenient. We like to know that there are mavericks and rule-breakers among us, but we want them at a tidy remove. We want them across the block and down the street. We are fearful of the contact that leads to contagion. All that "in your face" passion and volubility quickly wears thin. It's like a hot wind, pleasant and novel for a short while, but shrivelling and unnerving in the long run.

I knew him only slightly, but David Curnick stirred in me a strong reaction. He muddied my waters with both fascination and aversion. The more I thought about his eccentricities — his Robin Hood obsession especially — the more I wanted to learn about his story. His fanciful life. His brutal end. I would not have been able to venture into such hard territory had I not had the cooperation of three men who knew him well and whose friendship he valued. I am indebted to Graham Peat, who was the executor of his estate, and who kindly gave me access to his files and papers; to Dennis Pilon, who was one of David's students and who is now completing his doctoral work in political science at York University; and to Larry Killick, who was a long-time colleague at Gladstone Secondary School.

Larry, like most of the teachers at Gladstone, knew about David's all-embracing fondness for Robin Hood. David left full-time teaching in 1984, in favour of a half-time position, with the intention of devoting himself to the famous book. As well, he wanted to focus his attentions on a music business he had run for some years, a disc-jockey service, called Robin Hood Mobile Sound. The students were likewise apprised of his passion for all things Sherwood. Anyone who had Mr. C. as an English teacher soon learned that all his roads led to Nottinghamshire. He found ways of working the stories and films — especially the Richard Greene series — into his lesson plans. He justified their inclusion, when he was required to, by saying that folklore and mythology were part of the curriculum, and that the Robin stories were central to Anglo-Saxon traditions. The screen presentations, he said, enriched his students' vocabularies and were wonderful examples of tightly written narrative. And yes, there were quizzes.

Larry, like most of the teachers at Gladstone, knew that David was gay. He was discreet, but not secretive about his sexuality. He had written letters to the editor in support of gay causes. Some of his films had homoerotic themes. He belonged to an educators' gay and lesbian advocacy group. From all reports, he did not share this aspect of his life with his students, at least not in a direct way. Some may have drawn their own conclusions. Dennis Pilon recalls that there was a distinct campiness to his choice of classroom decorations, and his annual lipsynch extravaganzas held certain clues, particular drag-show references, for those who chose to find them. David had dallied with drag, had done a turn or two on stage in a club called BJ's. It was a lark, nothing more. It never became a lifestyle.

Larry was one of only a very few teachers at Gladstone who knew that David had once run a gay dating service called — no surprise here — Sherwood Forest Personal Introductions. That was in the mid-seventies. He may have matched a few true loves, but his interest was mostly in getting dates for himself. When he sold the business, he placed a running personal advertisement in a now-defunct sex-trade rag called *Star*. When that paper floundered, he transferred his allegiance to a weekly called *Buy & Sell*. He developed a niche-marketing strategy, and composed an ad that was a friendly, non-threatening come-on directed towards bisexual men, or to nominally straight fellows who might be in the mood for some experimentation. He used the usual catch phrases. First-timers welcome. Don't be shy. Give it a try. Call the Hotline. That was what he called it. The Hotline.

"David," remembers Dennis Pilon, "was a fan of all things British, a true Anglophile. It wasn't just Robin Hood. He loved such comedy series as *Yes, Minister*, and the *Carry On* movies. He was also very keen on espionage, especially the James Bond books and films. When he set up his Hotline, he actually installed a red telephone. Over the twenty years that he ran this service he met an astonishing number of men. More than anyone would have thought possible. Some would come over once, some more often.

"David never felt he was very good at presenting himself as an attractive commodity on the meat market, so he looked for other ways to meet sex partners. Like many people who spend years longing and never achieving, he got very fixed ideas about what he found attractive. He never got into that dialectic of sex, when your whole sense of attraction changes, when you discover that your partners don't have to be muscled, or hairless, or whatever. He became set in his ways. He liked big guys, muscular guys, Italianate guys. He liked them to be sort of menacing, but not very much so. He liked the illusion of rough trade, but was certainly not into getting hurt or pushed around. He was severe with anyone who got out of place, and he developed a remarkable set of skills for knowing who might be trouble."

Dennis and Graham Peat and David were part of a group of friends who would meet every Sunday for brunch. Often, David would regale them with stories of the "studs" he had met over the phone and whom he subsequently entertained in his home. These tales were received with a mixture of fascination and horror. Both Dennis and Graham warned David, as did Larry Killick in whom he also confided some of his adventures, that he was treading on thin ice. He was almost fifty. He was not a paragon of athleticism. He was putting himself in harm's way. David countered that he had taken the risks into account and that he took precautions to safeguard his person. He set an alarm when his visitors arrived, so that it would go off when they left unless he disarmed it. He kept a baseball bat under his bed.

He was lucky. Once or twice he had to eject a gentleman caller who was drunk and disorderly. Otherwise, there were no problems. There were plenty of guys who wanted what he offered, and for twenty years he enjoyed an active no-fuss, no-muss, no-obligations sex life. Little wonder he felt confident. He even began covertly videotaping his encounters, concealing a camera with a wide-angle lens in a stereo stand. His brunch buddies didn't mince words when they learned of this development. They told him such a tactic was both foolish and reprehensible. Many of the men he was meeting were insecure about their sexuality. Confidence, for them, was paramount. He was betraying a trust, and he was risking terrible consequences if he should be caught. David heard these concerns, but persisted. He had no intention of ever showing the tapes he made, and he further rationalized his actions by citing reasons of security. What if he were to be robbed? The videos could help identify the thief.

"POLICE THINK VICTIM KNEW HIS MURDERER"

That was the headline in the *Province* on February 2, 1994. And the police, it turned out, were right in their surmise. His name was Darin Young. David didn't know him well, but they had met on at least three occasions. They saw each other on the night of the murder, when Darin stabbed David repeatedly, in his own home, with one of his own kitchen knives, and they had seen each other earlier in that same week. Some six or seven years had elapsed between their second meeting and their first. They got together through the Hotline. Graham Peat remembers that David told him about that first meeting. He remembers that his friend was concerned. There was something about Darin that wasn't quite right. For one thing, he seemed rather young, even though he claimed to be nineteen. David was always, by every account, scrupulous about meeting only with callers who were of legal age. He activated his trouble-sensing radar, and his instincts proved spot-on. The boy called him again, not long after their first encounter. He'd changed his story. Now he claimed to be under age. He threatened to go to the police and lay charges of molestation unless they could agree on a cash settlement. David declined to play along. Darin never followed through. He disappeared.

When he resurfaced, some years later, he was fresh out of jail. He had served time for several misdemeanours, including violent misconduct. There was no longer any question of his majority. He was older, twenty-six, and his appearance was radically different.

"TATTOOED MAN SOUGHT IN SLAYING"

That was the headline in *The Province* on February 11, 1994. Why did Darin seek David out after so troubled a parting? Had he held him in his head the whole time of his incarceration? Or did he just happen on the ad again when he was flipping through the personals section of *Buy & Sell*, and call him up for old time's sake? On such arcane points as these, no one is clear. All that is sure is that they had a reunion. David, who was always sharing of such information, told his brunch companions that Darin was back on the scene, told them that he was now tattooed from stem to stern. They warned him against having any further contact. They told him the young man was surely disturbed, that he was bound to be trouble. "But he's terribly exciting" was David's answer.

Dennis Pilon says that David would engage in fantasy play with his Hotline friends. He would construct scenarios and have his friends act them out. He would ask them to pose for him, flex their muscles, encourage them to come at him in a threatening, but not too threatening, way. When Darin Young dropped by for the last time, on January 31, 1994, he went along with the prescribed scenario until it came time to turn on his host with mock menace. Then, he abandoned any pretense of play acting.

He left the apartment with David's wallet and chequebook. By the time the neighbours came to investigate the alarm, it was too late. "It's a terrible thing to happen at your own front door," one condo owner told a reporter, and she was surely right. The papers reported that David was stabbed more than a hundred times. And all the while, the video camera was taking it in. An unblinking eye. A terrible record. His final film.

David had been right all along about the utility of such evidence. In the end, he helped capture his own killer. The police released images from the tape to the papers. Darin's picture — his long hair, his muscled chest, his many tattoos — was published all over the country. He turned himself in in Kelowna, pleaded guilty, and was once again confined. Dennis and Graham attended the sentencing.

"David," said Dennis, "was my oldest friend, one of my best friends, and I miss him all the time. When I went to that sentencing though, all I could think was that there were two victims. Two tragedies. There was David, of course. And there was Darin. Here was someone who came from a background of terrible abuse, who was in and out of foster homes, who had sustained a head injury, who never really stood a chance, who held tremendous anger, and who, on top of everything else, got stuck with this uncertainty about his own sexuality in a society that hates gay people. And now where is he? In jail. And what kind of help will he get there? And in ten years when he's out, what's going to happen?"

What one wants, of course, is closure. What one wants is what one can't have, and that is the answer to the variations on the question: why? Why would anyone stab someone a hundred times? Why would David have willingly put himself in so vulnerable a situation with so dangerous a predator? Fatalism? Thrill seeking? Or was it just misplaced trust? A bad call? That's not so unlikely. Many of us can look back on an encounter that made perfect sense in the moment, and been appalled that it ever took place; shuddered at the prospect of what might have been.

It would not have been out of character for David to have met Darin with the hope of some kind of reconciliation in mind. Each of his friends told me, independently, that David was pathologically reluctant to let go of people who had passed through his orbit, to release them, or allow them to slip from his grasp and life. He knew that he could alienate people. He was always doing battle with some imagined foe, and he was argumentative and controlling by nature. He would fight with his friends, would give or take offence. There would be a sundering, a cooling off, and then a *rapprochement*. He would make overtures of friendship that were pleading, toadying almost. It was a familiar pattern. It happened time and again. He couldn't bear the weight of contempt. He wanted nothing more than acceptance. He wanted everyone to be his friend. He wanted to belong. He wanted to be part of a band of merry men.

Why did he love Robin Hood and the boys of Sherwood so much? Pick your reason. Because they were anti-authoritarian, and David felt he had been squashed by people who were in power. Because they stood up for the little guy. Because they looked great in tights. Mostly, all his friends agree, it was because they were naughty and got away with it.

David Curnick was a man who was lucky in his friends. They cared for him, watched out for him. They speak well of his accomplishments as both an artist and a teacher. They would like to see his films get wider attention. They were pleased when his family established a scholarship in his name. They want to see his memory and the several truths of his life preserved. They loved him for who and what he was. They loved him for his passion. For his naughtiness.

David was an adoring fan of Brenda Lee, Connie Francis, and Petula Clark. I imagine he might have enjoyed this little outing; would have enjoyed spending an afternoon here on the edge of these brooding woods — thicker than Sherwood — with Petula reprising yet again her hit of 1964. "Downtown," she sings, and it sounds like a good idea. This picnic is done. The country is another year older. St. Simeon Salus Day is withering on the vine. Even the cattle have taken a powder. I've always wanted to be able to say I wrote till the cows came home. Now I can.

Let's call it a day. It's time. The forest primeval is no longer

content to hold back its shadows. It's sending them out in our
direction. Look, look. Now they come. You can hear their steady
jackboot tread. Their merciless advance. I shiver and do what I
always do in moments of psychic distress. I close my eyes and
think of Kipling ("The Way Through the Woods"):

> They shut the road through the woods
> Seventy years ago.
> Weather and rain have undone it again,
> And now you would never know
> There was once a road through the woods
> Before they planted the trees.

Seventy years ago. Nineteen twenty-seven. The year Lillian
Alling began her walking. The year Letitia Reed made her big
decision, sat down at her desk and wrote, "To Whom It May
Concern, I am interested to know more about the courses
offered by the Marvel School of Cosmetology. I enclose a
stamped, self-addressed envelope for your reply." Nineteen
twenty-seven. The year Marius Barbeau, who would later write
down the story of Alexis Le Trotteur, recommended that Emily
Carr's paintings be considered as part of an exhibition of West
Coast art at the National Gallery of Canada. Nineteen twenty-
seven was the year the Gallery director, Eric Brown, went to
Victoria to visit Emily and see her work. He was overwhelmed
— as millions of us have been since — by their energy and heft
and vibrancy. He was charmed by the round little woman who
had seen the forest in so particular and striking a way, and who
lived with her dogs and her monkey called Woo, and was funny
and quick and odd, and embittered. At his request, she composed an autobiographical sketch. In 1927 she wrote:

"When I sent to an exhibition they dishonoured my work in
every way, putting it behind things, under shelves, or on the ceiling. My friends begged me to go back to my old way of painting, but [as] I had tasted the joys of a bigger way it would have
been impossible had I wanted to, which I did not. When ever I

could afford it I went up north among the Indians and the woods and forgot all about everything in the joy of those lonely wonderful places, I decided to make as good a representative collection of those old villages and wonderful totem poles as I could, for the love of the people, and the love of the places, and the love of the art, whether anybody liked them or not I did not care a bean.

"I painted them to please myself in my own way..."

The joys of a bigger life. Emily Carr achieved greatness before anyone had ever heard of her, but I don't suppose she could have known or imagined, as she wrote those anxious and defensive words, that her greatness was about to lead to fame. She was on the cusp of success. She would go to the east, and step into the warm light of approbation. She would feel the seductive tug of the centre. But she knew who she was, and where she belonged. She would never relinquish her claim on the margins. She would always be, in every way, eccentric.

In 1935, as though to renew those joyous, big-life vows, she painted *Scorned as Timber, Beloved of the Sky*. A tall and spindly fir is all that remains in a harvested forest. It was not worth the bother of cutting, not worth dulling the saw. There was no paper in it, no lumber. They passed it over. They left it where it stood, whole and uncompromised, paying the price of purposeful selfhood. Which is loneliness. Which is happiness. Which is communion with the sky. Scorned and beloved.

The breathless hours like phantoms stole away.

There's nothing left to do but pack away our feast. See? We've devoured so much, and so much still remains. It will always be like this. We need never fear famine. We need never know want. We can eat till we are bursting and our hunger will always be intact. We will always know the joy of wanting more. Praise the holy hunger in this blessed, blessed land. Praise as well the ending of this odd and lucky road. Amen, good friends, and thanks for coming. For look, now. Look. We are home.

An Alphabet of Suggested Kleiserisms for the Use of Critics

All the lesser lights paled into insignificance

As fresh and invigorating as a sea breeze

Browsing at will on all the uplands of knowledge and thought

A charming air of vigor and vitality

Comment of rare and delightful flavor

A cunning intellect patiently diverting every circumstance to its design

Delicious throngs of sensations

Endowed with all those faculties that can make the world a garden of enchantment

Every phrase is like the flash of a scimitar

Felicitousness in the choice and exquisiteness in the collocation of words

The flawless triumph of art

The fruit of vast and heroic labors

A gay exuberance of ambition

Generosity pushed to prudence

A heart from which noble sentiments sprang like sparks from an anvil

His words gave a curious satisfaction, as when a coin, tested, rings true gold

An ideal as sublime and comprehensive as the horizon

Ideas which spread with the speed of light

The idiosyncratic peculiarities of thought

Judging without waiting to ponder over bulky tomes

Justifiable in certain exigencies

Keen power of calculation and unhesitating audacity

A large, rich, copious human endowment
A man of matchless modesty and refinement
The maximum of attainable and communicable truth
The meticulous observation of facts
No longer shall slander's venomed spite crawl like a snake
    across his perfect name
Occasional flashes of tenderness and love
The oscillations of human genius
Plaudits of the unlettered mob
Prodigal of discriminating epithets
The purging sunlight of clear poetry
Questions and answers sounding like a continuous popping
    of corks
Quickened and enriched by new contacts with life and truth
Refreshing as descending rains to sunburnt climes
The romantic ardor of a generous mind
A spacious sense of the amplitude of life's possibilities
Startling leaps over vast gulfs of time
Through the riot of his senses, like a silver blaze, ran the
    legend
Touched every moment with shifting and enchanting beauty
Unforced and unstudied depth of feeling
Uplifting the soul as on dovelike wings
Voices that charm the ear and echo with a subtle resonance in
    the soul
Volcanic upheavings of imprisoned passions
Words were flashing like brilliant birds through the boughs
    overhead
Wrought of an emotion infectious and splendidly dangerous
Yearning tenderness
Zealous in the cause he affected to serve

Notes

I have made frequent and conspicuous use of Grenville Kleiser's forgotten masterpiece, *Fifteen Thousand Useful Phrases* (New York: Funk & Wagnalls, 1917). Kleiserisms are italicized throughout. Overwrought figures of speech that appear in roman type are, alas, my own. The *Dictionary of Canadian Biography* (Toronto: University of Toronto Press) was an invaluable resource. Biblical quotations are from the King James version.

1. Fugue

In writing about my childhood recollections of Glenn Gould (the *Reader's Digest* connection) I am not reporting facts but am giving an accurate account of my memories. As these are well over thirty years old, I would not be surprised to learn that they are not correct in their every biographical detail. Glenn Gould's appreciation of Petula Clark, "The Search for Petula Clark," appeared in *High Fidelity*, November 1967. It was reprinted in *The Glenn Gould Reader*, edited by Tim Page (Toronto: Lester & Orpen Dennys, 1984). His remarks about Toronto, originally part of a film-documentary script, were also anthologized by Mr. Page. Anna Brownell Jameson's *Winter Studies and Summer Rambles in Canada* was published in 1838, and released as part of McClelland & Stewart's "New Canadian Library" in 1990. *In Search of the Magnetic North: A Soldier–Surveyor's Letters from the North-west 1843–44*, by John Henry Lefroy (edited by George F. Stanley), was published by Macmillan, 1955. My thanks to Robert Rothon and Myron Plett for telling me about Messy May, whose story is included on their Tides of Men Web site.

2. Before We Go Further, a Parenthetical Word

The story of Esther Brandeau has been told in many different ways and places over the years. She is mentioned in Volume 2 of the *Dictionary of Canadian Biography*, and B. G. Sack's *The History of the Jews in Canada* (Montreal: Harvest House, 1964). Thanks to Thomas Walter Brooks, of Gravenhurst, Ontario, for the information on Sarah Emma Edmonds. Mr. Brooks is an American Civil War historian, and a keen participant in Civil War re-enactments. He is well known in Gravenhurst, Ontario, where he can often be seen riding about the town on his horse. They are an arresting sight at the Tim Horton's Drive-Thru, especially as Tom wears a Confederate army uniform every day of the year except Hallowe'en. Tom Brooks is the author (with Michael Dan Jones) of *Lee's Foreign Legion: A History of the 10th Louisiana Infantry*.

3. Begin
Chas. S. Robertson, of Kenabeek, Ontario, was the owner of what is now my copy of *Fifteen Thousand Useful Phrases*, and he did indeed mark particular similes with dates. Otherwise, I know nothing of his biography, and his story — as the reader will surely have deduced — is a fiction. Edith Sitwell's *English Eccentrics: A Gallery of Weird and Wonderful Men and Women* (Harmondsworth: Penguin Books, 1971) was first published by Faber & Faber in 1933. Henry Wilson and James Caulfield published *The Book of Wonderful Characters* in 1876 (London: Reeves). Glenn Gould's diet is discussed, in part, in Peter F. Ostwald's *Glenn Gould: The Ecstasy and Tragedy of Genius* (New York: W. W. Norton, 1997).

4. A Folly in Paradise
Any good hagiography, such as *Butler's Lives of the Saints* (4 vols), will make mention of the Simeons Stylites and Salus. For information on Charles Henry Danielle, I am especially grateful to Bert Riggs, archivist at the Centre for Newfoundland Studies at Memorial University. In reconstructing Danielle's story, I used the various clippings, brochures, etc. contained in the centre's files. I also used newspaper accounts; the papers of the day were full of stories about the goings-on at Octagon Castle. I made ample use of Danielle's own brochures. Both the *Dictionary of Canadian Biography* and *The Encyclopedia of Newfoundland and Labrador* have useful entries. As just one side of the Waugh/Brazill correspondence has been preserved (so far as I know), I can only guess at how these two men came into contact with each other in the first place. The italicized words in my text appear as underlinings in Waugh's letters. I found his candour about Danielle's

love of men surprising and moving. One of the Professor's fancy boys, he says, was a dentist, Dr. Harry Burnett. "Charles *worshipped* him. He was good looking and Charles' money was paid out for him like *water*. Charles afterwards told me that for all his kindness Burnett treated him like a *thief*. Charles got him there & introduced him & wrote out a fine lecture for him and afterwards Burnett made lots of money. You must have heard Charles speak of him. All of Charles' friends went back on him sooner or later."

The odd document in which Danielle, seemingly teetering on the brink of paranoia, writes of testing his servants' honesty reads, in part: "Believing that Mrs. Ryan is still stealing from me for Mr. Porter and others, toadying to their favours & opinions, I today, June 24 sent Adam McCamby & Mr. F. Brazill up in Porter's Room to see what was there from my Larder & this is their report. To wit, 2 sections of Rhubarb Pie, a lot of Rhubarb Jam, Half Doz Long's Biscuits all on a plate." Danielle instigated further investigations on July 15 and 27, on August 15, 26, 27, and 28, on which occasions his agents discovered bread, ham, chicken, and fancy cake. I don't know what punishments were meted out to the miscreants, but Mrs. Porter must have been forgiven her complicity as she was remembered in the will.

5. Devil among the Tailors
"Devil Among the Tailors" is a fiddle tune. All the tunes named are traditional, and are among those collected in *The Old Time Fiddler's Repertory*, Vol. 2. Compiled and edited by R.P. Christeson (Columbia: University of Missouri Press, 1984). The story of Pierre-Léon Ayotte appears in Volume 13 of the *Dictionary of Canadian Biography*. I did not interview Willie Francis Fraser in person, but spoke to him on the phone. His childhood visitation was reported by Bruce Erskine in the Halifax *Chronicle-Herald*, January 10, 1997. The story of Malcolm MacLean I learned from Barrie Fraser, of East Lake Ainslie, Nova Scotia. He related it in a letter he sent to the CBC Stereo program "As You Like It."

6. Shock
That a Mrs. Joyner was brushed by lightning, while in her room, and that she was unharmed, was reported in *The Toronto Daily Star*, June 23, 1906. The other facts of her life are unknown to me, and her story is an invention. I met Mr. Eddy R. Souris in the lobby of the CBC

building in Toronto, in November 1996. I have been unsuccessful in my efforts to contact him, and wish him well in his mousing around. The lyrics to "My Old Island Home" were written by Janette McLeod Morrison. The story of Modomnoc, who brought apiculture to Ireland, is contained in David Hugh Farmer's *The Oxford Dictionary of Saints* (Oxford: Oxford University Press, 1978). Hazlitt relates the story of the funeral party turned topsy-turvy by bees in his *Dictionary of Faiths & Folklore*, first published in 1905 by Reeves and Turner. Robert Dowie's story was assembled from material made available to me by the Prince Edward Island archives, as well as from contemporary accounts, reported in *The Islander*.

7. Ark

For dove and pigeon lore, I am indebted to Miriam Rothschild's *Butterfly Cooing Like a Dove* (New York: Doubleday, 1991) and to Iona Opie and Moira Tatem's *A Dictionary of Superstitions* (Oxford: Oxford University Press, 1989). Walter J. Weber's *Health Hazards from Pigeons, Starlings, and English Sparrows* was published in 1979 by Thomson Publications of Fresno, California. The curious tale of Merit Bean is taken from newspaper accounts (particularly *The Boston Globe*) kindly provided by the Yarmouth County Museum Archives. The story of Samuel Bean and the cryptogram gravestone is well known in the Kitchener–Waterloo area. The story of the *Royal Tar* and Mogul, the elephant, was cobbled together from 836 newspaper accounts of the disaster published in Boston, Yarmouth, and Halifax.

8. Food for the Phoenix

I have based my story of the sad death of Keith Pelton on an account contained in *Yarmouth Past and Present: A Book of Reminiscences* by J. Murray Lawson, published in 1902.

9. The Offending Hand

Lâche pas y'a toujours un moyen, by Jean St-Germain (Drummondville, Quebec: Les Editions Indépendantes, 1979.) The pyramid is located between St-Hyacinthe and Drummondville at 1447, rang St-Georges. This description of the forbidden pyramid, meant to be the largest in the world and scotched by the agricultural land reserve, was given in *La Presse*, August 24, 1988. "Pour financer cet audacieux projet, la corporation Citadelle de la paix prévoit vendre des emplacements pour des urnes funéraires de $1,000 à $9,250, les prix variants selon la hauteur achetée par la famille éplorée. Tout de béton, la pryamide comprendra 42 étages, dont 33 contiendront les 22 millions d'urnes. L'occupation des étages supérieurs n'est pas encore déterminée, mais il pourra servir, entre autres utilisations, de salles de recueillement pour les familles des disparus, etc. Au sommet, précise Saint-Germain, on trouvera un prisme de 42 tonnes qui projettra, par un puits de lumière jusqu'à la base, un arc-en-ciel de rayons lumineux d'y plus bel effet."

Alex Kolansky probably became fixated on Mark 9:43. "And if thy hand offend thee, cut it off: it is better for thee to enter into life maimed, than having two hands to go into hell, into the fire that never shall be quenched." How different his life might have been had Ecclesiastes, 11:6 become the focus of his attention: "In the morning, sow thy seed, and in the evening withhold not thine hand."

The Canadian Boy Scout, by Robert Baden-Powell (Toronto: Morang, 1911).

10. Past Forgetting
Margaret MacDonald's tale of bravery appeared in *The National Enquirer* in the summer of 1996.

There are, of course, many ways of charming a wart. A good source of spells and devices is Helen Creighton's *Bluenose Magic: Popular Beliefs and Superstitions in Nova Scotia* (Toronto: Ryerson Press, 1968).

I was fascinated by the possibility that Chas. S. Robertson, former owner of *Fifteen Thousand Useful Phrases*, might have known Nellee, inasmuch as Kenabeek is just miles from Englehart. While I was in the neighbourhood, I also looked into a letter I had received from one Mrs. Edna Hip, of Nanaimo. She wrote: "Growing up in Sudbury, I knew a number of eccentric individuals, as you can well imagine. Certainly the most eccentric of them all was an old farmer, Lester Kinos, who lived just south of the city. Old Les was as smart as they come, and was normal in all ways except for one peculiar trait. He believed the letter 'F' should be a vowel. He'd argue about this with anyone who cared to listen, and he even converted a few of the naysayers to his point of view. It was his plan to hold a civic plebiscite on this issue one day, but that never came about. 'Sure, I'm just an farmer,' he'd say, 'an farmer and an fool with lifelong ambition. But I have an dream,' he'd say, 'no wait…A dream…a dream to achieve justice for the letter 'F', the most misunderstood of all vowels.' Les's eccentric ways amused even old Roger Hope, the roofing contractor who wanted to replace capitalism with a small piece of wood."

Kinos is indeed a name that turns up in the Sudbury directory — it's of Finnish origin — and I called all of them to see if any knew of old Les, who was fond of "F." Everyone to whom I spoke disavowed knowledge. As there is no phone listing for Mrs. Hip, and as letters to her address (on a street that does exist) were returned, I have sadly and reluctantly come to smell a rat.

12. Some Good Shepherds
Jack Marriott's diaries, photos, and sundry papers have been housed in the Public Archives of Nova Scotia as the H.J.B. Marriott collection.

13. Job's Excellent Vacation
Paul Bog's story was reported in *People of the Interlake*, by Andrew Blicq, with photographs by Ken Gigliotti (Winnipeg: Turnstone, 1986). As well, there was an account of his life and times in *The Selkirk Journal*, June 24, 1996, written by Donna Delaurier.

14. Through the Hermitage Window
To protect his privacy, I have not revealed the name or location of the hermit K. The sad story of Helen Hatch and her icy plunge can be found in *The Canadian Alpine Journal* in its report of the 1908 camp.

15. A Woman Clothed with the Sun
A Little Treasury of Modern Poetry, edited by Oscar Williams, was published by Charles Scribner & Sons, 1949.

16. *La Belle et la Bête*
Eccentrics: A Study of Sanity and Strangeness is by David Weeks and Jamie James (New York: Villard Books, 1995).

17. Still and Moving Images
Alexis Le Trotteur, by Jean-Claude Larouche (Montreal: Editions du Jour, 1971).
The Kingdom of Saguenay, by Marius Barbeau (Toronto: Macmillan, 1936).

I found the photo of the Marvel girls in a store called Gardens Antique. A graduation diploma was part of the lot acquired by the store owners at an estate sale. The certificate was issued to Letitia J. Reed, and I have supposed that the photograph was also hers. The verses I copied or adapted from an autograph book that belonged to Lillian Godden. Lillian lived in Harbour Grace, Newfoundland. The Godden house was purchased and restored by Jerry Dick, who now runs it as the Garrison House Inn. Lillian lived in Boston for a time, and was part of a group of young women called "The Modern Priscillas." Most of the autographs are dated 1926 and were inscribed by other Priscillas.

18. The Forest Primeval
Lillian Alling's story is comparatively recent and often revisited. Even so, it has become impossible to separate fact from supposition and lore. It is not even clear whether she was Russian or Polish. What seems certain is that she started her journey in New York, and that she walked a very long way. I have based my truncated version of her story on materials supplied by the B.C. Provincial Archives and the Vancouver Public Library. For more comprehensive accounts of her extraordinary travels, see *Pioneer Days in British Columbia*, vol. 2, edited by Art Downs; "Lillian Alling," by Win Shivlock in *B.C. Historical News*, Winter 1992–93; and "The Long Trail to Home, Sweet Home," by J. Wellsford Mills, in *The Shoulder Strap*, vol. 1, no. 6. Emily Carr's *The Book of Small* was published by Irwin in 1942. Her biographical sketch, written in 1927 for Eric Brown, is quoted in *Emily Carr: A Biography*, by Maria Tippet (Toronto: Stoddart, 1979). Graham Peat, executor of the David Curnick estate, hopes to place his papers with the Special Collections Division of the UBC Library.

Acknowledgments

I thank from the bottom of my heart the men and women who agreed to be interviewed and profiled in this book. Meeting them was a privilege, and I am keenly aware that I have been able to draw attention to only a tiny aspect of their rich, rich lives.

My thanks to Louise Dennys and everyone at Knopf Canada, most particularly to the incredibly calm and patient Diane Martin who suggested this project to me, and on whose editorial guidance I have leaned rather heavily. Never did I see her flinch. Thanks, as always, to my agent, Dacia Moss. My friend and colleague Marg Meikle, who was born to organize, was an invaluable associate and collaborator during the information-gathering portion of the project, and ran Eccentrics Command Central while I was on the road. My partner, Wallace Robinson, kept the home fires burning and was the first to hear about it when I was frazzled nearly beyond repair. Sue Wagner was also a tremendous support, in many ways. I am grateful for research assistance received from Cathrine Wanczycki, formerly of Ottawa and now living in Vancouver; and from James Calnan.

I am indebted to my colleagues at CBC Radio, Stereo, and Television all across the country who provided many tips and leads. Thanks especially to my Vancouver co-workers who tolerated and accommodated my long absence and my subsequent distraction.

I was the fortunate recipient of kind assistance from librarians, archivists, and library workers at The Centre for Newfoundland Studies, Memorial University (Bert Riggs and Anne Hart); the St. John's Public Library (Joan Grandy); the Yarmouth County Museum Archives (Laura Bradley); the Argyle Township Court House Archives (Peter Crowell and Carmen Phinney); the Amherst Public Library (Beverly Prue); the Public Archives of Nova Scotia; the Halifax Public Library; the Public Archives of Prince Edward Island (Sharon Clark); McGill University Library; the Archives of the Canadian Jewish Congress (Janice Rosen); the McCord Museum of Canadian History (Eva

Burnham, Jacqueline Ross); the library of the Montreal *Gazette*; The National Library and National Archives of Canada (Sandra Bell and Mary Bond); the Toronto Public Library; Queen's University Library and Archives; the Provincial Archives of Manitoba; the Manitoba Legislative Library; the Winnipeg Public Library; the Saskatoon Public Library; the Moose Jaw Public Library; the library of the Whyte Museum of the Canadian Rockies; the Vancouver Public Library; and the British Columbia Provincial Archives (Ann ten Cate).

Thanks abounding to the following individuals for kindness shown along the way and for information freely given. In Newfoundland, thanks to Diane Tye and Phil Hiscocks of the Folklore Department at Memorial University of Newfoundland, and to Linda Badcock, Historic Sites Officer of the Department of Tourism and Culture, Government of Newfoundland and Labrador; to Kathie Housser, Ray Guy, Marjorie Doyle, John Gushue, Martha Muzychka, all in St. John's; to Jerry Dick and Company (fun-time guys, every one!) in Harbour Grace; to Johanna Rocco, of Garden Cove; and to Gilbert E. Higgins, of Stephenville. In Nova Scotia, thanks to Beatrice Desveaux, Lester Marchand, and the family of Joe Delaney, all in the Cheticamp area; to Hector and Eleanor MacKenzie, in Salem; in Amherst, to John McKay; in Wolfville, to David Sheppard and Jennie Sheito; in Halifax, to Stephen Archibald and Sheila Stevenson; and, in Yarmouth, to Brian Medel, Fred Hatfield, and Basil Pero. On Prince Edward Island, thanks to Annie Thurlow, Reg Porter, and Ed MacDonald. In Quebec, thanks to André Picard, Jim Boothroyd, and Philip Szporer, all in Montreal; and to Carol Froimovitch, in Chelsea. In Ottawa, thanks to Bridget Barber and Charles Gordon; in Englehart, to Jan Borecki, Dorothy Dupuis, and Merlin Black; also to Earl Houghton, in London; in Gravenhurst, to Tom Brooks and to the very kind people who stopped to extricate me from the snowpile at the side of the road and whose names I carelessly forgot to write down; in Guelph, to Richard Gorrie and the amazing Dr. Thut; in Toronto, to the gorgeous Elly May, to Geoffrey Pimblett and the staff of his restaurant, to the staff of Mount Pleasant Cemetery, to Robert Dante, Bert Archer, and Dennis Pilon, and to whoever abandoned his or her copy of *Fifteen Thousand Useful Phrases* that I might have it for my own. In Winnipeg, thanks as always to my parents, Stan and Peggy Richardson, for their quiet tolerance and hospitality; in Portage la Prairie, to Nick Kolansky; and, in Brandon, to Fred McGuinness. Thanks to Pat

Armstrong, of Sturgis, Saskatchewan, for a very pleasant afternoon; to Guy and Margaret Vanderhaeghe, in Saskatoon, for a very pleasant evening; to Moon Mullin, in Moose Jaw, for his amazing stories and the long loan of his tapes; and, in Willow Bunch, to M. Campagne, who took me on a tour of the closed museum and filled in some of the blanks concerning the Beaupré giant. In Vancouver, thanks particularly to bill bissett (thanks for the room, bill), Rosamund Norbury, Graham Peat, and Larry Killick.

Although I never aspired to anything like a comprehensive, coast-to-coast survey, I was disappointed to find that there were stories I had fully intended to include in *Scorned & Beloved*, but was unable to accommodate in so small a volume. I thank very much the following people who took the time to meet with me and willingly told me about their lives. Randy Lieb, a painter, writer, and fisherman who lives with his young family on Woody Island, in Placentia Bay. Randy, his wife, and their two daughters are the only full-time residents of an island that was depopulated during the resettlement. They live in a remarkable stone house of Randy's own design and construction. He was a very generous host when I visited there in November 1996. I thank as well the inventor and evangelist Lewis Roberts, of Bareneed, Newfoundland; the journalist and poet Elizabeth Cran, of Tignish, Prince Edward Island; Isabel Bayly, of Chelsea, Quebec, who is an authority in the area of wetlands conservation, and who welcomes a great many raccoons to her porch every summer and who described herself as "a brown paper wrapper of a person" but most certainly is not; and Margaret Kemper, of Ottawa, a writer, photographer, and homemaker who is a dedicated advocate of water conservation. During her life as Margaret Trudeau, she ruffled a great many feathers with the "dangerous spontaneity" she brought to her duties as Prime Minister's Wife. Thanks as well to Ron Ward, of Janetville, Ontario, who showed me his incredible parrots and spoke at some length about his ideas for deficit reduction. I am disappointed not to have found space for the story of Robert Dante, bullwhip master, publisher, and sadomasochist, and would have loved to have written about the late Noulan Cauchon. He was a city planner and dress reformer whose fearless, public showing of his knees, in Ottawa, in 1930, made it possible for men to wear short pants in the Capital, in the summer. I spent an entertaining morning with Kevin Torfason, in Peterborough. Kevin, who is not yet thirty, introduced the wearing of knee-britches to his Ottawa high school only a few years ago, and now creates fabulous period costumes which he sometimes wears around town. In Winnipeg, I visited with the family of Victor Leathers, who was for many years a professor of French at the University of Winnipeg, and who was recognized by students, staff, and faculty alike as an eccentric. Similarly, I wish I could have told the story of the late Ralfe J. Clench, whose many peculiarities endeared him to the community of Queen's University, and some of whose traces I sniffed out in Kingston. It was a pleasure to visit with Tam Bachalo in Portage la Prairie, and to hear about how she preserves Celtic pagan rituals, and about her aversion to wearing footwear. Jerry Kaiser, of Baildon, Saskatchewan, who lives just a few miles down the road from where the famous Sukanen "dust ship" is moored, spoke eloquently about his connection to the land, and showed me his beautiful, whimsical folk-art pieces. It had been my intention to write about the late mountaineer and snow appreciator Norman Bethune Sanson, who is a legend around Banff. And I had a lovely afternoon with Shawn Haley and his wife, Ellie, near Red Deer, Alberta, looking at their collection of Day of the Dead artifacts.

Similarly, space will not allow me to acknowledge individually the several hundred people who were generous enough with their time and information to contact me and tell me about eccentric personalities whose stories they thought I should investigate. I thank them each and every one, heartily, for steering me in all directions at once, and for helping me put the lie to a certitude of Reginald Hines, who, in his book *Hitchings Worthies: Four Centuries of English Life* (1932), said, "The age of the Eccentrics is over. We do not breed them nowadays. The world that made them possible has passed away." It is not. We do. We are living in it.

The impalpable presence of the new century rose like a vast empty house through which no human feet had walked.

Bill Richardson is a bestselling writer and broadcaster, currently the host of "Richardson's Roundup" on CBC Radio One. He is the author of *The Bachelor Brothers' Bed & Breakfast* (winner of the Stephen Leacock Memorial Medal for Humour); *The Bachelor Brothers' Bed & Breakfast Pillow Book*; and *The Bachelor Brothers' Bedside Companion*. He lives in Vancouver.